Praise for *Becoming Jewish*

"We learn in *Becoming Jewish* that converts to Judaism are to be treated as though they were at Mount Sinai with all of Israel when Moses received God's laws. But becoming a 'Jew by choice' is not as simple an undertaking as imagining oneself in the desert sprinting away from Pharaoh. *Becoming Jewish* masterfully guides the interested would-be convert through the myriad of complicated issues and choices that they will confront." —**William C. Daroff**, vice president for public policy and director of the Washington office, Jewish Federations of North America

"Throughout history, many Jews have pondered what it means to be Jewish, an identity that combines religion, ethnicity, culture, history, language, and other complex factors. In considering what it means to become Jewish, and why one would make that choice, the authors give insight into not only the conversion process but also Jewish identity itself. I highly recommend *Becoming Jewish* for both reasons." —**Aaron Eitan Meyer**, research director of the Lawfare Project; legal correspondent for the Terror Finance Blog; board member, Act for Israel

"With the growing debate about the connection between Jewish identity and Israel, *Becoming Jewish* serves as a useful reminder to all those who question the two and why it is so critical to see Judaism and Israel in tandem through the lens of conversation." —**Asaf Romirowsky**, Middle East analyst

"Written with clarity, wisdom, sunshine, and heart, *Becoming Jewish* is an essential mentor for anyone embracing the Jewish family or exploring meaning and faith. A treasure trove for the soul." —**Rabbi Zoë Klein**

"At a time when outreach has never mattered more, a sensitive, thoughtful, and eminently practical guide for those seeking to join the Jewish people." —**Rabbi Steven Z. Leder**, senior rabbi, Wilshire Boulevard Temple; author of *The Extraordinary Nature of Ordinary Things* and *More Money Than God; Living a Rich Life Without Losing Your Soul*

"*Becoming Jewish* deeply enriches the journey of anyone converting to Judaism but does so in a gutsy and refreshing way. I highly recommend it to those exploring paths to Judaism, those who are simply curious about the meaning of Judaism, those close to anyone becoming Jewish, or those concerned with the future of the Jewish state: Israel." —**Noa Tishby**, actor/producer; founder, Act for Israel

Becoming Jewish

The Challenges, Rewards, and Paths to Conversion

STEVEN CARR REUBEN
AND JENNIFER S. HANIN

ROWMAN & LITTLEFIELD PUBLISHERS, INC.
Lanham • Boulder • New York • Toronto • Plymouth, UK

Published by Rowman & Littlefield Publishers, Inc.
A wholly owned subsidiary of The Rowman & Littlefield Publishing Group, Inc.
4501 Forbes Boulevard, Suite 200, Lanham, Maryland 20706
http://www.rowmanlittlefield.com

Estover Road, Plymouth PL6 7PY, United Kingdom

Distributed by National Book Network

British Library Cataloguing in Publication Information Available

Library of Congress Cataloging-in-Publication Data

Reuben, Steven Carr.
  Becoming Jewish: the challenges, rewards, and paths to conversion / Steven Carr Reuben and Jennifer S. Hanin.
    p. cm.
  Includes index.
  ISBN 978-1-4422-0848-3 (cloth : alk. paper) — ISBN 978-1-4422-0849-0 (electronic)
  1. Conversion—Judaism. 2. Jewish converts. I. Hanin, Jennifer S., 1964– II. Title.
  BM645.C6R48 2011
  296.7'14—dc22   2011014083

♾™ The paper used in this publication meets the minimum requirements of American National Standard for Information Sciences—Permanence of Paper for Printed Library Materials, ANSI/NISO Z39.48-1992. Printed in the United States of America

To all those seekers throughout the years who have given me the privilege of being part of their personal journey to becoming Jewish and to my *Kehillat Israel* synagogue family for their constant love and support.

Rabbi Steven Carr Reuben, PhD

To Adam, my soul mate, whom I find endless reasons to fall in love with all over again. To Alexandra and Arianna, for amazing me with your unwavering energy, creativity, and knowledge of the animal kingdom and all things extinct. To each convert searching for a meaningful relationship with God, a synagogue that feels like home, and an extended family to break challah with every single *Shabbat*. Lastly, to my forever home, Israel—may you remain steadfast and continue showing the world what a small, innovative, Jewish country can do.

Jennifer S. Hanin, MA

Contents

Foreword

BY BOB SAGET

When I was asked to write this foreword for my dear friend for many years Rabbi Steven Carr Reuben, I was honored. Then I got concerned. It is a foreword. It precedes the manuscript that he and coauthor Jennifer Hanin have worked on for a very long time. And I am just writing a foreword. And not wanting to be too forward. There's an old show-business adage that there are two things that are suggested not to talk about if you do not wish to agitate anyone—religion and politics. And yes, with my sense of humor, ironically, those were my concerns with writing something appropriate for this book. Rabbi Steven is Jewish. So am I. He has also shared poignant moments in my life. He is an incredibly good man. A man that can be relied on. That is why, in this very foreword, if there is anyone who needs immediate information on Jewish history, Jewish holidays, the differences between Reform, Conservative, Reconstructionism, and Orthodox Judaism—anything involving Israel and the Jewish people—I would like right here and now . . . to publish Steven's cell phone number. I have just been edited. I had typed in his cell phone number. And they have removed it. It wouldn't have been a problem either. . . . No one gets good cell service in the Palisades in Los Angeles.

Okay, here's a short foreword so you can read this interesting and heartfelt book. I was born a Jewish boy. I was circumcised. Thank God by a professional. That is not something you want done by a novice. Or someone doing it for college credit. So I "became Jewish" instantly upon birth. I then went to religious school in Norfolk, Virginia, at a conservative congregation, became a *bar mitzvah*, and solidified my heritage—by working in a deli for four years throughout high school and college. The food of the Jewish people stays within me. It is still within me. I am writing this with a matzah ball inside me from 1975. It is next to the kishka. That will never leave. Let us pray. I have many fond memories of growing up Jewish. My Bube's gefilte fish, my Bube's chicken soup, my Bube's mandel bread. My Bube. My father's mother. She raised six children basically by herself. During rough financial times she would have an extra twenty people over and add breadcrumbs to whatever was being served—to feed everyone. That's what being Jewish meant to me growing up. About being generous of heart. About our family. Yes, food was important, but it was the cultural spirit that drew me in and kept me engaged.

My dear friend, Rabbi Steven Carr Reuben, and his friend, Jennifer Hanin, wrote this book, *Becoming Jewish*. And if anyone is thinking of doing so . . . Again, rather than hear me attempt to wax poetic on the subject, simply call Steven's cell. It's 310 . . . I have just been edited again. A good time to wish you well with whatever your spiritual and religious path is. It has been an honor to write this foreword for someone in my life that I treasure. Rabbi Steven Carr Reuben. His driver's license number is—

Acknowledgments

Becoming Jewish: The Challenges, Rewards, and Paths to Conversion evolved to give you (the convert) a gutsy guide to enter the tribe. It outlines the many paths to Judaism so you can avoid mismatched expectations and instead identify the denomination that best suits your life. You wouldn't choose a partner with tentacles and fins, so why bank on a movement that's as foreign to you as intergalactic space travel? Remember, each path is lined with plenty of challah, holidays, community, and God, so you can't go wrong as long as the level of observance works for you.

First, a world of thanks goes to our outstanding literary agent, Linda Konner, who connected us from the start. I can't say enough about her foresight, thoughtfulness, and expertise. Thank you, Linda, for doing what you do so well.

Our book would not be what it is today without invaluable insights from individuals who have touched our lives in many ways. Accolades go to Bob Saget for writing such a brilliant foreword. Many thanks also go to comedian Yisrael Campbell for allowing us to highlight one of his hard-earned conversion insights. Special thanks go to Rabbi Steven Morgan, Cantor Diane Dorf, and Rabbi Brian Strauss with Congregation Beth Yeshurun; Rabbi Richard Steinberg with Congregation Shir Ha-Ma'alot; Rabbi Dov Fischer with Young Israel; and Rabbi Drew Kaplan with Beach Hillel.

Loads of thanks go to editor, Sarah Stanton, and editorial assistant Jin Yu with Rowman & Littlefield, and everyone else contributing their time or talent to this labor of love. Their attention to detail and enthusiastic support and ideas made our book even better.

Heartfelt appreciation goes to Adam Hanin for spending countless hours reviewing chapters, generating illustrations, creating graphs, providing translations, and cheering us on every step of the way.

A warm embrace to Didi Carr Reuben for her constant love and support.

Most of all, our book would not be the same without the courageous converts who shared their personal stories. While we vowed to protect their anonymity and thanked them privately, they know who they are. They were humble, forthcoming, and generous enough to let others travel their path and see how they took the driver's seat. Their experiences are rich, compelling, and unique, and shed light on the multitude of issues that tug at the hearts of converts everywhere.

Introduction: The Inspiration for *Becoming Jewish*

Judaism first piqued my interest when, as a Catholic born-and-raised twenty-something, I bought a book called *The Jewish Book of Why* by Alfred J. Kolatch. At the time, I was working full time, dating a "holiday-only" Jew, attending graduate school, and searching for answers on how I could build a personal relationship with God.

Like lots of busy people, my life remained on autopilot until several forces collided to catapult me out of my comfort zone. One of the forces was a mother at my twins' nursery school. The other was a poorly timed holiday party. The third was none other than Mel Gibson. Let me start with the latter.

I had seen every *Lethal Weapon* movie and had always been a fan. Two years into my marriage, I even persuaded my Jewish husband to watch all four movies with me, making Adam a fast Gibson fan too. But my heart sank the day the 2006 story broke about Gibson's antisemitic tirade. Still technically Catholic, I stopped being a Gibson fan. Whether his rant was alcohol-induced or not, I felt betrayed.

Four months later, the secular nursery school our twins attended planned a holiday party. Usually, we would have been wildly supportive of this event until Sari, a Jewish mother, confided that she was offended the school planned a holiday party on the first night of Chanukah. My body tensed listening to the insensitivity I could no longer ignore, and I quickly became just as incensed as Sari. I emailed the director of Hearts Home at Bright Horizons as soon as I arrived home, letting her know that planning a holiday party on the first night of Chanukah was culturally and religiously insensitive.

As far as we were concerned, the timing of this party insulted Jews in the same way that Christians would take offense if the school planned the party on Christmas Eve or Muslims during Eid. All of these dates hold religious significance, and it would be offensive to suggest otherwise. Yet the school did it without much thought. This incident brought up a question: "Why did the school director and her planning committee totally disregard Chanukah?"

While the director claimed the poorly planned party was nothing more than a scheduling oversight, for my family it was the start of a religious refuge. During the initial conversation with Sari, she invited our family to a Chanukah puppet show at her synagogue. I told Adam it might be nice to visit a local synagogue (this would be a first for our twins and me), and the puppet show would be fun for our three-year-olds. Adam agreed.

We arrived at the *Shabbat yachad* (young-family service) at Beth Yeshurun in Houston, Texas, on December 15, 2007, and loved what we saw. Children were singing and dancing, parents were smiling and joining in, and an animated woman with a mane of hair led songs with a joyful heart. It was easy to determine this wasn't the puppet show Sari spoke of, but that didn't matter. My family had experienced a difficult year. For the first time, after losing three loved ones, as well as a family-owned business, and living in two states, three cities, and four houses, we finally felt at home.

I have always believed nothing in life is accidental, and stumbling into Beth Yeshurun was no exception. The people, the place—the warmth was extraordinary. The present we received that night compelled us to come back each *Shabbat*. And the impact it had on my life and that of our family is exactly what compelled me to champion a book that will impart insider's tips to those interested in Judaism.

Speaking to Rabbi Steven Carr Reuben helped me realize he was the right person to partner with on this book. While our agent first connected us, I soon learned we shared the same philosophies. One of the concerns when converting is that most converts want to stay deeply connected to family and friends who are not Jewish. I wanted to make sure that while I observed Jewish holidays with my family, my non-Jewish family felt comfortable inviting us to celebrate their holidays and vice versa. It was clear from Steven's ongoing work with interfaith families that he understood these concerns and knew just how important it is to keep ties to the past.

This book can enrich your journey into Judaism, but it is not a tool to persuade anyone to convert. Our objective is to deliver a book that gives insights into every facet of conversion to those who have already chosen to convert. There are many tips you can learn from an author/rabbi who has helped countless converts and from a coauthor/convert who has mastered conversion with children, become an adult *bat mitzvah*, and experienced a vow renewal/ Jewish wedding.

Our goal is to deliver a practical book with insider information that demystifies a religion still somewhat shrouded in secrecy with expressions, gestures, practices, customs, rituals, and a language that dates back over four thousand years. To do that, we put ourselves in your shoes to deliver the book I would have liked to read prior to my conversion (and one that Steven would want to recommend to prospective converts). Our aim from the start is to give you a guide that covers the conversion process and cultural transition. We don't tackle Jewish history, and for good reason. Conversion rabbis recommend countless books on Jewish history that prompt classroom discussion about key milestones of the Jewish People. Just as the historical books help you make sense of the past, *Becoming Jewish* helps you maneuver the present the way only a good friend that converted could.

For many, converting follows falling in love with someone Jewish. This interest may also include giving your children a single religious identity. For some, the attraction to Judaism may not be clear yet. And for others, *Becoming Jewish* holds essential information to guide you through the conversion process or help others gain perspective into a loved one's new life path. Some come from deeply religious upbringings, while others come from little or no religious affiliation at all. Still others find that their adult beliefs are more compatible with Jewish beliefs. Whatever the reason, we commend you for choosing our book to gain insight into what will likely result in a rewarding journey of personal and spiritual growth.

Becoming Jewish allows you to go through the conversion process with peace of mind. The book serves as a personal guide to fill in the gaps by providing insights, tips, resources, and the most meaningful and rewarding experience possible. We have organized the book to take you (the convert) on a step-by-step process through material that is largely unknown to those entering a conversion class. Our objective is to close this void and deliver a book that gives you clarity on every facet of conversion. This challenge involved breaking down the conversion process into what you need to know to make the time spent between "almost" Jewish and officially Jewish a more enjoyable one.

From the start, we wanted to make this book as personal as possible. There is no doubt that Judaism's face has changed over the years. Some of your rabbis are male, while others are female. While we have done our best to alternate between genders, there may be times when we refer to your rabbi as being one gender when *your* rabbi is really the other. We know that some of our readers may be in same-sex relationships or may not have a partner at all. While we may talk about partners as male and female, our book holds value for people in every situation. Some Hebrew words have multiple spellings, like *bedeken* or *badeken*, *chupah* or *chuppah*, *Chanukah* or *Hanukah*, or even *God* or *G-d*. In the end, we had to choose which versions of words—translations from Torah, Talmud, and Midrash—to use and remain consistent throughout, so be flexible if you notice some are slightly different than what you or your loved ones use. Ultimately, rely on your rabbi to introduce you to translations that are more widely accepted by the sect/movement of Judaism you choose.

We have structured our book to make your journey into Judaism seamless. Chapter 1 opens by explaining the conversion process and why becoming Jewish is challenging. Subsequent chapters discuss choices you will have to make before, during, and after conversion. There is no doubt that anxiety over what the *bet din* (Jewish rabbinical court) will ask is so universal among converts that it made sense to split your conversion day into two chapters: "Facing the *Bet Din*" and "*Mikvah* and More."

Each chapter offers insider advice on a variety of issues you will encounter and ends with a summary to help you consider steps as you master each milestone. Throughout, chapters feature key life-cycle events where Judaism plays a huge role. Because you will want to incorporate Jewish traditions and values into many (if not all) facets of your life, we have dedicated a number of chapters to what it means to live Jewish throughout your life. Since *tikkun olam* (repairing the world), *tzedakah* (charitable giving), social justice, and Israel are important to Jews worldwide, we discuss these fundamental beliefs in depth. To help you learn terms faster, we have italicized uncommon non-English terms, and in most cases these words will become part of your new

Hebrew or Yiddish vocabulary. Visit our glossary for terms you need definitions on ASAP. All italicized words that are not in English are in Hebrew unless we note otherwise. The book ends on a high note. You never have to guess what Jewish expressions and greetings mean thanks to a comprehensive glossary of terms.

Finally, our introduction would be remiss without mentioning the converts whose lives we interwove into our book. Besides graciously agreeing to tell their personal stories, each shares the same goals we do: to save you time, energy, and anxiety.

While we acknowledge there is a range of worship experiences among converts and no two are exactly alike, we are fortunate to provide many quotes that show why a particular convert ultimately chose Judaism. Because feeling "at home" in your synagogue makes all the difference, we want to ensure you choose the right one the first time around. Whatever path you choose, we hope this book increases your appetite for Jewish knowledge, makes your journey worthwhile, and gives you the license to laugh along the way. Conversion is a serious business, but it doesn't mean you need to down two pots of coffee to wade through it.

—Jennifer S. Hanin, *Chava bat Avraham v' Sarah*

1

Finding New Meaning

א

Attending synagogue is not that much different from attending mass. Except that instead of counting bald heads most Sundays with my grade school friends, now I thank God for *kippot* (yarmulkes). I can safely say that I never experience dome-inspired boredom since becoming Jewish. In fact, instead of staving off yawns, creating a mental to-do list, or playing mindless games, now I am surrounded by a philosophy that I embrace and a culture I enjoy, not to mention a sea of colors and patterns.

Jest aside, it's not the *kippot* that drove me to Judaism (although I'm all for it from a fashion perspective) but my childhood beliefs that no longer felt true to me. And I am not alone. There are many reasons to convert to Judaism. Just ask any of the two-hundred-thousand-plus Jews by choice in America. But there is one universal truth binding anyone reading *Becoming Jewish*—the search for new meaning. Finding new meaning will become evident as you explore the multifaceted aspects of what it means to become Jewish, including family, religion, *halachah* (Jewish law), culture, history, community, and so much more. (Jennifer Hanin)

The path to Judaism is rewarding but by no means easy. While achieving your conversion isn't as gut-wrenching as auditioning for *American Idol* (though the *bimah* may feel every bit like a stage), it does require discipline and dedication, especially if your rabbi requires you to learn Hebrew. Like running a marathon, training and preparation help you avoid potholes that some on the same path report. For instance, have you ever worried whether you would retain enough to pass a final? Ever flown overseas and felt pressure to speak the language? Ever had the hand-wringing experience of wondering whether a group of coworkers or in-laws accept you? Ever wonder if your loved ones will alienate you for your newfound belief? Ever fear the day when fellow Jews expect you to eat gefilte fish? That begins to sum up the challenges you face when converting to Judaism. But don't worry. This book can help you overcome all of these unknowns and more by guiding you step-by-step through the process. And about the gefilte fish? Get a dog.

MAKING THE TRANSITION

For Jennifer, making the transition from Catholic to Jew wasn't so hard. In fact, there are many similarities. The pope wears a yarmulke. There's lots of guilt. Family is a central focus. Food—lots of food—we're not saying it's good food, but there's plenty of it. Confession is present, but much more efficient; instead of going weekly, now it's annually—Yom Kippur. A good part of the formality feels familiar. Jennifer once asked her Catholic friend Beth what it was like attending synagogue with her Jewish husband; she replied, "It's just like a really upbeat mass minus Jesus." Beth couldn't have been more right.

A good way to approach converting is like anything else. Be prepared. Start by making room for all the new material your rabbi will ask you to cover. You'll also want to keep a journal, notebook, or personal computer handy to jot down thoughts or questions that arise throughout your conversion. Dedicating a file drawer plus a shelf or two for all the new books and articles you will read is highly recommended. This will keep you organized and acquaint you with Judaism and its rich history. Soon you will not only have the beginnings of what will be your Jewish library but also that of your future generations to come.

We had a significant number of Jews in my Masonic lodge, and I started talking to them about what Judaism meant for them, how they experienced it growing up, and how it dealt with many of the fundamental problems I had with Christianity. And it really felt more like home. I mean if you go back and look at most Christian hymnals, the music, the service, and the entire ritual is kind of a downer. Temple isn't like that. Bringing out the Torah feels like a celebration. One quote that has always stuck with me is a line delivered by Salma Hayek's character, Serendipity, in the movie *Dogma* (1999): "I have issues with anyone who treats faith as a burden instead of a blessing. You people don't celebrate your faith, you mourn it." (Chris, thirty-three, IT director)

WHAT DEFINES A JEW?

A descendant of an Israelite? A nationality? An ethnicity? A descendant of Jacob? A fan of Adam Sandler? A person claiming cultural or ancestral connection to Jewish People? Yes to all—but don't forget converts. Jewish converts have made far-reaching contributions to Judaism. Take Ruth, for example. She is one of the most well-known and well-respected converts and holds a high place in Jewish literature as the grandmother of King David, the most famous Jewish king (see page 124).

Likewise, the father of the most famous sage of the Talmud, Rabbi Akiva, converted. Some well-known converts from outside the Mediterranean include Khazars, Edomites, and Ethiopians, as well as many Arabs, particularly those in Yemen. Today, converting still puts you in a well-respected pool of people. Converts to Judaism in recent years include celebrities such as Elizabeth Banks, Isla Fisher, Ivanka Trump, Kate Capshaw, Marilyn Monroe, Elizabeth Taylor, and Sammy Davis Jr., as well as news personalities such as Campbell Brown, John King, Connie Chung, Mary Hart, Dr. Laura Schlesinger, and many others. Madonna? Hmmm . . . (see chapter 15).

In the past, *halachah* (Jewish law) defined a Jew as a person born of a Jewish mother. That has since changed, and those who convert and promise to believe in the most central belief of Judaism—God is one—can ultimately choose to be Jewish. This central belief is the *Shema*. Similar to Arabic, Farsi, and too many other languages to list, we read the *Shema* and any other prayers, songs, or texts in Hebrew from right to left:

The Shema

Hear, O Israel: The Lord our God, the Lord is one. (Deut 6:4)

Figure 1.1

There are a few other promises you will need to make as a convert, such as raising your children Jewish, obeying God's commandments (for example, honoring the Sabbath), and giving *tzedakah* (charity), but for the most part the key adherence is the belief that God is one. In fact, the first four commandments focus on this very theme: "Have no other gods before me" (see page 28). This alone validates the notion that God is one (not many). Besides using the word *Adonai* in place of the word *God*, some go as far as to print *G-d* to show respect and avoid taking God's name in vain. Spotting the words *Adonai*, *G-d*, or the *Shema* puts you a few steps ahead of most when entering *shul* (Yiddish for "synagogue" or "temple") for the first time.

WHY IS CULTURE SO IMPORTANT?

Most have heard Jews referred to as the "Jewish People," the "People of Israel," or the "Children of Israel," and possibly even have heard a reference to the "tribe." All indicate a unique identity and the notion of belonging to a group (see chapter 2). So just why is culture so important? Well, we would have to roll the history books back over four thousand years to show you a definitive pattern. But outside of visiting the nearest Holocaust museum (see Resources), the answer is simple. Groups all over the world have persecuted Jews for thousands of years, long before the Holocaust, a tragedy that is memorialized in museums worldwide of the lost hopes and dreams of six million Jews, as well as five million non-Jews, at the hands of the Nazis.

Continued persecution of Jews for centuries called for drastic measures. Emphasis on marrying fellow Jews, keeping kosher (see page 122), and observing the Sabbath and a host of High Holy Days and other holidays kept Jews in close proximity with other Jews, which incidentally helped preserve the bloodline. As our society became more mobile, organizations like the Anti-Defamation League gained prominence and lawmakers passed antidiscrimination laws. These events changed the face of Jewish families worldwide, making it more the norm to intermarry with non-Jews.

Reflecting upon my background as an adult, I recognize that I was fortunate enough to grow up in a very Jewish community and my best friends were all Jewish. My parents were divorced, and my family life was splintered, so I spent much of my time with my Jewish friends. My best friend for years during my adolescence was Rebecca, who came from a devout Jewish family. I spent much of my time with her, and

I recall every Friday her family observed the tradition of family *Shabbat* dinners. She would reluctantly participate, and I would join them regularly, as she and I were inseparable. For Rebecca, it was a dreaded ritual; however, for me it was a welcomed sense of family, a sense of tradition and belonging, and I always appreciated how her family welcomed me to be a part of it. (Renee, thirty-five, real-estate agent)

WHY CONVERT?

Marriage, raising children, and finding the right philosophy are some of the top reasons people give for converting to Judaism. Matzah ball soup is another. But while some rabbis (Reconstructionist or Reform) will marry interfaith couples, others (Conservative or Orthodox) won't. Many synagogues will not consider a couple Jewish if the non-Jewish partner does not convert. Chances are if you have decided to marry a Jew, you'll want to discuss your options regarding religion up front. Disagreeing on religion has not only put nations at war but also divided many would-be couples.

So what are your options? The easiest and perhaps emptiest choice is no religion whatsoever. Another choice is opting for one partner's religion over the other. There is a high probability if your partner grew up in an observant Jewish home, he will want you to convert. Some couples may opt for a slightly different but somewhat familiar experience and choose the mystical arm of Judaism—Kabbalah—or a philosophical religion like Buddhism. But the majority will vie for Judaism because it has such strong cultural ties to Jewish identity. That is just how powerful the Jewish community is for those who hold fond memories of their family's observance.

Many of the rules that I learned in Christianity, especially those enforced in my family, best fit in two statements: "Treat others the way you want to be treated" and "Life is not meant to be enjoyed, just suffered for the reward after death." While "The Golden Rule" made sense to my young brain, I couldn't believe that the gift of life was off limits to those who wish to live joyfully and responsibly. I also didn't feel the need for any go-between in my relationship to the creative and moral force called God. Jesus may have been a rabbi in his time, but he was also a child of God like the rest of us. (Judith, sixties, artist)

WHAT IS INVOLVED?

Eating bagels? Listening to Matisyahu? Shopping at Neiman's or Saks? Not so fast. Think books, and typically classroom participation along with a time commitment that runs as short as eighteen weeks or as long as eighteen months or more. Your rabbi will provide a list of books that cover most of the historical background of Judaism that we will only refer to occasionally in this book.

Think history. You will learn about some of the defining figures in Judaism like Moses, Maimonides, Ruth, David, and Esther, along with geographical markers of importance like Jerusalem, Masada, the West Bank, and the Dead Sea. Prepare to learn about the great Jewish-Roman war, the siege of Jerusalem, Jewish slavery in Rome and Egypt, the Holocaust, Israel, the Israeli-Palestinian conflict, *tzedakah* (charity), *halachah*, observance, *chavurot* (fellowship), social justice, *tikkun olam* (repairing the world), and much more.

Some say this is a big commitment, and they are correct. But some things in life are only worthwhile once much effort is put forth. Conversion is among them. The satisfaction that new Jews report after conversion completely outweighs the time they spent prepping for it. Many describe it as an extraordinary experience of personal and spiritual growth. Chances are good that your experience will be equally joyful.

While many people begin by taking a class, the primary experience of becoming Jewish rests upon private study with a rabbi. Candidates who are interested in conversion meet with a rabbi privately outside of class on multiple occasions. The content and duration of these meetings depend on the rabbi's requirements and the student's level of commitment. A student's conversion can only move forward once a rabbi determines that the student is ready to undergo the ritual elements of conversion.

Jewish tradition generally requires *mikvah* (ritual immersion) for men and women (not together, of course) and circumcision or ritual circumcision (drawing a drop of blood from an already circumcised foreskin) for men. Ouch! But don't let this scare you. Bikini waxing far outweighs any pain men might feel when receiving this ritual. Converts also meet with a *bet din*, which means "house of law." The *bet din* is a Jewish court that usually consists of three rabbis who examine the candidate's knowledge of Judaism and reasons for conversion. Keep in mind that not all liberal rabbis require their students to participate in every ritual, but the tendency is to perform all in some form.

CHOOSING A HEBREW NAME

For some, choosing a Hebrew name might seem odd. For others, it's no different than when a Catholic chooses a confirmation name, a rapper chooses a

street name, or an actor chooses a stage name. But considering that your Hebrew name is essential at three major stages of your life—conversion, marriage, and death—like the American Express black card, it carries clout.

This means you'll want to give careful consideration when choosing your
name. The Internet has plenty of sites where you can peruse Hebrew names,
learn their meanings, and select one that best fits you as a new Jew. There
are no rules for picking names. The only criterion that matters is that you're
comfortable with the name you choose. Converts choose names for all types
of reasons. Some choose names based on meaning; others choose names
based on pronunciation; still others choose names based on how they view
themselves.

There's plenty of time to choose your Hebrew name as your rabbi won't ask
for it until a few weeks before your class ends; however, the sooner you go
down this path the better. Since part of converting means developing a Jewish
identity, the sooner you identify with your Hebrew name, the easier the transition will be for you. Chances are good if you determine your Hebrew name
early, you will be ahead in the process both emotionally and psychologically.
Regardless of the criteria you use or when you choose it, the result should be
the same: a name that you're comfortable with and can wear with ease. For
instance, male Hebrew names like Moron, Tuwbal, or Dudu might not be the
wisest choice. One of the quickest ways to find a name that sticks is avoiding
those that stink.

While you have less control over last names (remember the movie *Meet the
Fockers*?), you do have final say over the Hebrew first name you select. But
while funny in a movie theater or on stage with a stand-up, a comical Hebrew
name is something you might not want to wear your entire life. Now, if you
feel that expressing a lighter side of your personality is essential, and you're a
Star Wars fan and a guy, there's still hope: Yoda is a Hebrew name.

While your Hebrew name won't replace your birth name, it is your official
Jewish name. The name you choose will likely only make an appearance at
major life events that involve you or your family and possibly on a few related
occasions like when your rabbi honors you with an *aliyah* (reciting a blessing
over the Torah). Nonetheless, your Hebrew name defines your Jewish identity,
and it should be a source of pride. Since a full Hebrew name includes your
parents' names, most converts get "adopted" by the first Jewish family when
converting, and their Hebrew parents become Abraham and Sarah.

GETTING STARTED

Conversion courses are an involved, albeit gradual, process that ranks right up there with exchanging vows or having a baby. Hard timetables won't apply as conversion is self-paced and your rabbi determines when you're ready. But not to worry. All rabbis are Jewish scholars and experts in Jewish law. Who better to oversee your conversion?

A rabbi's goal during conversion is to teach you the important aspects of Judaism and its history and confirm that you're on track. He will meet with you as needed to assure that you're comfortable with your progress. Your rabbi will have heard it all before, so feel free to ask him any question that comes to mind. Always let your rabbi know if you need more clarification or are experiencing any issue that might impede your studies. There are no wrong questions or situations. But he can only help you if he knows that you need it.

Once your class wraps up, your rabbi will assess whether you have demonstrated enough knowledge of Judaism to convert. He will want to know that you are committed to learning and upholding the teachings of the Torah (the five "Books of Moses") as well as the philosophies, beliefs, and practices of Judaism.

Your rabbi may encourage you to share your feelings and attitudes about becoming Jewish. Sharing your thoughts on this important life-step should relieve the uneasiness that can accompany practicing different rituals and philosophies than you did in your youth. Mastering your conversion will require you to make a commitment while developing patience, a desire to learn, a sense of humor, and the ability to ask tough questions.

Born Jews take a lifetime to master Judaism—and some never do. Try to be patient with yourself and your progress. No one expects perfection. Persistence, determination, and sincerity are the keys to getting through the process. Many converts buddy up with a classmate or two or organize informal study groups to discuss classroom lessons. Others prefer to study solo from the list of books that each class follows.

Keep in mind that the house of Israel is open to any who choose to enter it. In fact, part of the Midrash (the Jewish commentary on the Hebrew scriptures, written between 400 and 1200 CE) says that all Jewish souls were at Mount Sinai at the giving of the Torah and that converts to Judaism are those lost Jewish souls who have found their way back. Others believe that converts may have a Jewish relative somewhere in their bloodline. Either may explain why so many converts are unable to explain their strong attraction to Judaism and its people.

> I am Brazilian, and I moved to Florida in 1990. Luckily, I had the opportunity to live with a wonderful family—the Cohens—and felt an instant connection, one that I just couldn't explain. In fact, I felt such a strong sense of belonging that was missing in Brazil that I could not help but try to understand it. So I enrolled in school nine months later, began to learn the language and customs, and kept my feelings to myself.
>
> A decade later, I was running an art gallery and custom framing shop and a dear friend and customer confided in me about her wedding preparation and conversion process. That gave me the push to begin a conversion class.
>
> Two months after I completed my conversion, I called my cousin who had a fiancé in Israel. I told her that we could speak Hebrew soon because I was learning little by little after completing my Jewish conversion. Then she asked, "Why did you do that?" I answered with a pause. She quickly filled the silence, "We are Jewish from our paternal grandmother: the Correas from Spain. And where you are, it's the Cohens." (Marcia, fifties, business owner)

RABBI SHOPPING

Shopping for a rabbi is a lot tougher than finding that perfect pair of jeans. So where do you start? Referrals from friends are especially insightful. In this situation, it's best to ask those capable of giving you open and honest information: Jewish friends. Whether you know someone personally or have a Jewish acquaintance, don't hesitate to ask for a recommendation. You wouldn't buy a home or buy a new car without getting input from people. Why take a chance on a rabbi without hearing from those who can give you a sound opinion? Other options include contacting a local board of rabbis or other Jewish group such as a Jewish Community Center (JCC), skimming your telephone directory or Internet white pages for synagogues, or contacting one of the four Jewish denominations (see Resources).

Trying to find a rabbi on the Internet is not so easy. Unlike the barrage of "find a doctor" websites, you're more likely to find blogs, stories, rants, or jokes when surfing for a rabbi rather than a site of substance, though many are finding their way to Twitter and Facebook. Scouting out your local synagogues is a great place to start. Once you locate one, your best bet is to make an appointment for conversion information or speak with a conversion rabbi to discuss next steps. It's worthwhile to note that appointments are necessary as most synagogues take the threat of antisemitism seriously and as a result maintain tight security. Once there, you'll learn the synagogue's individual conversion requirements. Remember, it's essential to focus on your spiritual needs rather than on the process.

Before signing up for a class, you might consider interviewing a rabbi. Ask her if you can talk to others who have converted through her efforts. This is no different from talking to a college professor about her course material or interviewing a potential boss about a position that interests you. The difference is that, unlike a job, becoming a Jew is a lifetime commitment. This is why you want to be sure that you're converting for the right reasons. The ideal situation occurs when you decide on your own to convert without coercion from anyone else. Wanting to take this meaningful path will help you integrate Judaism and its values, ethics, laws, traditions, and wisdom into your everyday life.

FINDING COMMUNITY ONLINE

There has never been an easier time to let your fingers do the walking when you need information than with the array of computers, notebooks, tablets, and mobile phones available today. About 139 million consumers already do. But when you're surfing for synagogues, rabbis, and congregations, how can you find reliable information? Ideally, you'll want to start with official sites of organizations that oversee each movement (see Resources).

These sites can provide an overview of the movement, up-to-date information about its beliefs, and advice on how to find synagogues in your area. Most have zip code locators to make this a cinch. Be wary of sites that discredit, bash, or mislead you about Judaism. Unfortunately, some websites claim to represent Jews when they instead offer misinformation and practice conflicting beliefs. Gaining information from respected authorities, confirming credentials, and verifying references is the quickest way to bypass bogus sites when searching for potential spiritual homes.

One site that you won't want to miss is BecomingJewishBook.com. We created it to add value to your journey and have included numerous resources, daily Torah readings, additional updates, and an "Ask the Rabbi" section so you can gain answers to your questions and share information with others. We also created a *Becoming Jewish* Facebook page to give you an instant online community with converts worldwide.

THE RIGHT RABBI FOR YOU

Ideally, you'll want to identify traits in a rabbi that make you feel most at ease. This means finding an ordained rabbi in the movement of your choice that is able to devote time to guide you through your conversion and answer all your questions. Anyone who has ever had a subpar instructor tasked with guiding them through a project, research course, thesis, or dissertation knows just how important it is to find a first-rate mentor. It is helpful if he can consistently challenge you to learn more and advance your knowledge of Judaism.

Depending on the synagogue you choose, finding the ideal rabbi might not be so difficult. Some synagogues have made this easier by employing several rabbis and designating each for specific roles. For instance, synagogues serving large congregations may have a rabbi for conversions, one for youth services, and one as the senior rabbi, as well as one or more cantors (ordained leaders trained in Jewish music).

Keep in mind that rabbis are the gatekeepers of Judaism. Because Judaism is not a proselytizing religion, rabbis are selective and conscientious when it comes to conversions and only convert those that are sincere and ready in all respects. Knowing your intent is heartfelt is helpful to all before making an initial appointment with a rabbi. Once you have narrowed your options, you'll want to visit the synagogue and rabbi several times before deciding if they are a compatible match.

I grew up like many in the United States. I came from a middle-class family that made ends meet but did not have the wherewithal to be extravagant. Neither of my parents were particularly religious, and I had a fairly secular childhood until I started school. My mother wanted to give me the best education she could, so she put me in a private school that happened to be Episcopal. The education was great, although my teachers did not appreciate my inquisitive nature. I learned the usual: math, science, French, and English. But when it came to my religious studies class, things took a turn. They did not have an appropriate respect for the concept of "why."

When I asked, "If God only created Adam and Eve, and they only had three sons, where did the women come from to marry Adam's descendants?" or when I asked, "If *all* of us were really descended from the same two people, wouldn't that make us all inbred?" they did not really care for that. More importantly, they did not have an answer either, and I ended up leaving the school. That has been a common theme for me. But when I asked a rabbi why, he'd say, "I don't know. Let's figure it out together." That was really it for me. It sounds bizarrely cliché given the climate we're in, but Judaism offered me a way to reconcile the scientific side of my brain with the religious side. (Chris, thirty-three, IT director)

JEWISH DENOMINATIONS

Deciding what denomination to choose is not that difficult for most. Converts that wish to follow Jewish doctrine more strictly and join a synagogue that offers more services in Hebrew will likely choose either the Orthodox or Conservative movement. Those that wish to follow Jewish doctrine less strictly will likely choose the Reconstructionist or Reform movement. It's worth noting that the differences between Orthodox and Reform Jews are not that much different from liberal and conservative Catholics or Baptists.

While countries in the Diaspora (outside the Land of Israel) recognize multiple Jewish movements, the Israeli government only recognizes those belonging to the Orthodox branch. This probably won't present a concern unless you plan to live in Israel, where synagogues and the life-cycle activities widely available are all Orthodox. It's wise to explore each movement before choosing the one you want to embrace since each has its own philosophy, unique conversion requirements, and level of recognition.

Finding your religious home might be easy if you have fallen in love with a Jew who belongs to a synagogue. This may only present a problem if you find that you're uncomfortable with that particular movement. If you find yourself in this situation, it's a good idea to address it head-on. Talk with your love interest and to a rabbi in the movement that you most feel comfortable with, and see if there is a way to become Jewish in a movement that you can both live with.

While each movement has its own merits and varies slightly according to philosophy and interpretation, they are close enough that wiggle room isn't out of the question. It may be harder for an Orthodox Jew to adhere to the Reform movement or vice versa, but other than that, there shouldn't be too much discomfort in meeting in the middle. After all, leaving a faith behind is a big deal. Compared to that, trying a slightly different denomination in the same faith shouldn't be a showstopper. If it is, then it's time to rethink the compatibility of the relationship. Compromise needs to occur from both partners if a relationship is ever to be equal.

If you have already joined a synagogue, then feel free to skip ahead. It's important to know that synagogues in the same movement do not always offer the same feeling of "home" in different states or cities. Jennifer converted through a Conservative synagogue in Texas, yet the same movement didn't appeal to her family when they relocated to California. Others she interviewed reported the same thing. Again, it's key that you're honest with yourself about what you're looking for when it comes to religion. Those that feel strongly about following Judaism verbatim should follow their hearts. Others that want to worship and celebrate as a Jew but realize that their lifestyle, career, or values prevent them from strict observance should follow a less restrictive form of Judaism like Conservative, Reform, or Reconstructionist.

We wouldn't expect you to change your life to accommodate a religion but rather to find one that compliments your belief structure and lifestyle. After all, the majority of US Jews follow Judaism in a less restrictive way (Reform), while others need something in the middle (Conservative), and still others view Judaism as a progressively evolving civilization (Reconstructionism). We have outlined each movement so you can get an idea of what each stands for and where you fit in. We do recommend that you visit individual synagogues of the movements that interest you as the philosophy and overall comfort level varies across movements and even individual synagogues. Chances are good that nontraditional families will seek out Reform or Reconstructionist temples, for both encourage women to serve as clergy and embrace gay, lesbian, bisexual, and transgendered (GLBT) communities, whereas more traditional values are upheld in Conservative and Orthodox movements.

Orthodox

If you're considering Orthodox Judaism, then you're in store for a number of life changes. Besides following strict *kashrut* (dietary) laws, your rabbi will expect you to observe all thirty-nine *Shabbat* laws that come with it (see appendix 1). You'll also need to figure out which stream of Orthodoxy works for you: *Haredi* (also *Charedi* or *Chareidi*) Judaism (often referred to as Ultra-Orthodox) or Modern Orthodox. Many within the movement frown upon these terms as negative forms of labeling coined by the media. For instance, the term *Orthodox* is North American, whereas *observant* or *nonobservant* are terms the remainder of the world uses to describe levels of Jewish observance. The thought is that the term *ultra* is a way of saying "too rigid," and the term *modern* is a way of saying "better." While our society applies labels to differentiate, you'll want to bypass labels and focus instead on the path that's right for you.

Haredi Judaism

Throw all your designer duds and worldly possessions away if you're considering becoming *Haredi*. Modesty defines this stream of Judaism as most men are in black suits, beards, and wide-brimmed black hats. Women don long skirts, long sleeves, and high necklines, as well as some form of head covering if married, such as scarves, snoods, *shpitzelach* (headgear), hats, or *sheitels* (wigs). What unites *Haredi* besides their sixteenth-century attire is their steadfast reverence for the Torah, both the Written and the Oral Law, as the main determining factor in all aspects of life. Most don't embrace the secular world the way other movements do. Among *Haredi* Jews, there are two streams of spiritual and cultural Orthodox orientations: *Hasidic* and Lithuanian-*Yeshiva* from Eastern Europe, and Oriental Sephardic *Haredim*.

Modern Orthodox

This stream of Orthodoxy hails from Western Europe and follows strict observance of Jewish laws but embraces the secular world. For instance, Modern Orthodox will attend secular universities, go to movies, take in a plays or musicals, or attend sporting events. They participate fully in modern society yet remain Torah-observant because the benefits of doing both far outweigh the risks.

Modern Orthodox Jews are Zionists and hold a high national and religious regard for Israel and its people. Modern Orthodox Jews engage with those who are non-Orthodox in outreach efforts benefiting Israel and even participate in organizational and institutional cooperation. It's common to see Modern Orthodox give public lectures and televised interviews, submit articles to magazines/journals, publish books and/or blogs, or even maintain websites. Essentially, the only fundamental beliefs that separate the Modern Orthodox from other movements is that they, like *Haredi* (and Walter in *The Big Lebowski*), are *shomer Shabbos* (they follow all the commandments of the Sabbath literally, including *kashrut*).

Either your rabbi will likely mention the laws in class, or you'll read about it and ask. In Jennifer's conversion class, most of her classmates were interested in the law that pertains to tearing. There was good reason for this as toilet paper (and even paper towels) fall into this category by way of perforation. If you're considering an Orthodox conversion, you will need to have a sizeable amount of tissues or commercial pretorn toilet paper on hand. Luckily, there is a company that specializes in this product. There are also websites that offer tips on how to obey each law and advice on when you can disregard one (see Resources). To view the complete list of "work" activities prohibited on *Shabbat*, see appendix 1.

Reform

Reform Judaism believes that while preserving traditions is important, longevity depends on introducing innovation. Other criteria include embracing diversity while asserting commonality, affirming beliefs without rejecting those who doubt, and bringing faith to sacred texts without sacrificing critical scholarship. Reform Jews believe that all people were created in the image of God. The movement affirms the central tenets of Judaism—God, Torah, and Israel—even as it acknowledges the diversity of Reform Jewish beliefs and practices. Rabbi Isaac Mayer Wise is credited with founding the synagogue arm of the Reform Movement in 1873, and the Union for Reform Judaism oversees the movement.

Reform Jews believe in inclusion and unbiased equality rather than exclusion. The movement believes everyone is special and has something to offer the community. The Reform movement recognizes patrilineal descent and is committed to absolute equality of women in all areas of Jewish life. Of all movements, Reform Judaism was the first to ordain women rabbis, invest in women cantors, and elect women as synagogue presidents. The movement welcomes gays and lesbians fully in synagogue life as well as society at large.

Tikkun olam is an important part of being a Reform Jew, as is encouraging Jews by choice and interfaith families to embrace Judaism, do *mitzvot*, and become *mensches*. Reform Jews consider children Jewish if they have a Jewish mother or father so long as the children are raised Jewish. The movement has a fair amount of Hebrew in its services, yet typically includes transliterated texts for non-Hebrew speakers. The Reform movement is now the largest Jewish movement in North America, with more than nine hundred congregations and 1.5 million people (see Resources). Reform synagogues accept nontraditional families, interfaith families, and conversions from all other movements.

Conservative

The Conservative movement came about as a moderate choice between Orthodox and Reform Judaism. It combines a positive attitude toward modern culture while conserving traditional elements of Judaism, including encouraging Torah study, preserving Hebrew as the language of prayer, observing *Shabbat*, and maintaining strong ties to Israel and her restoration, among others. Conservative Judaism believes that scholarly study of Jewish texts indicates that Judaism continues to evolve to meet the needs of the Jewish People in varying circumstances, and that a central *halachic* authority can continue this evolution. Conservative synagogues recognize Orthodox conversions and acknowledge conversions from other movements on a case-by-case basis. You'll want to see if the synagogue you choose has additional conversion requirements. Many Conservative synagogues accept interfaith families as long as children are brought up Jewish.

Founded in 1913 by Dr. Solomon Schecter, the United Synagogue of Conservative Judaism oversees seven hundred affiliated Conservative congregations in North America (see Resources). Most have a considerable amount of Hebrew in their services and vary according to their expectations—some are closer to Orthodox, where most women wear head coverings, and others are more like Reconstructionist or Reform, where most women don't.

As a Conservative Jew, action is encouraged. Your rabbi will encourage you to get involved, to make a difference and not follow the crowd. He might encourage you to add a new *mitzvah*, do more *tikkun olam*, or find opportunities to recite *berachot* (blessings), or even work toward observing *kashrut*. Other ways to contribute are to participate in social justice programs, give *tzedakah* regularly, volunteer for homeless shelters, or make *bikur cholim* (visiting the sick) a habit.

Reconstructionist

Reconstructionism believes Judaism exists for people—people don't exist for Judaism. While the movement is rooted in Jewish tradition, it evolves to meet people's needs. As a Reconstructionist, you would reject the idea of a supernatural God who "chose" the Jewish People. The movement's founder, Mordechai Kaplan, views "chosenness" as a "vocation." In other words, the movement believes that Jews were not "chosen from all other peoples" but were called to do God's work.

Reconstructionist Judaism is a modern American-based Jewish movement that views Judaism as a progressively evolving civilization reflecting peoplehood, community, history, the arts, and ethics. Founded in 1955, the Jewish Reconstructionist Federation (JRF) oversees the Reconstructionist movement, serving more than one hundred congregations and *chavurot* across North America.

The Reconstructionist movement was the first to endorse the idea of patrilineal descent and recognize a child as Jewish if his or her father is Jewish as long as the child embraces a Jewish identity. As a result, Reconstructionist congregations are egalitarian, inclusive, and welcoming to interfaith and nontraditional families. Unlike other movements, *halachah* is not considered binding but is treated as a valuable cultural remnant that should be upheld unless there is a valid reason not to (see Resources). Reconstructionism accepts conversions from all other movements.

DO YOU NEED TO LEARN HEBREW?

All converts are welcome to learn Hebrew. In fact, knowing the language will open more doors later since there will be times when others greet you in Hebrew or a rabbi speaks it during services. Speaking it will help you make friends quicker since you'll be able to communicate in the language that many born Jews know conversationally. Consider attending a service on *Shabbat*. The two traditional sayings that a Jew might greet you with are *"Shabbat shalom"* (Hebrew for "Have a good Sabbath") or *"Good Shabbos"* (English/Yiddish for, well, "Have a good Sabbath"). If you reply back "Hello" or "Hi," it might not endear you to that congregant and may impede your ability to make friends or acquaintances because it indicates a lack of effort on your part (now you know how the French feel when faced with well-meaning Americans). Besides *Shabbat*, just about every holiday has its own traditional sayings in Hebrew that you will want to learn (see chapter 5).

But being required to know Hebrew depends on the movement you choose. Those converting into Conservative or Orthodox movements will absolutely have to know it. Those converting into Reconstructionist or Reform are encouraged to learn but are not necessarily required to master beginning Hebrew.

WILL YOUR CHILDREN NEED TO CONVERT?

Converts' children in Orthodox or Conservative congregations are required to go through their own conversion process. Commonly, daughters are present in the *mikvah* when their mothers are immersing themselves in the ritual bath. All are required to recite prayers (as long as the daughters are old enough to do so). Young boys are also required to immerse in the *mikvah* and recite prayers (if old enough) before being accompanied by either parent to the *hatafat dam brit* (circumcision for those already circumcised). Older children are required to meet with a rabbi to determine when they are ready to complete their conversion. Obviously, the process varies depending on the rabbi and the movement.

USING THIS BOOK

Mazel tov! By picking up this book, you've taken the first step in making Judaism your new spiritual home. When used often, this book can be an indispensible partner to help you through the process. Besides having eighteen chapters (a lucky number in Hebrew that stands for *chai*, or "life") and an extensive glossary, this book shares everything you need to know for a successful conversion.

For many, the experience is deeply rewarding and invigorating. Those that lack a support system can find valuable resources to deal with the wide range of emotions that occur with conversion (see chapter 3). Most can attest that conversion added a new dimension of richness to their life and report intensified feelings of love and closeness to family. Now take a few moments to enjoy the energy and commitment that you're bringing to the tribe. And let's get started.

CHAI NOTES

- There are more than two hundred thousand Jews by choice in America.
- Prepare by setting aside space for books and starting a journal.
- Some denominations of Judaism—Reform and Reconstructionist—recognize patrilineal descent (born of a Jewish father).
- The most central prayer of Judaism is the *Shema*—stressing that there is one God.
- Only Reconstructionist and Reform rabbis marry interfaith couples.
- Prepare to learn history, Jewish law, Jewish philosophies, and basic Hebrew in conversion class.
- Jewish tradition generally requires *mikvah* immersion for men and women and circumcision or ritual circumcision for men.

- Choosing a Hebrew name early will help you develop your Jewish identity faster.
- You are ready for conversion when your rabbi decides you are ready.
- Pick a synagogue and rabbi you feel most comfortable with when converting.
- The four primary denominations of Judaism are Orthodox, Reform, Conservative, and Reconstructionist.
- Children of converts in Orthodox and Conservative congregations will also have to convert.

2

Belonging vs. Believing

ב

One thing is certain about becoming Jewish. Soon you'll have two opinions on everything. In many cases, you'll even have a third. But seriously, your religious identity will undergo a transition, so you'll want to understand the process. Three *B*s sum it up: *believing*, *belonging*, and *behaving*.

BELIEF-BASED RELIGION

If you live in North America or any country greatly influenced by Western civilization, your religious identity likely evolved from a Christian mindset that emphasized *belief*. For example, Christians believe Jesus is the Son of God who died for their sins. If you grew up Christian, you probably learned about heaven and hell, sin and repentance, and the role that God plays in your salvation.

As an expression of your particular beliefs, you engaged in *behaviors* that reflect those beliefs. These include attending church services, celebrating holidays, taking communion if your denomination celebrates the Eucharist, and partaking in certain rituals that reflect your beliefs such as baptism, confirmation, and those related to marriage and death. Then you practiced those rituals, customs, and celebrations in a specific church or religious community. For instance, you may have felt a sense of *belonging* to a particular house of worship, like the Palisades Lutheran Church or the First Baptist Church of Houston or St. Patrick's Cathedral in New York City.

BELONGING-BASED RELIGION

The same concepts of *believing, behaving,* and *belonging* apply to Jewish iden-tity, except Jews value a slightly different order and importance. For Jews, identity does not spring from belief at all. Instead, what gives us identity is *belonging.* It's our sense of belonging to the Jewish People, being part of an ancient and extended spiritual family of Jews, that forms our primary sense of religious identity.

Judaism is a spiritual family that extends back in time to the matriarchs and patriarchs of the Torah. We trace our ancestors to Abraham, Isaac, and Jacob and to Sarah, Rebecca, Rachel, and Leah. Their children became the original twelve tribes of Israel. For nearly four thousand years, we have continued to be a family that new members have joined in one of three ways: they are born into it (Jews by birth), are adopted or convert into it (Jews by choice), or marry into it (Jews by association).

It's this sense of belonging to the Jewish People that is fundamental to all Jews and how most define themselves if asked to name the most important factor of their Jewish identity. This is why so many nonobservant Jews are still passionate about being Jewish. Just as you may skip church as a Christian, yet decorate a Christmas tree, exchange gifts, drink eggnog, hang lights, sing car-ols, and sit on Santa's lap. This is how most Jews experience their relationship to Judaism and the Jewish People.

Since *belonging* is what gives us the foundation of our religious identity, the *behaviors* of Judaism include acts like eating matzah on Passover or potato latkes on Chanukah, attending services on the High Holy Days, or fasting on Yom Kippur. Even speaking Yiddish is a behavior—*Oy gevalt!* All of these actions have meaning in Judaism and as a result strengthen our Jewish identity. Simply put, behaving reinforces and strengthens be-longing.

For most Jews, *believing* takes a backseat to belonging and behaving when it comes to Jewish identity. In fact, most Jews will tell you that the single most important Jewish belief is the idea of "one God." This concept is universal despite language or words anyone might use to name, describe, or refer to God. It holds true regardless of the wide range of attributes that anyone might identify as belonging to God or what specific religion any person may claim to adhere to. For Jews, God remains the same one true creator of all life. That is what we mean when *we* say that we're all God's children regardless of language, religion, race, or culture. There is always more that unites us than there is that divides us because we're all fashioned by the same creative power in the universe that we call God.

The easiest way to understand Judaism is through the lens of its four-thousand-year-old culture and its evolving religious community. Like any civilization, Judaism contains multiple attributes of language, literature, art, history, culture, customs, music, ethics, holidays, celebrations, hopes, dreams, and aspirations, as well as a common spiritual homeland.

Throughout contemporary times, many have attempted to create a definition of Judaism. Since it's a natural human tendency to understand things in relation to what we already know, people try to pigeonhole Judaism into categories occupied by other societal groups. That is why, depending on the author, Judaism falls into the following categories:

- religion
- nationality
- people
- culture
- race
- civilization

In fact, *all* of these definitions except *race* are accurate. Although Jews were originally Semites from the smallest segment of the Caucasian race, today Jews are among nearly every race worldwide. Most Jews you meet experience their identity primarily through what most people see as Jewish culture. This shows how *behavior* helps create a bond with the Jewish People, where our sense of *belonging* gives us the identity of being Jewish in the first place. It's also why we feel Jewish when eating a bagel, latke, or gefilte fish. It's why we feel Jewish when we hear jokes or read stories about Jews. It's why we feel Jewish pride when we hear a Burt Bacharach song, watch an Adam Sandler movie, see a Barbra Streisand concert, or witness Steven Spielberg walk away with yet another Academy Award. We're even proud (in a motherly way) of Howie Mandel.

In general, Jews that identify themselves as *cultural* Jews wouldn't describe their behavior or attitudes as being particularly religious. This is because they generally accept the prevailing stereotype that *religious* refers to those that are observant on a regular basis.

WILL JEWS ACCEPT YOU AS A CONVERT?

Acceptance varies widely depending on the congregation and openness of the community; however, the Torah instructs Jews to welcome converts. In fact, the Torah emphasizes accepting converts so much that it does so thirty-six times, more than any other commandment. In other words, the Torah places a great burden on Jews by birth as well as on Jews by choice when it comes to conversion.

For the most part, Jews born into the faith are wildly accepting. In fact, many Jews by birth say some of the most devout Jews are converts. Why? Choosing has its advantages. When you choose to be Jewish, chances are you're going to work harder than those who see it as an entitlement via birthright. Converts usually approach Judaism with a real desire to learn and embrace a philosophy that fits with their current belief structure. Beliefs can change as you age, so what you believed in when you were ten or twelve (e.g., Santa, the Easter Bunny, the Virgin Mary, or even the Immaculate Conception) might not necessarily be the same as when you're twenty-five or thirty.

Thanks to two rabbis in my town who guided me to books that explained Judaism from several points of view, I found that all Jewish theology I read aligned with the basic tenets of my beliefs. It was then that Jews as "they" became "we." A friend who observed the reading I was doing gave me more information and invited me to his home where I saw *Shabbat* ritual and joy celebrated. At last, I had a name for what I was: a Jew.

It wasn't as easy as that, though. For some time, I read and studied, visiting with the two rabbis who answered my questions and asked even more questions. No mention was ever made of my need to convert by the rabbis. I was there to learn. This open exchange of ideas was a radical departure from where I had come from. Any idea was fair game for discussion and questioning. It was a thrilling revelation—questioning was good, reading and learning from many sources were good, and life was good and meant to be explored and enjoyed. Finally, I announced that I wanted to convert formally, do whatever it took to be officially a Jew. And I followed the path to the *mikvah*. (Judith, sixties, artist)

Another reason converts do well in conversion class is that they are at a point in their life where they take religion seriously. Most converts realize it's a lengthy commitment, and they have years of catching up to do. So many converts to Judaism throw themselves into it, which helps when learning Judaism's history and the basics in Hebrew, for instance.

Conversion takes work, and most Jews appreciate the fact that you had the *chutzpah* (Yiddish for "nerve") to do it. In fact, it's common for synagogue members who learn of your conversion to congratulate you with a handshake and verbal well wishes. Expect to hear *mazel tov* (Yiddish for "congratulations") many times.

WILL FAMILY AND FRIENDS ACCEPT YOU?

Let's hope so, although it's common to worry about alienating loved ones when you convert. This concern is so universal that we devoted the next chapter to it. It's even stronger when your parents are alive and it's clear they won't support your decision. More often than not, friends remain and family members who voice strong opposition turn a corner with time. There are situations where parents' religious philosophies differ so much from converts' that they refuse to have any contact. But those situations are few and far between, and honestly, if the parents in doubt thought about it, they would realize that their own religion does not support their unsupportive stance. Sometimes it's difficult for parents to see that another religion has replaced their efforts. Many parents see conversion as a sign of personal failure on their part and view it as an act of rebellion that will incite gossip and possibly ridicule from their peers.

In situations like this, heart-to-heart talks are necessary. Telling your parents just how essential Judaism is to you and how it in no way lessens their parenting skills is incredibly important. It might help them understand that adopting a new philosophy is a personal choice that has no bearing on them. If that doesn't work, it might be possible to confront your parents with other supportive family members and friends. It's worth seeing if they change their mind once they notice that the rest of the room supports your wishes.

Often it takes a gathering of supportive people to make stubborn views subside. Other times it takes having children to bring families together. Quite often the realization that parents may not have any relationship with their grandchildren makes the most inflexible parents succumb. Then again, these situations are atypical. Usually, most parents are overjoyed to see their adult children find their own way.

WHAT DOES "RELIGIOUS" MEAN?

Ralph Waldo Emerson once said that if the sunset occurred only once every ten years, we would be so awed that we would certainly describe it as a miracle. But since it happens every day, we dismiss it. The soul of a religious person remains awed by sunsets, enchanted by rain, overjoyed by laughter. In short, being religious should include having the courage to solve the world's ills and the vision to see the miracles that surround us daily.

Guess what? *Religious* isn't a label that is reserved for those that frequent a temple, church, or mosque. It's a broad category that includes striving to make sense out of difficult times and the struggle to impart values that move the world closer to our collective dreams. Judaism is the result of the Jewish People's march through history, as each generation struggled to make sense out of the world and share those results with one another and their children.

That is why we have no trouble calling many Jews religious when they see themselves as cultural. Being religious isn't dependent solely on specific rituals, services, ceremonies, holidays, or customs that you celebrate. It's an all-encompassing approach to life, people, family, relationships, and the world's well-being that we express in a number of ways. Some of those ways include the rituals, customs, and holidays that the Jewish People have developed throughout our history. But the main point isn't the rituals or the prayers; it's the values they symbolize. The rituals are cultural reminders of our most important historical events and ethical values—they are group-building symbols that help bind us together as members of the Jewish civilization, but they are not all-encompassing in and of themselves.

LABELS BELONG ON PRODUCTS

As a society, we're often too concerned about labels. Whether we're checking ingredients on food products or comparing designer shoes, we are a label-conscious society. Leave it to Madonna to get it right with her 1984 *Material Girl* album. But people don't walk around with labels stuck to their foreheads. Our best advice: leave labels at stores (or the nearest trash can will do just fine).

Other than for the purpose of affiliation and pubic identification, labels and categories of Jewish identity are often divisive. In a world where there are

2.1 billion Christians, 1.6 billion Muslims, and only about 15.3 million Jews, the Jewish People constitute less than one tenth of one percent of the population. We would be stronger, more united, and more supportive as a community if we emphasized the elements that we have in common rather than those that fragment us.

Labels tend to categorize arbitrarily in broad strokes that leave little room to understand the individual nuances of Jewish identity that result from personal choices about being Jewish. People too often say of others, "Oh, they are _____ Jews" (e.g., Reform, Reconstructionist, Conservative, Orthodox, Secular, Israeli, or any other label you choose), as if that single label somehow captures the reality of their Jewish lives.

There are Reform Jews who keep kosher, Reconstructionist Jews who won't drive on *Shabbat*, and Conservative Jews who wear *tefillin* (leather boxes with prayers inside that are wrapped around the head and arms) every morning. What separates them isn't easily identifiable to a casual observer, yet too often the labels of Jewish identity categorize how we choose to express our faith.

MORE THAN A RELIGION

Above all, Judaism is more than a religion for Jews; it includes a way of life. Judaism defies narrow definition because its history includes religious strivings, national aspirations, cultural artifacts, practiced rituals, spiritual celebrations, and philosophical ideals that Jews throughout the world have experienced. It is the living context within which individual Jews and the Jewish People as a whole work to create meaning and purpose in life. Judaism allows its adherents to articulate the highest ideals of the human spirit, inspiring them to search for answers to the profoundest questions the human heart and mind can confront.

The rich diversity of Jewish practice, ritual, custom, theology, and philosophy that is available to the average Jewish family allows them flexibility to create their own Jewish lifestyle that is right for them. Just as Jewish civilization itself is in a constant process of evolution, so are Jewish households as they choose their own unique collection of holidays and celebrations, rituals and customs, folklore and traditions, to embrace each year.

Soon you will adopt the Jewish traditions that best fit your lifestyle (see chapter 10). Years ago, there was a wonderful movie by Touchstone Pictures starring Richard Dreyfuss called *What About Bob?*. Dreyfuss played a character who wrote a bestseller designed to help people cope with the overwhelming demands and confusing choices of life. It was titled *Baby Steps*. Baby steps are exactly what you need as you find your Jewish foothold. Try to avoid feeling discouraged by congregants who know the ins and outs of thousands of years of Jewish history. That's not important. Instead, take baby steps. Or think of yourself like the character Jake in James Cameron's movie *Avatar* who had to learn about the Na'vi on the fly. Either way, it's best to approach Jewish culture one step at a time.

YOUR JEWISH INHERITANCE ROOM

Imagine you suddenly found a secret door to your attic that you didn't know you had and upon entering discovered that it was your own personal "Jewish inheritance room," filled with everything the Jewish civilization has produced throughout its history.

Suddenly, you'd find artifacts and ritual objects from every country on earth, wherever Jews have wandered, put down roots, and allowed their civilization to flourish. Seder plates for Passover; candlesticks, wine cups, and challah covers for *Shabbat*; dreidels and menorahs for Chanukah; sacred books written in Hebrew and Aramaic. Then you uncover commentaries on the Torah in French and Arabic, as well as Torah scrolls from Spain, Iraq, Germany, England, Poland, Israel, and Yemen. Books of folklore from throughout the world, instruments and music written by Jews in many languages and styles, every Jewish custom, superstition, recipe, tradition, and costume ever created. *And it all belongs to you.*

Becoming Jewish means gaining a lifetime key to this inheritance room, and having a desire to learn about all that the room has to offer. It means sharing your knowledge with family and friends, figuring out what you like and what you don't, what adds meaning and joy to your life and what doesn't.

It's unlikely that you or any Jew will grasp all there is to know about all the artifacts in that room no matter how long you live or how much energy you put toward it. But you can accept the challenge of constantly updating and expanding your personal Jewish life skills, knowledge, and cultural competence by experimenting with the vast collection of Jewish culture that belongs to you.

The challenge is to embrace this process as a lifelong adventure in self-discovery and belonging. The more you play in that room, the more you will feel connected to the rituals, customs, and traditions of Judaism. The more time you spend uncovering details about Jewish culture, the more you will feel a sense of belonging to the Jewish People. Creating your own Jewish lifestyle complete with your own unique collection of rituals and customs is an exciting and empowering opportunity.

For instance, if you're Italian, you can serve Italian meatballs along with matzah balls on Passover. If your family is Irish, you can say a Jewish prayer in Gaelic in addition to one in English or Hebrew. The possibilities are endless. Making your own traditions can enrich your life in significant ways and can often bring you and your family closer.

DEVELOPING YOUR OWN JEWISH CUSTOMS

Many converts wonder how to start creating Jewish customs. It's easier than you might think. Each time you celebrate a holiday or participate in a Jewish ritual, you create a custom. In other words, the best way for you to understand the cultural component of Judaism is simply by participating. It's the same for any children you might have as well. Children learn about Jewish culture in the same way Jake did when learning about the Na'vi in *Avatar*—by living it.

Keep in mind there is practically nothing you can do wrong (except maybe yelling "cheeseburgers" or "bacon-wrapped shrimp" during services). Jews all over the world approach Judaism and Jewish culture in so many different ways, we are confident that you will find ample validation for most *any* choice that you make. Besides believing that God is one, the most essential step is to become willing to choose in the first place. The act of making a decision to *do* something about creating a nurturing Jewish environment in your own home can inspire you to realize that you *can* take charge of your own spiritual, religious, and cultural destiny.

Creating a Jewish cultural environment in your own home doesn't happen overnight. It takes time to find those elements of the culture that are compatible with your own internal needs, beliefs, and values. It takes time to become familiar with the options that are available to you and to find out which best fit your lifestyle. In many ways it's a lifelong experiment. It's a process where you'll want to consider incorporating new aspects of Jewish civilization into the fabric of your daily life in small but meaningful increments. Usually the greatest problem is simply knowing where and how to begin. Don't let the fear of being overwhelmed by thousands of years of Jewish history and civilization prevent you from taking one step at a time to create your unique Jewish life-style. Millions have done it before you, and we have no doubt that you can too.

CHAI NOTES

- The three *B*s sum up developing religious identity: *believing*, *belonging*, and *behaving*.
- For most Jews, believing takes a backseat to belonging and behaving when it comes to Jewish identity.
- It's not the label (e.g., cultural, religious, observant, secular, Jew by choice, etc.) you attach to your Jewish identity that's important, but rather how you live your life.
- Being religious isn't dependent solely on specific rituals, services, ceremonies, holidays, or customs that you celebrate.
- You're creating a custom each time you celebrate a holiday or ritual.
- It's a good idea to expand your life skills, knowledge, and cultural competence by experimenting with the vast collection of Jewish culture.
- Taking small, meaningful baby steps is by far the best way to develop your Jewish identity.

3

Telling Family and Friends

ג

For Jennifer, telling family and friends was a no-brainer. She was already a wife of five years with two-year-old twins and no one was going to tell her how to worship. Look, if the twelve-foot snowman in her yard complete with fake snow, a Santa Claus, and a Christmas tree inside didn't mind that their days were numbered, then who would? Besides, gaining feedback from her parents would have required years, or at the very least a Ouija board, since one was being held captive in a brown metal box and the other was six feet under. But that's a whole other book. So what did her siblings say? Not much. Her sister Liz already paved the way when she wed a Muslim just out of college, so the shock value was zip. And her friends? They were supportive without question. She was lucky.

But this isn't the case for everyone who becomes Jewish. Sharing your conversion plans with those close to you can bring up some degree of apprehension. Will they be happy? Put off? Upset? Angry? Indifferent? Or will they distance or disown you all together? Some families will be delighted, while others may be disappointed. Some may congratulate you, while others may cut off all communication.

Whatever occurs, you need to gain perspective by way of other life events that have given *you* pause. Consider when you heard the news of someone close to you that chose to marry, divorce, or remarry. Maybe you supported the decision or maybe you didn't. Maybe you disapproved but didn't exactly know why. Sometimes change takes a while for people to warm up to, and most will have no experience dealing with religious conversion. There are no glossy magazines or reality shows geared toward the family of a convert, so many times parents are at a loss when they hear the news—and it may surface as frustration, annoyance, disappointment, or even anger.

Those close to you expect you to share the news, especially if they are used to seeing you at the same church, Buddhist temple, or mosque. This might be easier than you think if your family and friends are open-minded enough to respect your wishes. But the news can also put you in the center of a perfect storm if public opinion is not in your favor. So what can you do to avoid confrontation? Lots.

TOPICS CONSIDERED TABOO

As Bob mentioned in the foreword, there is a reason many consider politics and religion taboo in social circles. People can get downright ornery when someone voices a belief that differs from theirs. Sometimes there isn't any immediate remedy to relieve concerns family and friends might have when you discuss conversion, especially if they're of the mindset that you're disgracing the family or you won't end up in heaven. But don't despair. There are several ways to lessen the shock value before having that heart-to-heart discussion.

Consider your parents' concerns. They might wonder if conversion will exclude them from a great deal of their current or future grandchildren's lives. Part of this concern is real and critical to address. Most parents raise their children in a religion that they hope their kids will follow. A Christian grandparent may feel a huge loss if they can't shower their grandchild with gifts at Christmas or hide colorful eggs at Easter. They may know of Chanukah but may feel intimidated or like a third wheel. The thought of learning Hebrew might bewilder them, or they may blow concerns out of proportion like worrying over not having a kosher kitchen.

Muslim grandparents may have similar concerns. They celebrate Ramadan, Eid, and other holidays and may have always dreamed of accompanying their grandkids on the pilgrimage to Mecca called *hajj*.

Ditto for Buddhist grandparents. They celebrate their New Year for three days and observe other holidays like the birth, death, and enlightenment of

Buddha. Many may wish to pass on Buddhist holy days or festivals but may feel that their influence is simply not wanted.

The thought of not adding value or passing on longstanding generational traditions thanks to a new religious barricade might present a pink elephant in the room. So what should you do?

BE HONEST

Letting your family see that you're attending synagogue is by far one of the best ways of dropping the hint of where your intentions are heading. Once you start celebrating Jewish holidays, you can discuss the meaning with them. It becomes less of a shock if they see that you are committed to Judaism. If you are participating in synagogue activities, you might want to share this with them also.

Keep your family involved by letting them know when you're ready to sign up for an introduction to Judaism class. Imagine if you came home and told your parents you're getting married next week. This would jolt them out of their comfort zone, and they would probably feel deeply hurt and extremely over-looked. But if they see you becoming more serious with someone, they will de-velop an expectation that you might take your relationship to the next level.

Converting is no different. While you're not marrying Judaism, you are making a lifetime commitment. Unlike you, your family may have no refer-ence for Judaism, and it might be as foreign to them as if they boarded a rocket to Mars. Gradual changes give you the best possible chance of helping your family adjust without feeling alienated. Honesty is always the best policy.

Be heartfelt. Let them know that you love them, and that synagogue is where you feel most comfortable. Some of us were born to be Jews, and we don't always know why. For instance, Jennifer came from a smallish Texas town and only knew three adult Jews well, all friends of her parents. She had always wondered about other religions besides Catholicism and even attended other services, but none ever felt right. The moment she entered a synagogue service, everything fell in place.

FIND A NEUTRAL SETTING

If a friend confided in you that she was planning to drop the divorce bomb-shell on her husband, you probably wouldn't suggest that she does it at the roast his buddies are throwing him or at his company holiday party. Well, the same thing goes for talking to your family about conversion. While there are many ways you can approach the subject, the best is always a private, neutral setting. Judaism is not the same as a divorce, but in some respects, your family might feel that way. If religious holidays were always a big deal in your family, there is a chance that they may feel slighted and even mourn the thought.

It's a good idea to discuss your conversion in person with your family if geographical distance isn't an issue. One of the first questions your family might pose is if you're converting for your love interest. This is a natural concern and one you will want to be prepared to answer. Having your partner there can help reassure your family that this decision is 100 percent yours so they don't build up any unfounded resentment at your partner.

If geographical distance is an issue, then a thoughtful letter might do the trick. Given the way email can sometimes sound more abrupt than the sender intends, you might want to avoid this one. Calling on the phone is the next best thing to being there, so this is another way to discuss conversion. If you happen to have a Skype account and a computer camera, you can hold a teleconference at home and gauge how your family is taking it. If your family doesn't own a computer camera, this might be a worthwhile gift since you can share the coursework you're doing so that they can feel involved in the process. Remember, talking to your family about converting is no different than telling them you're adopting a child from another country or that you're getting a divorce. Yes, it's a big change in the beginning, but given the right circumstances, most families are resilient and bounce back quickly. In time, they too will see that they had nothing to worry about and that learning about another religion is actually fascinating.

I can recall telling my mother I was going to convert to Judaism, and her response was, "Sure, go ahead." Of course, at the time, I had no idea where to begin, so it would be a long time coming.

So here I stand now, at thirty-five, beginning. Years of life experience have brought me to this point, longing to feel connected once again with God, as I did lying in bed with my grandmother at the age of five. I can recognize that this world can be a very lonely place without faith, guidance, and a genuine connection with God. I sought out Judaism as the faith that had always spoken to me personally. Judaism embraces a way of being, not simply believing. It values a sense of community, tradition, family, which have always been values that I hold dear to my heart. Judaism recognizes that God can be abstract and even elusive at times. There is freedom in Judaism to question our notion of God, for the focus is more centered on the way in which we live in the world than on analyzing the nature of God. For this reason, embracing the Jewish tradition was a natural choice for me. (Renee, thirty-five, real-estate agent)

GAINING SUPPORT

It's possible that you won't need support outside your spouse, significant other, rabbi, or classmates. But some do. If you find that your family is unable to accept your conversion, disowns you, or harbors antisemitic feelings, then you'll want to gain as much support as possible. Talk to your rabbi to understand what support groups are available at your synagogue. She may know of others in similar situations that can share how they dealt with family alienation or similarly offensive responses. Like any life change, conversion can certainly overwhelm even the most tolerant family and can take some getting used to. Be patient. Changing religions is a huge transformation and impacts families in different ways. Try not to get down about it or judge your family too harshly, but understand that everyone has limitations. Be a role model. Continue making contact in a respectful way.

KEEPING PAST TIES

All transitions in life risk alienating those who might see the change as too big an obstacle to overcome. Your task is to make sure those you love understand that becoming Jewish won't alter your relationship but may add some interesting dimensions to it. Offer to educate your family and friends about Judaism and its traditions. Some may voice opposition, but those that really care about your happiness will want to know more. Most parents are pleased to know that you have found a religion that you feel strongly about. Some converts invite their family to attend services and even synagogue dinners just to ease their mind about this new transformation. Doing so works best if those close to you have accepted your decision and are not planning to sabotage you or use this as an opportunity to rail at the rabbi. This is something only you can gauge since you know your family and friends the best.

DO IT FOR YOU

Giving up traditions that you loved as a kid can be hard if you're becoming Jewish for someone else. Losing Christmas—the tree, the lights, the songs,

Santa Claus, and so on—has to be for you, or you will harbor resentment (see chapter 7). But that goes for everything in life. Jennifer's husband worked part time as a dive master years ago and taught a number of women that were earning their open water certification because their boyfriends wanted them to. This was *not* a good idea. Most were tense, frightened, and had a hard time completing basic skills like clearing their masks. Some even gave up before earning their certification. Bottom line? Do it for yourself and no one else. If becoming Jewish comes from the heart, then you will have no hesitation whatsoever. Remember, reservations are for dinner, not for conversion.

Sometimes family or friends may try to talk you out of a decision, and becoming Jewish might fall into this category. Be resolute. They will be less likely to talk you out of it if you are firm about your decision. If you're hesitant about telling them or seem unsure in how you talk about conversion, they might mistake it for uncertainty on your part or transfer their uneasiness onto you.

Showing that you're committed by attending services and getting involved with synagogue activities might help you gain confidence to talk about converting with conviction. But you might find that some degree of distancing is required depending on how your family reacts to your conversion decision. Detaching yourself from your old religious identity is often necessary when families are having a difficult time letting go. Family dynamics occur in such a way that there is often a tendency to sabotage change when it's uncomfortable for the entire family. For instance, when an alcoholic detoxes, counselors often recommend sessions for the entire family because, once an alcoholic becomes sober, family members often lose power and subconsciously rebel. Don't get pressured or guilted into worshipping your former religion to make your family comfortable. Adults have the right to choose every aspect of their lives, including where and how to worship.

MORE THAN YOU BARGAINED FOR

There are times when nothing you say or do seems to work when those you care about have negative preconceived notions of Jews. In fact, you might even get surprised. Your conversion may uncover that some of your family is anti-semitic (anti-Jew) or anti-Zionist (anti-Israel). Don't be alarmed. They may have hidden these feelings in some dark place only to unleash them at the thought of you becoming Jewish. Those feelings belong to them and have no bearing on you. As long as you can separate the two, you should have no problem distancing yourself until they come around.

Even more prevalent are cases where nothing you try works with family members who don't embrace Jews. Often these standoffs occur between well-meaning individuals after one communicates something that the other family member finds offensive or even unbearable. Consider some of the more public family feuds, such as television celebrity Tori Spelling and her mom, Candy Spelling. They drifted further away from each other when Tori divorced her first husband, Charlie Shanian (coincidentally Jewish), and married Dean McDermott (not) around the same time her dad's health was failing. But in December 2009, Tori and Candy ended their three-year estrangement. Another public celebrity feud that comes to mind is that between Angelina Jolie and her father, Jon Voight (neither is Jewish, though Voight is an ardent advocate for Israel). Heck, if these two can make up after a nine-year estrangement with six grandchildren Voight never hugged, anyone can. So hang in there!

THOSE AWKWARD MOMENTS

You try to avoid them. You want to run. You want to hide. But there's a 99 percent chance that you'll experience an awkward moment or two once you become a Jew. It might come from well-meaning relatives that redecorate their home with big crosses after you convert. It might come from good friends who insist on sending Christmas gifts even though your children celebrate Chanukah. It might come from colleagues who ask you what you did for Easter, Eid, or some other holiday that you don't celebrate anymore. Then again, it might come from a place you least expect, like a routine doctor's visit.

Jennifer felt the need to bolt when she visited a prominent Houston plastic surgeon who rambled on about his missionary work and how important his church was, then veered the conversation into whether she had kids. Once she confirmed this, he asked the question she had hoped to avoid: "What school do they attend?" This normally would be a proud moment, but it became a sticking point when she revealed her twins attended a Jewish day school. The next question was obvious: "So you converted?" Jennifer stated yes and how it was one of the most meaningful experiences of her life. Her answer was met with silence and a syringe of Botox pointed directly between her brows. As he injected it, he asked, "Do you take Jesus Christ as your savior?"

Well, hopefully the health care professionals you come across will be more professional. Bottom line is that it's hard to predict who will make catty remarks or when these situations will arise. The best advice we can give is to prepare for anything. People react in strange ways when they perceive a threat to their worldview. You have the choice to address a loved one in a way that lets them know you care about them and that disparaging remarks hurt your feelings, discount your holiday, or whatever transpired. Most people mean well, so our philosophy is to give them the benefit of the doubt and talk to them if it's a relationship you value or a colleague you see on a regular basis. If the awkward moment occurs with a service professional or doctor like in the last example, do what Jennifer did: find another.

START LIVING IT
Living Judaism means attending synagogue regularly, getting involved with some of the groups or activities your synagogue offers, and observing Jewish holidays (which on many levels means leaving former holidays behind). It *doesn't* mean that you can't go to a family member or friend's home for their celebration. It just means there is a distinct difference between *attending* a loved one's celebration and *observing* their holiday. Many new Jews have relatives who practice other religions, and no one expects you to stop socializing with them just because you converted. Much the opposite. But it's probably a good practice to draw the line at attending your former place of worship. Some may get the idea that you're rethinking your decision, and others may spend overtime trying to convert you back.

But like anything else in life, the more you start living your life as a Jew, the more those close to you will respect your decision. Think about the people you respect. Most have steadfast opinions and are not the wavering types. We can't think of anyone that we admire that fits into the wishy-washy category. Can you? So do the same. Avoid being indecisive when you talk about your decision. Instead, demonstrate your resolve through your actions. But hold on to your family and friends that are not Jewish even if they're not receptive initially. Trust us. There is room for both Jews and non-Jews in your life.

CHAI NOTES
- Drop the hint that you're interested in Judaism and that you're attending synagogue.

- Gradual changes give you the best possible chance of helping your family adjust.
- Let your family know you love them, but that synagogue is where you feel most comfortable.
- Tell your family when you have signed up for an introduction to Judaism class.
- Approach the subject of conversion with your family in a private, neutral setting.
- Having your partner there can help reassure your family that this decision is yours.
- Leaving the lines of communication open is essential to continuing a positive relationship.
- Talk to your rabbi to learn what support groups are available at your synagogue.
- Be patient, as changing religions is a huge transformation and impacts families differently.
- Show that you're committed by attending synagogue and getting involved in activities.
- Keep ties to your past since there is room for both Jews and non-Jews in your life.

4

Hitting the Books

ד

"Look to your right, look to your left—one of them won't be here next year." I remember thinking that exact sentiment when I gazed at my fellow Jews-to-be—all forty-six of them—wondering how many would really stick it out until their conversion day. Fortunately, many did, but there were some that determined midstream that either the timing or a yearlong commitment just wasn't in the cards.

It was, in many respects, a weekly religious boot camp with lectures, reading assignments, ample discussions, and healthy debates on Jewish history, along with tips on how to be, think, and observe like a Jew. But for me, it came with all the bells and whistles because, like many of my classmates, Judaism just made sense and learning, reading, and debating about it afforded us pleasure rather than pain—especially for those of us who grew up in faiths where questioning was not encouraged and had become accustomed to watered-down versions of "well, that's just the way it is." (Jennifer Hanin)

This isn't to say that converts don't enter the class with varying expectations. Some are eager to absorb as much as possible regardless of the time commitment involved. Others are enthusiastic, but their hectic schedules may press them to consider a fast track. Luckily, among the four movements there is something for everyone. Some conversion courses are longer and more intensive than others, so it's up to you to decide (if you haven't already). Orthodox courses last about two years, Conservative courses are about a year, Reconstructionist courses are about four months, and Reform courses are about four and a half months (see appendix 2). Each rabbi differs in observance requirements. Some may also require a year of observing major Jewish holidays and some monthly synagogue attendance, while others may be less demanding. All movements require you to meet with your sponsoring rabbi periodically to assess progress and answer questions.

Whether you're a student or a seasoned professional, becoming Jewish means you are the proud owner of about a dozen new books. Most offer historical accounts of Judaism, while others ponder what it means to be Jewish. Few detail the process, which is why this book is indispensable to complement any course you might take.

Now, you're probably wondering why becoming Jewish is less like a standard dunking that you might find with a Christian conversion and more like completing the Ironman Triathlon. There is no doubt that converting to Judaism is a lengthy and involved process, which seems counterproductive since the number of Jews worldwide—15.3 million—hasn't risen much since the 1950s. So what's the rub?

Simple. Becoming Jewish is a lifetime commitment that rabbis want to make sure you don't take lightly. Yet the anticipation, hesitancy, and excitement of starting a new class can be overwhelming. Fortunately, your own guidance and that of your rabbi are just as essential to your class as history and tradition. Remember that Judaism is fundamentally a religion of learning, questioning, and determining your place in the world. Your rabbi knows you can't learn *everything* there is to know in your conversion class—think of it as a doorway that leads to a whole new path of lifelong learning.

Some converts report that other life courses help prepare them for conversion. Those that enable you to think about the world around you and how to solve ongoing problems in particular seem to complement our Jewish belief in *tikkun olam*. Here's one convert's recollection of how a life-changing course led to her decision to convert:

> When I took the course, it taught me how people have had the same ineffective conversation for the last three hundred years. It has nothing to do with religion or

conversion, but it has to do with changing the course of humankind by solving the world's biggest problems through discourse. It teaches you how to go beyond the beyond, meaning that you have to learn how to stand in the unknown and do it for longer periods. Then, like a ship going out to sea, you will go so far out that you will lose sight of the shore. Essentially, you go so far out that you will never come back to the same place. It's a little unsettling perhaps, but it teaches you to confront the unknown and be okay with it. The distinctions in this course helped me go through conversion class because at that point I was just exploring my spirituality and hadn't decided on a religion yet. For me, the class really applied to converting because once you go out that far and explore what's out there, you can never really go back. (Laura, fifty-three, financial consultant)

CHOOSING YOUR PATH

Take a careful look at your syllabus. This is the GPS for your journey. It should clearly lay out the dates and times of your classes, the topic discussed in each, and perhaps some questions to consider before class. It may also identify readings, written assignments, and even field trips you may need to attend to gain full credit for your class. You'll want to leave this document in a safe place and ask for one via email in case it collides with your caffeinated drink one day (or your dog decides it's homework). Some might even consider placing it in a clear report cover if their class is a year or longer, but it might be easier and cheaper to print another copy. Your syllabus in many cases will be your lifeline to upcoming readings, questions to ponder, and preparation for field trips and other class activities.

Now for the reading list. This part may be the biggest surprise for the uninformed. Because Judaism values lifelong learning, your rabbi will likely give you a long list of books to purchase. You may have a temptation to use the library or do without, but try to avoid this. It can be a bit costly upfront, but use your conversion book list as an opportunity to begin building your own personal Jewish library. If you are like most conversion students, you'll find that over time you will add more books on Jewish life, history, culture, religion, practice, and maybe even recipes. Your rabbi will start you off with reading recommendations based mainly on her experience with Judaism, along with her favorite Jewish mentors and scholars. You'll rarely get a better recommendation than that.

Don't let the quantity or thickness of the books scare you. Remember that you have more than four thousand years of catching up to do, so you'll find comprehensive history books, Torah analyses, cultural analyses, and perhaps some Talmud for good measure. You'll also probably have a book or two on the conversion process (like this one) and on living a Jewish life.

Finally, you may have an "introduction to Hebrew" book on your list. Some classes even give out CDs or recommend software or e-learning classes to help with Hebrew. If your movement requires Hebrew or if you've elected to take it, your introduction to Hebrew class would be separate from your introduction to Judaism class. This is because both classes have independent material and goals that they want you to run with. Given its importance to Judaism and prayer, we have devoted chapter 5 to learning Hebrew.

SEEING WITH A JEWISH SET OF EYES

Your reading list will be lengthy and the books will be heavy, but there is some upbeat news. Unless you want to, you won't have to read every page. That's not to say that there's not value in every word the authors penned (obviously there is, especially in *this* book), but your rabbi doesn't expect you to read everything. Think of your collection of Jewish tomes as vast resources you can mine over time. Your rabbi *will* expect you to read assigned chapters prior to class and share your perspective, but it's not likely that she will expect you to know the differences between how Rabbi Hillel's followers tied their *tzitzit* versus how Rabbi Akiva's followers did. There's a lot of fascinating but arcane knowledge in Judaism, but much of it is simply not critical to know. Your rabbi will determine what *she* feels is important for you to know, and that's what you should focus on. There will be plenty of time after conversion to learn the rest.

On the other hand, if reading and soaking up knowledge is an area you excel at and you want to cover as much ground as possible, go for it. Nonetheless, once you get into the groove of class, you may find you want to read more about a particular subject. Go for it! The best time to learn is when your mind is open to it. This is what is so wonderful about tools like the Internet and search engines like Google. If you want to know more about Maimonides, the Second Temple, the Israelites all the way to modern-day Israel, or even Yemenite Jewish jewelry, you are only a few keystrokes away. This is a unique time in your life, so enjoy each minute of it. You are voluntarily going "back to school"—take advantage of that.

Now for writing. Many rabbis and students have already discovered that a valuable resource for converts is a personal journal. Shop for a bound book that interests you (most journals come in all different fabrics and colors) and keep it handy. When you have a thought about class, Judaism, conversion, life, God, food, whatever—write it down. Try to summon your thoughts and write daily, even if it's just to say hello to your future self (because someday you will go back and read the journal). You might surprise yourself and find what you write is quite interesting. You don't have to write a lot, just write something. There are many reasons this will help you in the conversion process. Often, journals like this reflect your thinking process pre-conversion and show gradual changes until you officially become Jewish.

A journal can help you develop your Jewish identity and pinpoint how you wish to express it once you become Jewish. It also helps highlight any issues you are having, and it's a good starting point to speak with significant others or your rabbi. The last thing you want to do is go through all the motions and realize later that you have some significant reservations. It will all be there in black or blue (or whatever color pen you use), so make sure you address your feelings head-on. The other benefit is that your journal will start helping you realize what kind of Jew you want to be. Are you concerned about *tikkun olam*? Is it social justice? Is it *tzedakah*? More than likely, whatever keeps you up at night will likely surface in your journal. Take this as a clue to follow up on it later and incorporate it into your life somehow. Once you look back, you're likely to see a whole slew of Jewish endeavors that you can get involved in at your synagogue or in your community. One of Jennifer's favorites was selling *hamentashen* (triangular filled pastries) at the Purim carnival.

First, conversion is a spiritual and emotional process. You'll find as you begin to write that it's easy to capture thoughts and feelings on paper that you might not express otherwise. Because you are writing for yourself, you'll be more open, introspective, and insightful. You may find when you are done that your writings become a valuable reminder of your experiences and are something you'll refer back to many times.

Second, writing helps you think and learn. There have been studies that demonstrate this. The reason is simple. When we learn, our brain stores information in neurons and actually builds connections between related neurons so that you can recall the memory or piece of information easier in the future. When you write, you cause your brain to create more connections between the parts of your brain that control thought and action. This allows you to increase the amount of neural connections surrounding each concept. More connections mean more relevance and better recall. This is something we all want, right?

Finally, journaling your thoughts will allow you to go back at the end of class and really see what you've learned and how you have changed—and you *will* change. Many converts say they began to see things through a "Jewish set of eyes"—that for the first time they began to see antisemitism and anti-Zionism and even found themselves more concerned about the Middle East conflict and developing a love for Israel. By cataloging your feelings, you will learn about your journey a bit more. Your rabbi may even ask you to write a few paragraphs about your conversion journey. Your journal is an ideal vehicle for this.

Unlike Jews by birth, this is your opportunity to learn a religion from the ground up. From fundamental beliefs to practices and prayers. From dietary laws to Sabbath rituals. From "*Shanah Tovah*" to "*Shabbat shalom.*" You'll learn all these practices and greetings, but more importantly you'll learn *why*—or at least discuss it. After all, many customs don't really have a "why" answer. They are because they are. This is where debate comes in handy.

You've probably heard that questioning and debating issues and concepts is a central tenet of Judaism. Now you have the opportunity to question things deeper than "why" (and your rabbi will expect that you will). Questioning issues and debating them helps you come to an answer that makes sense to you. This is one reason Judaism is such a personal and denominational religion. Different movements of Jews over time have asked, "Why?" This freedom to question helped Jews develop insights and answers that have led not just to different streams of Orthodoxy (Modern, *Haredi*, and *Hasidic*) but also to additional movements including Reform, Conservative, and Reconstructionist (see page 18).

By now it's probably clear to you that you are not going to be attending straight lectures. Your rabbi expects you to participate in class as much as possible. Your insight will be as valuable as hers for your own personal growth and that of your classmates, so don't be afraid to share, ask questions, speak your mind, and give your perspective. You'll get more from the class and more satisfaction to boot.

Obviously, you'll want to support your classmates and encourage their participation as well. This may be hard at first, but over time you'll find your class becomes just like a large extended family. You'll know each other well, will high-five each other's accomplishments, and will have shared a very personal and rewarding experience with them. In some cases, you might just be the person that your classmate leans on when they're having a difficult time with a family member, friend, or colleague that doesn't quite understand their need to convert. Hint: If your classmate feels comfortable confiding in you, consider this an honor.

TMI!

It would be hard to write this chapter without at least one acronym that describes all the content that your rabbi will throw your way, and "too much information" seems fitting. In fact, you'll likely realize partway into your syllabus that you've only scratched the surface of the vast Jewish knowledge you now own. While correct, it's simply no cause for concern. You'll have many more years to mine these volumes and discuss them with others. Until then, it's often helpful to take advantage of tips others found useful to complete the course.

> It was helpful for me to discuss each topic with my husband or my friend (both Jewish) after reading the material. I've found that if you study material and mull it over with a partner afterward, it starts to make more sense. Once I read a section, I would chat over dinner with either of them, and it helped solidify what I was learning and at the same time gave me a little more real-world perspective on it. It really helps you grasp material quicker once you start debating an issue and discussing all the ins and outs. (April, thirty-three, attorney)

Having the right mindset always helps too. Unlike sitting in a freshman history course because it's required, you're electing to convert, so that puts you way ahead in terms of being open to learning rather than taking it solely because it's a prerequisite. Other facts to remember are that you're not the first or the last to convert and, more importantly, you're not doing it alone. Many have embarked on the path you are taking, and honestly, if they can do it, can't you?

We already mentioned keeping a journal, but it bears discussion again. Frustrated? Happy? Excited? Write it down. Frightened? Motivated? Exhilarated? Write it down. It will help you remember the high points and get through the low ones. And while you're writing, why not write down new words, concepts, or ideas? Your new glossary is a great way to keep track and

memorize all the new words you're learning. While this book has a very comprehensive one for your reference, you should still add to it. It will definitely
help you in the end. Some even find it helpful to write a letter or prayer to God
as it crystallizes beliefs, goals, and expectations going forward.

Another approach that will help is to create a study group. Ask the classmates you feel most comfortable with to meet outside of class a few times a
week. Then go over the things you're learning. Ask questions. Debate. Discuss.
Do whatever it takes to make learning work for you. Don't understand something? Say it aloud. A concept that may be over your head may be just the
thing a classmate can explain easily. You may find that you excel on another
topic or in learning Hebrew, for instance. Work together. This isn't a competi-
tion for grades; it's an opportunity to broaden your horizons and enhance
your spiritual self.

For the more disorganized or frazzled, setting aside a specific time to study
is a great and easy way to build the habit into your lifestyle. After all, our lives
are full of routines. The trick with finding time to do something is dedicating
time to it. It may take sacrifice. *American Idol, Dancing with the Stars*, or whatever your favorite TV show is must wait. But in the end it will be worth it. And
if you have a DVR device, you won't really miss any of it anyway.

JUST DO IT

Finally, the beauty of your conversion class is that it's ultimately about experiences. Learn by doing. Attend every event or service you have an opportunity
to. Whether community, cultural, or religious, you'll be learning. Your first
time in synagogue as a new Jew should not be your first time in a synagogue.
Go to Friday-night services and welcome *Shabbat*. Go to Saturday-morning
services and become comfortable with the practices and prayers around the
Torah service. Attend a morning *minyan* (a quorum of ten people for prayer)
to see what it's like. Experience the richness and variety of Jewish holidays and
festivals. Hear the *shofar* on Rosh Hashanah and Yom Kippur. Pray and eat in
the *sukkah*. Dance with the Torah during *Simchat Torah*. Light the menorah
on Chanukah. Dress in costume and drown out Haman's name on Purim. Attend a *seder* on Passover. Study all night on Shavuot.

Don't underestimate your attendance. It's critical for you to become a part
of the Jewish People, and your rabbi will not only notice your presence but will
welcome it. Attending synagogue regularly will help you transition into your

synagogue's community and at the same time help you learn what to do and how to act in *shul*. It will no doubt be the beginning of lifelong friendships, especially if you have the opportunity to stay in the same community. Part of attending on a regular basis is feeling connected to your synagogue community, and you will only feel that way if you make an effort to participate in functions and make friends.

CHAI NOTES

- Luckily, among the four movements there is something for everyone.
- Remember, you have more than four thousand years of catching up to do, so give yourself a break.
- Your class is driven as much by history and tradition as by your guidance and your rabbi's.
- Think of your collection of Jewish tomes as vast resources that you can mine over time.
- Creating a glossary is a great way to keep track and memorize your new vocabulary.
- Questioning issues and debating them help you reach an answer that makes sense to you.
- Don't be afraid to share, ask questions, speak your mind, and give your perspective.
- Your rabbi determines what you need to know, and that's what you should focus on.
- Whenever you have a thought about Judaism, conversion, life, God, food, and so forth—journal it!
- Create a study group. Ask questions, debate, discuss—Judaism encourages it!
- Attending synagogue regularly and participating in its functions helps you transition faster, connect with the community, and make friends.

5

Learning an Ancient Language

ה

Talk about a test of will. Hearing that you have to learn Hebrew as a Jewish convert is akin to parachuting out of a plane or mastering public speaking. Luckily, only the latter applies for some. For most, though, the idea of learning Hebrew is intimidating. Try listening and pronouncing it in a room full of Texas accents. That was Jennifer's experience, and it proved to be one that was colorful and well worth the effort. Trust us. Hebrew, like all languages, can be either easy or difficult depending on your instructor's approach, the course materials assigned, your support networks (family, friends, and classmates), and whether or not you actually practice. Don't worry about acing all of these. Three out of four will work just fine.

REALLY? IS HEBREW REQUIRED?

There is no denying that Hebrew is an important aspect of being an observant Jew as most of the greetings, prayers, customs, ceremonies (life events), and of course the Torah are in Hebrew. In fact, there is a good chance that you will have a fuller observant life if you understand even basic Hebrew. Think of it this way: if you moved to France for an extended stay, chances are you would want to learn the language to communicate with the locals. Nothing says "tourist" like speaking English when those in the marketplace are haggling in their native tongue.

Learning Hebrew serves a dual purpose. It provides (1) a more fulfilling religious life and (2) greater opportunities to develop a richer social life within your Jewish community. Some movements place more emphasis on Hebrew than others. There is no getting around learning Hebrew if you are converting to the Orthodox or Conservative movement. Honestly, you'll feel like a third wheel when others around you are repeating the *V'ahavta*, the *Aleinu*, or the *Kaddish* (which is one of the few prayers in Aramaic) and you're speechless. Those converting into the Reconstructionist or Reform movements are encouraged to learn but are not necessarily required to master Hebrew. Even so, there are many more blessings to receive from knowing the language than from not.

Hebrew is a beautiful and mystical language that held up for centuries before Eliezer Ben-Yehuda resuscitated it, dusted it off, and standardized it for popular use. Once a dead language, today Hebrew is spoken by some six million people in Israel, where it is the official language along with Arabic. The mere fact that you can read a scroll thousands of years old if you know Hebrew is more proof that as a new Jew this language deserves your time and consideration.

LANGUAGE OF THE TORAH

One of the main reasons to know Hebrew is that it's the language of the Torah. The word *Torah* comes from the Hebrew root *yaroh*, which means "teaching," "instruction," or "law." Soon you'll see that rabbis and congregants treat the Torah with the utmost respect. This is because one of the central beliefs in Judaism is that God gave Moses the first Torah on Mount Sinai. Moses plays a key role in Jewish history (along with his brother, Aaron, and his sister, Miriam) because God handpicked him to lead the Jews on their exodus from Egypt. The traditional belief in Judaism is that God revealed the entire Torah (Genesis, Exodus, Leviticus, Numbers, and Deuteronomy) to Moses, who wrote each of the five books as God instructed him. This also includes prophecies and history that are in other books of scripture, and the entire oral Torah, the oral tradition of interpreting the Torah that later became the Talmud.

All Torah scrolls you see are handcrafted replicas of the very first Torah. Under strict supervision, a specially trained scribe (*sofer*) hand-prepares each Torah on parchment in attractive Hebrew calligraphy with "crowns" (crow's-foot-like marks coming up from the upper points) on many of the letters. This style of writing is called STA"M (an abbreviation for *Sifrei Torah*, *tefillin*, and *mezuzot*).

CURL UP WITH THE DEAD SEA SCROLLS

Most have heard about the Bedouin boy that accidentally uncovered seven of the Dead Sea Scrolls near Qumran while searching for his goat in 1947. But did you ever imagine that you could actually read them? Well, here's your chance. Most of the scrolls contain ancient Jewish texts in Hebrew, not Aramaic, which was the common spoken language in the region at the time. Once you can read Hebrew, there are many manuscripts at your disposal. Excavation of Qumran caves continued through 1956 and involved ten additional caves that yielded eight hundred manuscripts in all, dating from approximately 200 BCE to 68 CE. One of the scrolls is nicknamed the "Temple Scroll" as over half of its content pertains to the construction of the Second Temple in Jerusalem.

HELP!

Just like learning any new subject, there are plenty of things you can do to make learning Hebrew easier. Perhaps the simplest way to learn is to commit to it. If you are serious about conversion (and if you're here, we assume you are), then just reminding yourself that learning Hebrew is important for your success may be enough. Dedicating regular times to study and practice is critical, as is ensuring that you are honest with yourself about where you need improvement.

But for many, dedication alone is not enough. This is why there are countless great products available in specialty stores and online that can make learning Hebrew easier and even fun. Some are free, some you'll have to buy, but all focus on helping you achieve your goal of reading Hebrew. How can you find them? Well, you can visit our Resources section, or simply search online for "Learning Hebrew." You'll find a vast array of audiobooks and podcasts, interactive websites and sophisticated software tools.

We can't recommend any specific tool because new tools become available regularly, and more importantly, because different tools appeal to different people. What works great for another might bore you to tears and vice versa.

Read the descriptions, try a sample of the material, and see how you respond to it. Many software packages are final sale items, and stores that sell them will not entertain returns or exchanges, so reading reviews or gaining personal recommendations might help you choose. Of course, if you have frequent access to Hebrew speakers and a friend, spouse, or in-law to study with regularly, you might find that you can forgo software products and audiobooks for traditional in-person study work. After all, this is exactly how you would master a foreign language years before language tools were invented.

Making this transition is easier if you have a support network as you work through the conversion process. If you don't, see if one or more of your classmates would be comfortable forming a study group with you. Hebrew can be challenging even for those who grew up hearing it, so you can expect some degree of frustration along the way. Another way to get ahead is to see if your teacher will spend a little extra time with you before or after class. Many times Hebrew teachers will even have a list of tutors and may encourage you to call one. Often the progress you can make with a tutor one-on-one far outweighs what you can do on your own or with your teacher. It's just a matter of dynamics and personalities, but there is something empowering about learning from a tutor who is solely dedicated to enhancing your abilities during the hour or so you practice together. Tutors usually charge by the hour, so ask for recommendations and compare prices before deciding what route is best for you.

When Jennifer was learning, her husband (a nearly fluent Hebrew speaker) helped her. They got to the point where he would only stop her reading if she made an error, so that she wasn't getting used to constant feedback of "yes," "good," "perfect," and so forth. While it's nice to know you're doing well, it's better to continue when you're doing well and save the high fives for later.

To learn the letters, try flash cards. They've been around seemingly forever, and for good reason: they work. Practice with a support person or a classmate. Try naming the letters you see, and then try pronouncing the sounds. Use the flash cards to build words. Bring them with you and look through them when you have a spare moment. You'll soon find the letters come naturally to you.

Transliteration can help you learn in a pinch, especially when it comes to memorization of prayers. It can be a little addictive when you realize you're spot on with pronunciation, but don't let it fool you. Being able to pronounce Hebrew via the English alphabet is not the same as learning Hebrew. Many synagogues have the transliterated version in English across from the Hebrew version like this:

Le-chah do-di lik-rat ka-lah   לְכָה דוֹדִי לִקְרַאת כַּלָּה.

As you can see, it's easy to read and pronounce but it can interfere with how fast you grasp Hebrew if you rely on it too heavily. Learning the Hebrew alphabet and vowels, and becoming comfortable reading them, are your real first steps to speaking the language. Transliteration is a half step to help you with pronunciation immediately, but not everything has it, so you will feel a little out of sorts if you don't know actual Hebrew.

BUT IT LOOKS SO DIFFERENT

א ב ג ד ה ו ז ח ט י
כ ל מ נ ס ע פ צ
ק ר ש ת

Hebrew looks much different from English for many reasons—most importantly because it *is* different. Unlike English, Hebrew is an ancient language. The oldest known Hebrew writing is more than three thousand years old, and while it has changed a bit over time, Hebrew we use today is still very close to the text our ancestors wrote. The differences between Hebrew and English are quite significant. Unlike English, anyone writing Hebrew writes it from right to left, which means that Hebrew books open with the spine on the right. Some may say (or think) that Hebrew books open "backward." Yet that's like visiting Israel and calling Israelis foreigners, or saying that in England people drive on the wrong side of the road.

YOUR SECRET DECODER RING

But there are other distinct differences between Hebrew and English. Take the alphabet, for example. Hebrew uses a very dissimilar alphabet than English, with only twenty-two letters in comparison to twenty-six letters in English. Hebrew also does not have vowels in standard written text. Yes, there *are* vowel symbols, but they are not regularly used. In fact, the Torah has no vowels in it, and if you visit Israel, you'll find that most printed material, signs, and so forth do not use vowels either.

One trick to learning Hebrew is to imagine you are deciphering a code. Remember the old decoder rings so many of us (or your parents) had as kids? On them, a letter or symbol matched up against an English letter and replaced it in a coded message. If you knew which symbols replaced which letters, you could actually read the otherwise random symbol string. Well, each Hebrew letter corresponds to a distinct sound. So if you can get comfortable matching the letter to its sound, you'll find you can actually break the code and start reading.

That's not to say you won't come across a few snags here and there. In all likelihood you will, as most adults do when they study a foreign language. One thing that might throw you off is that two Hebrew consonants are silent. Yes, there are words that feature letters that have to be there but have no sound of their own. But remember the vowel sounds we mentioned earlier? The way Hebrew works is that you pronounce the letter/consonant first, then add the vowel sound attached to it. This means silent letters adopt the sound of the vowel they sit above.

Yet another complication is with the sounds themselves. Certainly, there are some standard English-like sounds. But there are other sounds in Hebrew as well, some unlike anything you've heard before—like *ch* or *kh* (think *Bach*, but more guttural, not *chow*)—and some more subtly different—like *tz* (think the *z*'s in *pizza*). Even the letter *r* is pronounced slightly differently. It'll take good listening skills and practice, but eventually most people can pick up these truly unique sounds.

Finally, Hebrew (like English, we'll note) has some letters that share the same sound; there are two *s*'s, two *t*'s, two *k*'s, and two *ch*'s. Unlike English, Hebrew has some letters written differently when at the end of a word (suffix). These are final letters, or *sofit*. There's one for the *ch*, *m*, *n*, *f*, and *tz* sounds.

But in the end, the decoder principle still works. If you know the sound the letter makes (and the vowel associated with it), you can sound out the word. With practice, this will become second nature.

Learning to read Hebrew is different in so many ways. It's structurally different because the letters themselves are unfamiliar. But it's also physiologically different. As we mentioned earlier, we read Hebrew right to left *and* up down, up down, up down for vowel sounds. This is the opposite of English. You really have to train your eyes to do that kind of tracking. And even then it takes practice because some of the letters and some of the vowels look similar. The key is practice. It's better to practice ten minutes a day than practice an hour a week. The continuity that comes with studying daily is so important for learning a new language. You won't retain it or track properly if you wait a week between practice sessions.

NOTHING VENTURED, NOTHING GAINED

In learning a new language, most converts are afraid of making a mistake. For that matter, who isn't? Maybe you're worried sick over your accent, or that you just won't sound right. Other fears that often arise are the pressure to keep up with fluent speakers or that your inexperience with the language will cause fellow Jews to chuckle or simply reject you. Nothing could be further from the truth.

Most Jews are well meaning, but let's face it, there are always reasons to laugh. In fact, studies have shown that laughing triggers endorphins, which are good in their own right. Remember the saying "Nothing ventured, nothing gained"? This applies completely to learning a new language. No one expects perfection, and you can't expect that of yourself or give yourself a timetable.

The goal here is simple: communication. Even if you sound deliberate, talk slower, miss a word, or use several wrong words or sounds, you need to commend yourself for trying. We still know what someone is saying when they're trying to master English, even if it's choppy at best. The wonderful thing is being able to communicate and understand each other. The alternative is much worse: speaking two different languages to each other and not understanding anything.

The good news is that most Jews you speak Hebrew with as a convert to Judaism will speak English fluently. The main goal here is to get you acquainted with the language of the Torah and many of the prayers and hymns as well as the traditional sayings on *Shabbat* and the holidays. Embracing Hebrew early on provides you with richer experiences as you and your family develop your own traditions and transition into a Jewish way of life.

People learn at different paces, so instead of comparing yourself to your classmates, only compete with your last personal best. In other words, benchmark your current progress against where you were a week or two ago. Steady self-improvement is what you should aim for. Doing so will eliminate peer pressure and allow you to focus on consistent progress. Giving yourself a break here will go a long way. Learning a new language as an adult requires patience, practice, and a sense of humor. For example, as a new convert, every time Jennifer saw or pronounced the Hebrew word *bereshit*, which means "in the beginning" and is the first word of the Torah, she had to stifle back a giggle because she kept looking at it and thinking about the old saying about a bear in the woods. But situations like this are common. After all, you laugh when you see or hear something that you don't expect. For her, it was *bereshit*. For you, it's wide open. (Hint: If you want to see your Hebrew teacher blush, ask about the multiple meanings of *zayin*, the seventh letter of the Hebrew alphabet. Google it or just refer to our glossary.)

The same goes for when native speakers hear your first attempts at Hebrew. You've probably giggled or stifled a laugh when someone tried to speak your native language but butchered it inadvertently. Most of us have. Again, give yourself a break here.

Put yourself in a Hebrew speaker's mindset. If you speak Hebrew, but you pronounce words differently than someone born and raised in Tel Aviv, do you think they'll think any less of you? Probably not. The fact is, you may very well sound like a New Yorker or Southerner speaking Hebrew, but you are still communicating. Israelis are happy to know what you have to say. Ditto for God.

So while it's admirable to work toward sounding exactly like your Hebrew teacher's intonation, it's more productive to work on reading and speaking clearly. In the end, you'll bring your own character and personality to the words, and that is what will make Hebrew *your* language too.

WORTH THE EFFORT

For many, learning a new language often starts out as a love-hate relationship. Most revel in their accomplishments while silently cursing their failures. Hebrew is no different in that regard. Luckily, there are turning points where everything falls in place. Soon your furrowed brows and deep sighs will fade into head nods and high fives.

Jennifer's Hebrew instructor always recommended studying at least ten minutes a day as a great way to keep everything fresh. She was right. When you break that down, it's about the same amount of time you spend on a phone call or a walk around the block. The idea behind her wisdom was that it's not about the length of the study session but rather the frequency. The more you practice, the more comfortable you get. Recognizing letters and the sounds they make gives you that much more confidence when reciting prayers and greetings.

Once you've mastered the basics, you're well on your way to becoming conversational. Take some time to enjoy your accomplishment and consider whether taking more classes or studying independently is right for you. There are a wide variety of tools at your disposal if needed. The great news is that you can do much of it from your own home in the comfort of your pj's (though we wouldn't recommend that for private tutoring sessions). Speaking the language will not only make you an instant hit when you visit your eternal homeland, Israel, but it also gives you yet another reason to plan a trip.

CHAI NOTES

- Try to keep an open mind and not let the idea of learning Hebrew intimidate you.
- Grasping any new language is easier when you like your teacher and the course materials and have good support networks.
- Learning Hebrew provides you with a more fulfilling religious life and the ability to develop a richer social life within the Jewish community.
- Dedicating regular times to study and practice are critical to ensure you're making progress.
- Transliteration helps with memorization of prayers, but don't rely on it.
- One trick to learning Hebrew is to imagine you're deciphering a code.
- Ten minutes (or more) a day is highly recommended to study Hebrew.

6

Honoring *Shabbat*

ו

When most people think of holidays, they think of special days that come once a year. Passover and Chanukah are yearly, and so are birthdays, anniversaries, and most other joyful occasions we celebrate. For Jews it's the opposite. Our most important holiday is one that comes weekly: *Shabbat*. Your rabbi might say its English name: Sabbath. But there's more to this holy day than most let on.

ROCK STAR STATUS

What makes *Shabbat* a rock star is that it's the only day God mentioned in the Ten Commandments (the fourth, to be exact). That alone makes it a hall of famer among holy days. But while *Shabbat* is the holiest day in every sense of the word, it also suffers from the same overexposure celebrities often face. Because *Shabbat* makes a weekly appearance, it's often the best known and least understood holy day. This is why it makes sense to take a closer look at this sacred day so you can develop a greater sense of appreciation for it.

Jews observe the Sabbath on the seventh day of the week. This follows the biblical commandment: "Six days you shall labor and do all your work, but the seventh day is a *Shabbat*" (Exodus 20:9–10). But it's not Sunday, if that's what you're guessing. Try Friday at sunset until Saturday at sundown (or, if you want to get technical, until the appearance of three stars, according to traditional Jewish law).

In fact, all Jewish *days* begin at sunset. No, it doesn't mean that you need to switch your breakfast with your dinner or turn your schedule on its head. But what it does mean is that the concept of evening being day and day being evening is probably as foreign to you as dating an angler fish. So why the reversal? Simple. It's based on the biblical story of creation (Genesis 1:5) and emphasizes the two words ending this phrase: "And there was evening and there was morning, *one day.*" Since evening comes before morning in the phrase, rabbis concluded that all days begin and end in the evening.

Throughout civilization, the Jewish People welcomed *Shabbat* with open arms. Jews considered it their favorite day of every week, a time when they could put aside their struggles and frustrations and focus on family, study, prayer, and meditation. Like a vacation day away from a stressful job, *Shabbat* brought them peace of mind, contentment, and joy.

Many rabbis equated *Shabbat* with the observance of all laws of Judaism. In fact, it is so central to Jewish life that a great Jewish writer and thinker, Ahad Ha'am, once said, "More than the Jewish people have kept the Sabbath, the Sabbath has kept the Jewish people."

What is it about *Shabbat* that kept this rock star of holy days unique, sacred, and special for thousands of years? The key is found in a famous Midrash (rabbinic story) when rabbis bequeathed *Shabbat* with mystical power to foreshadow world peace. The Midrash describes God's actions before giving the Torah to Jews on Mount Sinai.

> God: My children, I have something precious and wonderful that I would like to give you for all time, if you will accept my Torah and observe my commandments.
>
> Israelites: Ruler of the universe, what is this precious gift that you have for us?
>
> God: It is the world-to-come, the perfect messianic age.
>
> Israelites: Please show us a sample, a model of the world to come.
>
> God: I will give you *Shabbat*. *Shabbat* is a sample of the world to come, for when that world comes, it will be one long Sabbath of joy, fulfillment, and peace.

Shabbat trumps all holy days for its starring role as a symbol of the perfect life. But you may wonder how this can be when we're bombarded by CNN and unrest in many areas around the world. Simple. This messianic age is when people realize their potential. It's when peace, security, justice, and compassion rule the hearts of all humanity. *Shabbat* is such a symbol because it provides a weekly reminder that we have the power to create a mini-version of that perfection in our own lives. It's also a reminder that we can *achieve* a perfect world. Judaism has always empowered individuals to make choices that have a profound difference in how the world supports, nourishes, and sustains human life. *Shabbat* symbolizes that empowerment and the daily choices that we make.

It isn't study, worship, or meditation that matters. It's the idea of *Shabbat* that has always resonated for Jews. When a Jewish person spent *Shabbat* in study and prayer, it reinforced essential values that underlie Jewish civilization. That reinforcement occurred simply by participating in a religious service where prayers focused on peace, freeing the captive, healing the sick, clothing the naked, housing the homeless, and spreading justice and compassion.

The same is true when Jews study Torah on *Shabbat*. The lessons center on creating the kind of world we want. Worship, meditation, and study helped traditional Jews create a weekly ritual that fortified their resolve to help bring about this messianic age. Texts reinforce the values we teach and cherish, our personal responsibility and power to manifest those values in daily life.

The key for you lies not necessarily in worship or study (although you will want a synagogue whose philosophy, theology, and style of worship suits you), but in discovering those activities, rituals, and experiences that make *Shabbat* meaningful to *you*. The truth is that *Shabbat* comes weekly whether you do anything special to acknowledge it or not. Recognizing *Shabbat* in a special way is totally up to you.

MAKING *SHABBAT* YOURS

How do you get started? Some Jews light candles each *Shabbat* with traditional prayers, their own prayers, or both. Others may host a *Shabbat* dinner and serve challah and wine (grape juice for kids). Some go to synagogue on Friday evenings and others go Saturday mornings. Most report that *Shabbat* has greater value when it adds something unique to their life. This means adding a ritual or activity that brings an extra sense of purpose into your life and your family.

Each week is an opportunity to create a moment in time that somehow reminds you that the world *can* be the kind of place you've always imagined.

Think of it as the twenty-four-hour period that renews your focus on growth, creativity, inspiration, and love. This is why it's considered a blessing, or double *mitzvah*, to make love with your spouse on *Shabbat*. After all, *Shabbat* has lasted four millennia to tell us what matters most is up to us. *We* can make a difference in the quality of life on our planet, and *Shabbat* reminds us that we have another chance to discover how.

Some synagogues place their emphasis on Friday nights and others on Saturday mornings depending on the stream of Judaism and temple. No two are exactly alike. Soon you'll discover that each has its own unique spiritual tone and feeling. Friday-night service might be the main community time for spiritual gathering. Your synagogue may feature speakers on Jewish or contemporary topics and services for young families or seniors with live music followed by dinner.

But in some synagogues the main emphasis and time for spiritual gathering is on Saturday morning. Here is where the majority of the community comes to pray and study, welcomes *bar* or *bat mitzvahs* (except in most Orthodox communities, where there are only *bar mitzvahs*) into Jewish adulthood, and make the day of *Shabbat* meaningful. In either case, the idea is to set aside time for family and community to gather, pray, study, and reinforce the idea that one of our primary challenges and tasks in life is to be holy and bring more holiness into the world. It's our challenge to imitate God as the source of holiness, just like the opening words of Leviticus 19 suggest: "Be holy because I, your God, am holy."

To make something holy is to set it apart from other things, to make it special and ultimately important. That is why the Torah tells us, "Remember the Sabbath day and keep it holy" (Exodus 20:8). Is it doable? You bet. Being holy is easier than you think. All of us can belong to a synagogue, attend religious services, or read the Torah regardless of our religious background or Jewish education. Each of us has virtually an unlimited range of possibilities for making the Sabbath *holy* in a personal way. Avoid those that say that one way is better, more acceptable, more "correct," or more appropriate than another. If what you're doing brings that perfection we're trying to achieve with *Shabbat* closer to reality, then however you choose to celebrate *is* the right way.

THE THREE TRADITIONAL *SHABBAT* RITUALS
Naturally, certain rituals for celebrating *Shabbat* have become commonly practiced over the course of Jewish history. The three most important take

place on Friday night: (1) lighting and reciting a blessing over candles, (2) reciting a blessing over wine, and (3) reciting a blessing over challah (twisted egg-bread prepared for *Shabbat*). Jews perform these three rituals in the following manner.

Lighting *Shabbat* Candles

It's customary to light at least two candles on *Shabbat*, although some households light a candle for every family member. Traditionally, the woman of the house has the honor and recites the blessing, although it's perfectly permissible for a man to do it. In the latter members take turns leading each of these *Shabbat* blessings while everyone joins in. Traditionally, after lighting the candles, the person performing the ritual "pulls" the warmth of the lights toward herself by waving her hands three times over the flames. Then she covers her eyes so she does not yet see the flames, and recites the blessing:

בָּרוּךְ אַתָּה יְהוָה אֱלֹהֵינוּ מֶלֶךְ הָעוֹלָם, אֲשֶׁר קִדְּשָׁנוּ בְּמִצְווֹתָיו,
וְצִוָּנוּ לְהַדְלִיק נֵר שֶׁל שַׁבָּת.

Baruch ata Adonai, Eloheinu melech ha-olam, asher kid'shanu b'mitzvotav,
v'tzivanu lehadlik ner shel Shabbat.

"Blessed are You, Source of Light our God, the Sovereign of all worlds, who makes our lives holy through *mitzvot*, and commands us to kindle the *Shabbat* light."

Since lighting the candles marks the "official" beginning of *Shabbat*, at the conclusion of the blessing many wish each other "*Shabbat shalom*" or "Good *Shabbos*."

Many Jews set aside a special set of candlesticks that they only use on *Shabbat*. Others rotate them depending on season or mood. Feel free to use the candlesticks that you and others in your home feel most comfortable using. You might even encourage your children to participate by letting them have or make their own as part of their contribution to make *Shabbat* special. Jennifer and her husband gave their daughters their own *Shabbat* candlesticks at age six and let them help with the candle lighting and prayers each week. Another way to make *Shabbat* special is to paint a challah plate at a local pottery store or sew a challah cover. Some Jews go as far as decorating a matchbox that they use only for *Shabbat*. There are endless ways to make your *Shabbat* celebration unique.

The Blessing over Wine

The second *Shabbat* ritual involves reciting a blessing over wine (or techni-cally, the "fruit of the vine"). Wine is a traditional part of every Jewish holiday or festival because it's a symbol of joy and sweetness. *Shabbat* is supposed to be a time of joy, and in fact there is a rabbinic saying, "In the end of time, we will be brought to judgment for all the opportunities for Sabbath joy that we had which we passed up."

Usually, sweet red wine honors *Shabbat*, but since *you* are the one drink-ing it, use whatever wine or nonalcoholic grape juice you like. The special blessing over the fruit of the vine on *Shabbat* is the *kiddush* (sanctification), and it is traditionally recited or chanted by the man of the house, but a woman can equally do the honors. In many homes, the entire family says the blessing together.

בָּרוּךְ אַתָּה יְהֹוָה אֱלֹהֵינוּ מֶלֶךְ הָעוֹלָם, בּוֹרֵא פְּרִי הַגָּפֶן.

Baruch ata Adonai, Eloheinu melech ha-olam, borei pri ha-gafen.

"Blessed are You, our God, Sovereign of all worlds, who creates the fruit of the vine."

In some homes, each person has his own cup of wine for the blessing, and in others a single cup is blessed and then passed around for everyone to share. Many families use special *kiddush* cups made of silver, ceramic, pewter, or glass. Naturally, you can use any cup that is available, since when you use it to bless the wine on *Shabbat* it automatically *becomes* a *kiddush* cup. Be creative and flexible. There are certainly hundreds of ways that one might decorate or make a *kiddush* cup.

One way of personalizing *Shabbat* rituals is to have each family member (or friends if present) mention one joy from the past week that they are willing to share. These joys are then symbolically placed in the *kiddush* cup and create an atmosphere of happiness that pervades the entire *kiddush* experience. Once you (or the designated person) recite the prayer, it is as if you are blessing all your collective joys as well as the joy of *Shabbat* itself.

Remember, it's usually best to add one ritual, idea, celebration, or experi-ence at a time to your family's *Shabbat* repertoire. In that way, no one ritual seems overwhelming, and it's easier to integrate a new idea into your ritual whenever you choose to do so.

The Blessing over Bread

In traditional Jewish practice, every meal begins with a simple blessing over bread. Bingo, if you guessed challah. Of course, if you don't have challah, you can recite the blessing over any bread you have. Challah is available from some bakeries and supermarkets, and also from many delicatessens. Additionally, there is a delicious frozen challah dough that you finish baking in your own oven made by a company called Kinneret that is available in many supermarket frozen food sections.

The blessing over the bread, *Motzi* (prayer signifying bringing forth bread), is usually recited by the entire family, or given as an honor to a guest or older relative. Some Jews also recite this blessing before any meal, any day of the week:

בָּרוּךְ אַתָּה יְהֹוָה אֱלֹהֵינוּ מֶלֶךְ הָעוֹלָם, הַמּוֹצִיא לֶחֶם מִן הָאָרֶץ.

Baruch ata Adonai, Eloheinu melech ha-olam, hamotzi lechem min ha-aretz.
"Blessed are You, our God, Sovereign of all worlds, who brings forth bread from the earth."

Many families pass challah around first so everyone at the table can tear off a piece prior to reciting the blessing. The custom is to tear the challah rather than cut it because *Shabbat* is a time of peace and Jews considered knives instruments of war. Tearing the bread instead of cutting it symbolizes our rejection of war and bloodshed, and our desire to create a world free from the need for weapons of destruction.

It's an interesting fact that the Hebrew words for bread (*lechem*) and war (*milkhama*) come from the same root. This reminds us that bread—sustenance—has often been the root of war throughout the course of human history. When the day comes when we have created a world providing sustenance for everyone in abundance, perhaps wars will cease.

A BLESSING FOR CHILDREN

Although the three blessings over the candles, wine, and bread form the core of a *Shabbat* celebration, one of our favorite rituals involves a blessing over children. A wonderful Jewish custom on *Shabbat* is that after the other three blessings are recited prior to the meal, parents stand beside their children (one at a time, if you have several) to give them their own blessing.

Some prefer to recite in Hebrew (transliterated here) while others prefer standard English. This is for you to decide.

For Boys:

יְשִׂימְךָ אֱלֹהִים כְּאֶפְרַיִם וְכִמְנַשֶּׁה.

Ye'simcha Elohim ke'Ephraim ve'chi Menashe.

"May God make you like Ephraim and Menashe."

For Girls:

יְשִׂימֵךְ אֱלֹהִים כְּשָׂרָה רִבְקָה רָחֵל וְלֵאָה.

Ye'simech Elohim ke'Sarah, Rivka, Rachel ve'Leah.

"May God make you like Sarah, Rebecca, Rachel, and Leah."

For Both:

יְבָרֶכְךָ יְהֹוָה וְיִשְׁמְרֶךָ

יָאֵר יְהֹוָה פָּנָיו אֵלֶיךָ וִיחֻנֶּךָּ

יִשָּׂא יְהֹוָה פָּנָיו אֵלֶיךָ וְיָשֵׂם לְךָ שָׁלוֹם.

Ye'varech'echa Adonai ve'yish'mer'echa.

Ya'ir Adonai panav eilecha vichuneka.

Yisa Adonai panav eilecha, ve'yasim lecha shalom.

"May God bless you and watch over you.

May God shine the Divine face toward you and show you favor.

May God be favorably disposed toward you and grant you peace."

Jennifer and her husband use the traditional blessing in Hebrew with their twins and bless both simultaneously in synagogue, and afterward they discuss what they give thanks for that week and what they liked best about the service. But Steven and his wife always created their own *Shabbat* blessings for their daughter that reflected their thoughts that week and included goals, dreams, hopes, and desires for their daughter and her life. When you discuss what you're thankful for or what touched you in the service, or even incorporate your own personal blessings each week, you'll find that your kids never get bored and it promotes positive family discussions.

DO-IT-YOURSELF *SHABBAT*

Shabbat is definitely a do-it-yourself experience. Beyond the traditional blessings we have shared, the rest is up to you. Your challenge is to find ways of making *Shabbat* fit your family's lifestyle. No two families are exactly alike, and no two have exactly the same background and interests. It's no surprise that different families put their own touches on how they celebrate *Shabbat* in their own homes.

Another custom that many families adopt is to empty their pockets of change and put it into a family *tzedakah* box before lighting the *Shabbat* candles. *Tzedakah* means "righteousness" in Hebrew, but most Jews think of it as "charity." In Jewish tradition, *tzedakah* isn't exactly charity, because it is seen as a moral obligation, an expectation of righteousness that is incumbent upon everyone no matter how rich or poor. In this way, we remember that celebrating *Shabbat* is a time to rededicate ourselves to share our blessings with those less fortunate— only then will the world come closer to its messianic potential.

Making a *tzedakah* box is a fun project to take on if you have kids as it's an important first step in helping them realize that it's a Jewish obligation to take care of others. Jennifer remembers when her twins started a *tzedakah* box (really, a can) at day school, then brought it home to enlist help with the finishing touches. Four years later, their *tzedakah* cans are still in use and often prompt discussion about helping others.

Be creative and enlist the help of family and friends. Ask the rest of your family to come up with suggestions for adding something special or unique to your own way of celebrating *Shabbat*. The most important element is your own involvement and participation in the process of creating the kind of *Shabbat* experience that you and your family will share. The details of exactly what you do or how you choose to celebrate become far less important than the idea that you are making your *Shabbat* experience your own.

WEEKLY FAREWELL PARTY

But that's not all. Unlike most holidays where celebrations occur during their duration, *Shabbat* is so important that some throw this rock star among holy days a weekly farewell party. A *Havdalah* service marks the end of *Shabbat*.

Those conducting the service, which can be done in synagogue or at home, use a wine glass, a special braided *Havdalah* candle, along with *besamim* (spices) stored in a decorative container. Smelling the spices is believed to revive us after losing our extra *Shabbat* soul (see page 174).

Often Jewish day schools will help their young students make a spice container as an art project. Jennifer's twins made one at age three, and her entire family attended their first synagogue-led *Havdalah* service. She recalls the wonder of using all five senses—to taste the wine, smell the spices, see the flame of the candle, feel its heat, and hear the blessings. When the candle is extinguished in the wine, *Shabbat* is over. Bidding *Shabbat* farewell with prayers, candles, wine, songs, and spices are about as close as most Jews get to any real ties with Kabbalah.

Above all, the Torah tells us to rejoice in the Sabbath and call it a delight. The more you make *Shabbat* meaningful for you and your family, the more it becomes just that.

CHAI NOTES

- The most important holiday in Judaism is *Shabbat*, and it occurs weekly.
- *Shabbat* is the only day mentioned explicitly in the Ten Commandments (the fourth).
- All Jewish days begin at sunset.
- *Shabbat* provides an opportunity to take a break from the workweek and focus internally.
- *Shabbat* is often described as a representation of the Messianic age to come.
- Common traditions at *Shabbat* include lighting candles, reciting the *kiddush* over wine, and reciting the *Motzi* prayer over challah.
- Jewish parents typically bless their children on *Shabbat*.
- *Tzedakah* is an important obligation, and many collect change on *Shabbat*.
- The *Havdalah* service marks the official end of *Shabbat* each week.

7

Holidays and Holy Days

‫ז‬

Most Jews experience Judaism primarily through celebrating holidays. In fact, even those who go out of their way to let you know that they aren't particularly "religious" usually still light candles on Chanukah or show up for a *seder* on Passover. For such Jews (and in fact, for all Jews), setting aside these moments as special "Jewish times" is one of the primary ways they reinforce their sense of Jewish identity. Each year, these holidays not only link them emotionally with past events in Jewish history but also connect them with Jews worldwide that are celebrating the same holidays at virtually the same time.

The most important values in Judaism come to life through its customs, holidays, and traditions that fill the Jewish year. These traditions, some going back thousands of years, provide a concrete, hands-on approach to expressing Jewish identity. Perhaps that's why so many of our celebrations center on simple family rituals that can be carried out by adults and children at home, regardless of the level of their formal Jewish training. In many ways, the challenge you face as a new Jew centers on your ability to integrate Jewish holidays into your family's life.

The key is to find appealing ways of marking these special days that encourage participation. Our goal is to help you find creative, time-saving ways to make holidays fun, easy to understand, and joyful to all. It's a tall order, but it's doable. First, let's briefly review the Jewish holiday calendar before we zero in on the most celebrated holidays: the High Holy Days, Chanukah, and Passover.

EARLY OR LATE?

The standing joke among Jews each year is the perpetual question, "Does the holiday come early or late?" For non-Jews, the question doesn't even make sense. How can a holiday be early or late? Doesn't it always fall on the same day each year? For example, everyone knows that Christmas is always December 25, and it never changes. But for Jews, the question is a bit more complicated than that (surprise, surprise). Everyone knows that Chanukah falls near Christmas, yet some years the first night of Chanukah might be December 1, and other years the first night might be December 23.

How can that be? It's simply because the Jewish calendar and the American "secular" calendar don't match. The American calendar (the Gregorian) that most people use is primarily based on the cycles of the earth around the sun, and it has arbitrarily made each month twenty-eight, thirty, or thirty-one days. To compensate for the fact that these numbers do not exactly reflect the earth's yearly rotation around the sun, every four years we have a leap year and add a day to the month of February. (Unless the year is divisible by one hundred; however, if it is divisible by *four hundred*, then we *do* add an extra day. But you knew that, of course.)

On the other hand, the Jewish calendar is based not only on the rotation of the earth around the sun (yearly measurement) but on the revolution of the moon around the earth (monthly measurement) and on the rotation of the earth around its own axis (daily measurement). All of this together creates a rather complex formula of counting days in a month. That formula takes into consideration twenty-nine or thirty days, since the lunar cycle is twenty-nine and a half days, plus months in the year as the solar cycle is 12.4 months, then adds an entire month periodically in leap years to make it all work.

What that means on a practical level is that Jewish holidays are always on the same day of the Hebrew calendar (e.g., Chanukah is always on the twenty-fifth of *Kislev*), but the timing of the Hebrew months shift from year to year against the Gregorian calendar, sometimes by almost an entire month. That is why in 2008 Rosh Hashanah fell on September 20, in 2009 on September 19, and in 2010 on September 9. The Hebrew date was always the same—the first day of the month of *Tishri*—but the secular date was different.

Even though Jewish holidays always fall around the same time of year, the only way you'll ever know *exactly* when our holidays occur is to consult a Jewish calendar. If you are really interested, there are many applications for computers, netbooks, handhelds, and even smart phones of all kinds that include Jewish calendars where the Hebrew dates and holidays simply appear right alongside your secular date. Even Microsoft Outlook has a Hebrew setting on its calendar, and Jennifer uses it on her desktop and laptop to plan for upcoming holidays.

MORE HOLIDAYS THAN YOU CAN SHAKE A *LULAV* AT

Jewish holy days kick off each year in fall with Rosh Hashanah (the Jewish New Year), Yom Kippur (the Day of Atonement), and the ten days of repentance that connect them, *Yamim Noraim* (Days of Awe). Unlike secular New Year celebrations, Jewish civilization has always understood the New Year to be one of introspection, self-renewal, and spiritual and ethical assessment. It is a time to look into the moral mirror of our own conduct during the prior year and judge how we fared against our own best intentions and communal standards of ethical behavior. It's also time to blow into a hollowed-out ram's horn, or a *shofar*, as most Jews call it. You'll likely see someone at your synagogue blowing the *shofar* on both Rosh Hashanah and Yom Kippur. Typically, your rabbi will designate someone at your synagogue to blow it at four particular occasions in the prayers on Rosh Hashanah, and to mark the end of the fast at Yom Kippur. The *shofar* has four distinct sounds:

1. *Tekiah*: One long blast with a clear tone
2. *Shevarim*: A broken, sighing sound of three short calls
3. *Teruah*: The alarm, a rapid series of nine or more very short notes
4. *Tekiah gedolah*: A single unbroken blast, held as long as possible

Then we have the daunting task of resolving to change for the better so that we can become the spiritually self-actualized person we strive to be. This season is marked mainly by participating in synagogue services and reading from the *machzor* (communal prayer book) to lift prayers for repentance, renewal, and spiritual rebirth to God.

Most realize that this season is also infamous for something else: attendance. This is where the phrases "holiday-only Jew" or "yearly Jew" come into play. It's these holidays where you may not find a convenient parking place. It's these holidays where you forego work to attend. And it's on these holidays that you will see faces you haven't seen all year.

In other words, the High Holy Day season is a yearly opportunity to reconnect with the best within and make a personal and communal pledge to be better in the year ahead. It is a fundamental acknowledgment that God passed Jewish tradition to the Jewish People (and ultimately all people) from the time of the Ten Commandments until today. It's the principle that, because we're all created in the image of God, what we say matters, what we do matters, and who we are *really* matters. This sacred season is the time each year when we are reminded that we do not accept an impersonal life that is simply "fated." Instead, we recognize that each of us is responsible for the quality of our choices and are a result of the quality of our lives.

Throughout this season, your rabbi and cantor wear pure white vestments. The Torah scrolls also wear white covers. Some Jews follow the tradition wearing white during these holidays and avoiding wearing leather or other animal products on Yom Kippur under the belief that it would offend God to ask for Divine forgiveness while wearing something made from one of God's creations. We greet each other with *"Shanah Tovah"* (Happy New Year), *"L'Shanah Tovah Tikatevu"* (To a Good New Year where you are inscribed in the Book of Life), or simply "Good *Yontiff*" or *"Yom Tov"* (Happy Holiday). On Rosh Hashanah we eat round *challot* to remind us of the circular nature of the year.

Yom Kippur is one Jewish holiday definitely not known for its food. In fact, it's best known for the *lack* of food, as Yom Kippur is a day of fasting and repentance. And when we say fasting, we mean it! No coffee or water or any food. Imagine what happens when you put an entire congregation in one room for an entire day, have them constantly stand, then sit, then stand again, sometimes physically beating their chests, and you don't feed them? Oy! Remarkably, you end up with a community focused on repenting the sins of *all* Jews, so that God allows us all to live for another year.

MAKE YOUR *SUKKAH* SHINE

Five days after Yom Kippur comes yet another holiday, *Sukkot* (the Festival of Booths, or Feast of the Tabernacles). *Sukkot* in biblical times was known as a thanksgiving celebration for the fruit of the harvest. Two special guest appearances of this holiday are a *lulav* (a closed frond of the date palm tree, along with sprigs of myrtle and willow) and an *etrog* (fragrant yellow citron). Rabbis recite a daily blessing over both during the holiday, or families often do this at home. Jennifer recalls the first time her family attended an informal synagogue dinner under a *sukkah* (a temporary "booth" built for *Sukkot*) and how her twins delighted in reciting the blessing with the rabbi, touching the bumpy, perfumy *etrog*, and waving the *lulav*.

Over the centuries, *Sukkot* has continued to be a fall celebration showing gratitude for food and its nourishment, yet less emphasis is now placed on harvesting. *Sukkot* in the twentieth and twenty-first centuries has become a time to teach empathy for the homeless and hungry in our society as it's celebrated by spending time over a week in a simple, homemade booth or hut. Most families either build or buy a pop-up *sukkah* online and decorate it by hanging fruit, vegetables, and children's artwork.

The *mitzvah*, or religious obligation associated with *Sukkot*, is "to dwell in the *sukkah*" and traditionally to invite spiritual guests (called *ushpizin*) like Abraham, Isaac, Jacob, Moses, Miriam, Sarah, Rebecca, Leah, or any other biblical figures or those from Jewish history to share your *sukkah*. This can become a wonderful opportunity for families to share their values, ask others to join their *sukkah*, and invite any others alive or from history.

Sukkot lasts for seven days according to the *Torah* and Reform and Reconstructionist Jews, and eight days for Conservative, Orthodox, and other traditional Jews who add a final day called *Sh'mini Atzeret* (or the eighth day of celebration). This eighth day culminates in the holiday of *Simchat Torah* (celebrating the Torah).

Simchat Torah is the day we celebrate by reading the end of Deuteronomy and follow it with the first lines of Genesis to demonstrate that the annual cycle of reading the Torah never ends. Jews read a section of these five books in synagogues worldwide in a continuous annual cycle. *Simchat Torah*, the name of which literally means "joy of Torah," is a very joyful holiday. Every Torah scroll is removed from the ark, and worshippers carry the scrolls around the synagogue seven times, dancing and singing. Often, mini-scrolls appear for children to carry, and many children also bring or make their own flags to carry and wave during the processions.

In December, Jews celebrate Chanukah (the Festival of Lights), which means "dedication," to commemorate the first recorded fight for religious freedom in 165 BCE. This is when our Jewish ancestors defeated the Syrian army. But more on that in a few pages.

Tu B'shvat (New Year of Trees) marks the next Jewish holiday of the year. It's the fifteenth day of the Hebrew month of *Shvat*. The holiday marks the time each year when Jews plant trees in Israel and in their own communities as a reminder of our need to revive nature by making *mitzvah* toward the earth. Long before there was an Earth Day, Jews had Psalm 24, which teaches, "The earth is God's and all its fullness." We created *Tu B'shvat* as the "birthday of the trees" to teach one another that one of our most important jobs in life is to take care of the earth and its environment that we oversee as a sacred trust.

Purim (meaning "lots") usually falls in February or early March. It is a holiday of costumes and carnivals, and celebrates the Jewish victory in ancient Persia over the villain Haman, who schemed to murder the Jewish community. Jennifer recalls a funny story of when her three-and-a-half-year-old twins were mesmerized by a Purim play that featured larger-than-life costumed characters at their Houston synagogue. Haman, oddly, was represented by a large stick. When Jennifer's brother, Paul, asked about the play the next day at her synagogue's Purim carnival, one daughter joyfully offered a description of King Ahashueras and Queen Esther. When Paul asked, "What about Haman?" Jennifer's other daughter passionately interjected in a loud and far-reaching voice, "Haman was a BIG —ICK!" But instead of the *ST*, insert a *D*, and you'll get it (after all, this is a book about religion). Needless to say, the story told on the synagogue grounds in Texas made it all the way to Oregon, proving converting often comes with a wide range of firsts that you *never* could have imagined or expected. This is why we believe the key to dealing with the data download that accompanies conversion is to give yourself license to laugh along the way. Now, back to the holidays.

A month after Purim comes the festival of Passover (*Pesach*), which celebrates the Jewish Exodus from slavery in Egypt. Remember the classic movie *The Ten Commandments* with Charlton Heston, Yul Brynner, and an overacting cast of thousands? This was one of Jennifer's favorites growing up. God, through Moses, brought ten plagues upon the Egyptian Pharaoh and led the Jewish People into the Sinai desert on the way to receive the Ten Commandments, and then to the Promised Land of Israel. Passover is a weeklong holiday that Jews celebrate more than any other Jewish holiday of the year, primarily at a ceremonial ritual dinner called a *seder* (order). We'll go into much more detail on Passover in a bit.

Shavuot (the Feast of Weeks) occurs seven weeks after Passover and marks the giving of the Torah to Moses and the Jewish People at Mount Sinai. Typically Shavuot is commemorated by studying Torah or other important Jewish issues late into the night. Some synagogues sponsor classes and lectures that run until midnight or even into the next morning.

Tisha B'av is a sacred day that falls in the summer on the ninth day of the Hebrew month of *Av*. This holiday commemorates the destruction of both the First and Second Temples in Jerusalem, and the anniversary of the edict to expel all the Jews from Spain by Queen Isabella and King Ferdinand in 1492. The latter is important because most Jews were painfully forced to convert to Christianity or, worse, tortured and sentenced to death. Many times both occurred.

Besides these ancient and traditional Jewish holidays, new holidays and communal celebrations have graced the calendar as a result of the triumphs and traumas of twentieth-century Jewish life.

Yom Ha-atzmaut (Israel Independence Day) occurs on the fifth day of the Hebrew month of *Iyar* and marks the anniversary of the declaration of Jewish statehood that Israel's first prime minister, David Ben-Gurion, enacted. Often Jewish communities hold parades, festivals, and parties to celebrate this day.

Yom Hashoah (Holocaust Remembrance Day) takes place eight days before Israel Independence Day. It's obviously a day of great sadness; Jews around the world honor the edict regarding the Holocaust to "never forget."

THE MIRACLE OF RELIGIOUS FREEDOM

Chanukah is undoubtedly the best known of all Jewish holidays in America. It owes this fame, in no small part, to its annual proximity to Christmas. Originally a relatively minor holiday in Jewish tradition, Chanukah has grown in importance during the past century as Jews have felt a need to compete with the glamour and attraction created by the commercialization and heavy promotion of Christmas. The two holidays have virtually nothing in common except that they both utilize the symbolism of light. Christmas trees and decorations that adorn houses during the holiday season are aglow with multicolored lights, and Chanukah is the Festival of Lights. But the lights of

Chanukah are lights of a different nature, lights that represent a radically different reality from that of Christmas.

For Christianity, Christmas marks the moment when God adopted human form (Jesus) in order to provide people with the means of solving the problems they had created on earth. The lights of Christmas represent the divine light that, according to Christianity, Jesus brought into the world via his birth, and the promise of the divine light of grace symbolized by his voluntary death. For the Jewish People, the lights of Chanukah symbolize the light of religious freedom.

In the year 167 BCE, the Syrian emperor Antiochus decided to unify his kingdom by insisting that all people, including Jews, adopt a single religion: idol worship. He outlawed circumcision and teaching or practicing Judaism, and ordered Jews to abandon the Torah and publicly embrace paganism. This meant sacrificing pigs and bowing to idols.

Many Jews were sentenced to death, but one named Mattathias, along with his five sons, refused to accept this repressive policy of Jewish self-destruction and took to the hills in revolt. They inspired others to join them in a struggle that lasted for three years. Though the Jews were vastly outnumbered by the Syrian army, when the torch of leadership passed upon the death of Mattathias to his son Judah the Maccabee (the hammer), Judah led a brilliant campaign of guerrilla warfare. His wartime strategy retook the road to Jerusalem and ultimately climaxed in routing the Syrian army and the liberation of Jerusalem and its sacred Temple.

Chanukah is the celebration of the Maccabees' victory (as the entire rebel army came to be called) over the Syrian army and the rededication of the Temple in Jerusalem to its rightful place as the center of Jewish worship. The legend surrounding this remarkable victory describes how when the Maccabees entered the Temple for its rededication, they could only find a small jar of oil, enough to light the Temple menorah (candelabrum) for one day. Miraculously, it burned for eight days, which allowed them to prepare enough ritually pure oil to complete the rededication ceremony and keep the sacred menorah lit continuously.

Jewish tradition has taught that in commemoration of this miracle of the lights, we celebrate Chanukah for eight days. Many modern scholars point out that this story was overstated long after the victory of the Maccabees to emphasize God's role in our deliverance from the genocidal plan of Antiochus, and to deemphasize militarism and armed struggle. Regardless of whether you believe the oil burned eight days or not (remember, Judaism encourages questioning), the true miracle we celebrate on Chanukah is the miracle of religious freedom.

Chanukah is an annual reminder that religious freedom is a precious gift. It reminds us we must be vigilant to ensure that everyone, regardless of religion, continues to enjoy the right to practice and celebrate as he chooses, free from the tyranny of coercion. It's a day that also raises one of those crucial questions that all of us are confronted with during our lives, namely, "What is worth fighting for?" The celebration of Chanukah is an opportunity to wrestle with the implications of this question for you and your family each year.

As you may know, the main way we celebrate Chanukah is by lighting a candle each night for eight nights. Most people use a menorah (*chanukiah*) with colored candles, but some create their own or use lamps that burn olive oil. Creating your own menorah can be a wonderful family project, as it gives you the opportunity to express your family's thoughts on freedom as you create together.

The traditional way of lighting the menorah is to light one candle on the first night (plus the *shamash*, or "helper," candle), and add one candle each night until the entire menorah is filled on the last night. Some families have a separate menorah for each member. Others take turns lighting candles on a single menorah each night. Whatever way works *best* for your family is fine.

A special ceremony accompanies the lighting. Customarily, candles are placed in the menorah from right to left and lit from left to right. This means you'll light the candle that signifies the current night of Chanukah first. After the candles are placed, the *shamash* is lit first and then used to light the others.

Now to the ritual itself. Either before or while lighting the candles, the following two blessings are traditionally recited:

בָּרוּךְ אַתָּה יְיָ אֱלֹהֵינוּ מֶלֶךְ הָעוֹלָם
אֲשֶׁר קִדְּשָׁנוּ בְּמִצְוֹתָיו וְצִוָּנוּ לְהַדְלִיק נֵר שֶׁל חֲנֻכָּה.
Baruch atah Adonai Elohaynu melech ha-olam,
asher kid-shanu b'mizvotav v'tzeevanu lehadlik neyr shel Chanukah.
"Blessed are You, our God, Divine power of the universe, who makes our lives special through commandments, and commands us to kindle the Chanukah lights."

בָּרוּךְ אַתָּה יְיָ אֱלֹהֵינוּ מֶלֶךְ הָעוֹלָם
שֶׁעָשָׂה נִסִּים לַאֲבוֹתֵינוּ בַּיָּמִים הָהֵם בַּזְּמַן הַזֶּה.
Baruch atah Adonai Elohaynu melech ha-olam,
sh'asa nisim la-avotaynu, ba-yamim ha-hem bazman ha-zeh.
"Blessed are You, our God, Divine power of the universe, who performed
miracles for our ancestors in days of old at this season."

On the first night of Chanukah only, the blessing known as the *Shehecheyanu* is
recited. It marks the beginning of every holiday or special time. You'll likely
repeat it during your conversion. Reciting the *Shehecheyanu* gives thanks for the
fact that we have lived to be able to celebrate this occasion, and it goes like this:

בָּרוּךְ אַתָּה יְיָ אֱלוֹהֵינוּ מֶלֶךְ הָעוֹלָם
שֶׁהֶחֱיָנוּ וְקִיְּמָנוּ וְהִגִּיעָנוּ לַזְּמַן הַזֶּה.
Baruch atah Adonai Eloheinu melech ha'olam
she'hecheyanu v'ki'y'manu v'higiyanu lazman ha'zeh.
"Blessed are You, our God, Ruler of the Universe, who has granted us life,
sustained us, and enabled us to reach this occasion."

Jewish tradition teaches that menorah candles are lit in order to publicize the
miracle of Chanukah. In olden days, Jewish families lit menorahs outside the
front of their home so that passersby would see the lights and remember the
miracle of Chanukah. Today, Jews traditionally place the menorah in a win-
dow (without curtains, of course) to serve both as a sign of the miracle of
Chanukah and as a symbol of pride in being Jewish and having holidays to
celebrate.

If you live alone, you can celebrate the holiday by lighting the candles yourself each night and perhaps pausing to name one freedom you cherish today.
If you live with others, you might ask each to name their own cherished freedom. If you write down the freedoms you name each night, eight nights later
you'll have a beautiful reminder of the liberties you cherish and the powerful
lessons this holiday can teach you each year. Don't be surprised if your children name their favorite toys, movies, Wii games, candy, and so forth. You
might even record each child's responses in a Chanukah notebook, and by the
time they become an adult you'll see how those liberties changed over the
years. Expect some great laughs!

Celebrating Chanukah becomes one of the most joyous family times of the Jewish year. It's a time to exchange presents (many families give one present each night for eight nights), a time to sing songs about Chanukah and freedom, a time to play games and eat special holiday foods. It's customary to invite others to your home to join your celebration, and the proximity of Christmas provides a wonderful opportunity for Jews and non-Jews to share each other's holidays and learn about each other's customs.

The most famous Chanukah game is called dreidel. It uses a special four-sided spinning top with a different Hebrew letter on each side that together stand for the phrase "A great miracle happened there." In Israel, one letter is changed and the phrase reads, "A great miracle happened here." One person spins the top, and depending upon which letter is face up, the spinner either wins the pot, which is usually *gelt* (gold-foil-covered chocolate coins), takes half, gets nothing, or has to put in more.

Two special foods that are associated with Chanukah are latkes (potato pancakes) and *sufganiyot* (jelly donuts). Both became Chanukah foods because they are fried in oil and remind us of the jar of oil that lasted eight days and allowed the rededication of the Temple in Jerusalem to take place after the Maccabee victory.

You can celebrate Chanukah any way you wish. The most personal way is to be creative and add something new and different of your own each year. For example, Steven remembers as a child with his sisters making their own Chanukah decorations, drawing pictures of their favorite freedoms on large paper and hanging them around their house. Try doing the same on a simpler (or, for that matter, more ambitious) scale in your own family. Pick one activity each year and add it to your celebration repertoire. If you have young children, you can ask them to help make latkes or *sufganiyot* (of course, driving to the donut shop is quicker!). Other ideas include drawing pictures of Judah Maccabee, a dreidel, a menorah, a jar of oil, or any other Chanukah scene to post as decorations. There are also many commercially made Chanukah decorations that you can buy to create a festive ambiance in your home. Use your imagination, don't be intimidated by a lack of Jewish experience, and you'll discover that Chanukah can be one of the most wonderful and loving family experiences of the year.

THE THREE-HOUR MEAL

Passover is not only the most widely observed holiday but also the one that often prompts loved ones to discretely eye their wristwatches. Interesting enough, it's also one that fascinates young and old alike. It's a special time when families gather to share a festive meal that revolves around odd foods, four cups of wine, and the story of how our ancestors were liberated from slavery in Egypt.

Rich with rituals and symbols, songs and stories, it's all designed to remind us that, for the Jewish People, freedom is most important of all. Passover is the quintessential home holiday. Its celebration centers around the family dinner table, where an elaborate dinner party called a *seder* takes place.

The meal is called a *seder* because there is a definite order to the various rituals, foods, and stories that are told. Participants follow a guidebook called a *Haggadah* (telling), which gives step-by-step instructions regarding which foods to eat in what order and their meanings, the stories to tell, when to drink wine, and even which songs to sing.

Passover's universal themes of liberation from all forms of bondage, freedom from hunger and want, and the rebirth and renewal of spring touch the hearts of everyone. It's a holiday that's most fully appreciated when shared with others, whether it's extended family, friends, or a community. In fact, the beginning of the *seder* contains a phrase in Aramaic that states, "Let all who are hungry come and eat. Let all who are in need come and share the Passover with us."

It's easy to see why Passover has always served as a concrete lesson in responsibility and interrelatedness. One cannot share a *seder* meal without realizing the importance of all people being freed from the oppression of hunger and poverty, homelessness and want. At every turn, the rituals teach us that Judaism believes freedom and justice is the natural, God-given state human beings were meant to enjoy.

In a sense, learning and teaching the moral lessons of Passover is the easiest task of all. To do so, all you need is to participate in the *seder* itself, sharing the unusual Passover foods and hearing the stories of slavery and freedom, and you and your children can't help but learn its moral imperative. The holiday is a self-contained educational experience, which in each generation has taught us its crucial and powerful lessons.

The name *Passover* comes from the biblical story where death passes over the houses of the Israelite slaves during the tenth and final plague. The story teaches that although Pharaoh had decreed that all Israelite baby boys were to be thrown into the Nile and drowned, this tenth plague caused the death of all firstborn Egyptians instead. It was only then that Pharaoh's spirit was broken and he allowed the Israelites to go free.

Passover is the celebration of this freedom after four hundred years of slavery in Egypt. In it we retell the story of our slavery and liberation, and we pledge to do whatever we can to see that all people are free. If you're looking for family movies other than *The Ten Commandments*, try the animated *Prince of Egypt*. It's often a good way to introduce the story and talk to your children about it before you hold a *seder*.

One of the most fascinating aspects of Jewish civilization is that we remember and connect to the slavery of our ancestors. Most people long to forget the poverty and degradation of their past, obscuring it from memory and glorifying instead the successes and heights to which their people have risen. On the other hand, Jews treat our past slavery as a constant lesson for the present and future. In fact, Jewish tradition goes so far as to command every Jew to recall our slavery as a *personal* experience. Even our *Haggadah* states, "In every generation, each person is obligated to feel as if he or she personally went forth from the slavery of Egypt."

This personal experience of slavery is our collective way of ensuring that we never become too complacent. It ensures that we never get too comfortable and think that freeing the world from slavery, poverty, and injustice is someone else's responsibility. Passover reminds us each year that we have a duty to help those enslaved because we know the pain of slavery. It reminds us that we must help strangers in our land because we know what it's like to be a stranger in a foreign land.

Each year, as we celebrate Passover, we have another opportunity to teach these lessons to our children. Simple step-by-step guides are available online or at most bookstores if you need help with the structure. Some are geared toward adults and others are great for families with young children. Local synagogues often have workshops and one-time seminars designed for those who want to learn how to lead their own *seder*.

Matzah, *Charoset*, and *Maror*, Oh My!

For many years, the *Ten Commandments* always aired on television around the same time as the *Wizard of Oz*. Because this was Jennifer's other favorite movie growing up and because what's on the *seder* plate can be a little eye-opening, we couldn't resist subtitling this section after the classic film's famous line, "Lions, tigers, and bears, oh my!"

On to Passover. Besides having a *seder* in your home, many Jews also have one on the second night, either in their homes again or at their synagogues. The second-night *seder* can be different from the first if you focus on a particular theme like freedom for Jews or others, ecology, an end to human trafficking, women's liberation, release of kidnapped Israeli soldier Gilad Shalit, and the like.

The primary symbols of Passover are found on the ceremonial *seder* plate that usually sits in front of the leader:

1. Roasted shankbone symbolizes the Passover offering brought to the Temple in Jerusalem in ancient times (when animal sacrifices were a normal part of religious ceremonies). It also reminds us of the biblical phrase that God redeemed us from slavery "with an outstretched arm." Furthermore, it's a reminder that on the actual night of liberation from Egypt, Israelite slaves had enough faith in the power of freedom to slaughter lambs, which symbolized Egyptian gods, and smear blood on their doors. That took *chutzpah!*

2. *Maror* (bitter herbs), usually grated horseradish root or romaine lettuce, symbolizes the bitterness of slavery.

3. *Karpas* (parsley) or any green herb or vegetable, represents spring, renewal, rebirth, and hope for the future. During the *seder*, the parsley is dipped in salt water (a symbol of the tears of slavery) to remind us that despair must always be mixed with hope. It's also a reminder of how our ancestors used a leafy vegetable as a brush to smear the blood of the lambs on their doorposts on the night of their liberation.

4. Roasted egg symbolizes the continuing cycles of life (since it's round); it also serves as a reminder of the special holiday offering brought to the Temple in Jerusalem in ancient times. Some people see it as a symbol of the Jewish People's will to survive. Just as an egg becomes harder as you boil it, so too do the Jewish People continue to emerge from the heat of persecution and oppression, stronger and more resilient than ever.

5. *Charoset* (a mixture of nuts, apples, wine, and cinnamon) serves as a symbol of the mortar that the Israelites used for making bricks during their slavery to build cities for Pharaoh.

6. Matzah is the best known of all the symbolic foods of Passover. Matzah is simply unleavened bread that is used both during the *seder* meal and

throughout the week of Passover, since the chief commandment of the holiday is to avoid eating anything that is leavened (*hametz*).

Besides preparing the *seder* plate, you'll need to place three ceremonial pieces of matzah in the center of the table (or in front of the leader). They represent the two traditional loaves of bread that were a part of every holiday. They also serve to remind us that God provided a double portion of food for our ancestors during their forty years of wandering in the desert each Sabbath so that they didn't need to work to gather food. Plus, you place an extra matzah to symbolize Passover itself. Today many people set out a fourth matzah, "the Matzah of Hope," to remind us of Jews and non-Jews who live in countries where they are still not free to worship as they choose.

Matzah is first mentioned in the Torah in Exodus 12:34–39, where we learn that the Israelites left Egypt in such a hurry (wouldn't you if you were heading to your freedom?) that they simply slapped their dough on their backs and it baked in the hot desert sun without rising. This is why we eat matzah on Passover: to remind us of our rush to freedom. Matzah is also called the "bread of affliction" since slaves eat only the simplest of foods, such as bread made with flour and water, like matzah. Each time we eat matzah, it recalls both our slavery *and* our freedom, and this makes it the perfect ritual symbol for the entire Passover season.

Toward the beginning of the *seder*, the middle matzah (of the ceremonial three) is broken, and the leader hides half called the *afikomen*. It's customary that once it's hidden, children in the house have to find it at the end of the meal. This is often a highlight for children as, once it's located, they can bargain with the leader for prizes, money, candy, or gifts before returning it since the *seder* is technically not supposed to end without it.

The Four Questions

One of the most important elements of the *seder* is asking questions. The *seder* is designed to provoke questions, especially from children, who sit and wonder about the peculiar foods, the elaborate *seder* table, and all the excitement of the evening. Almost everything is designed to stimulate questions, answers, and discussions. In fact, Jewish tradition states that the longer you talk about the experience of being slaves and going free from Egypt, the more praiseworthy you are. Prepare for a long night!

The most famous of all questions during the *seder* are "The Four Questions." They are traditionally asked by the youngest child who is able. The purpose of the questions is to make us aware of the unusual elements of the evening and invite the leader (or anyone who wants to join in) to retell the story of our Exodus from Egypt. The four questions are kicked off with this initial question: "Why is this night different from all other nights?" The four questions are as follows:

1. On all other nights we eat leavened or unleavened bread. Tonight, why do we eat only unleavened bread?
2. On all other nights we eat all kinds of vegetables. Tonight, why do we eat only bitter herbs?
3. On all other nights we are not required to dip at our meal. Tonight, why do we dip two times?
4. On all other nights we eat either seated upright or reclining. Tonight, why do we all recline?

The remainder of the *seder* is really a response to these four questions. They form the framework around which answers are given, and the stories that unfold carry with them the essence of the lessons contained in the festival of Passover.

Elijah, You There?
One of best-remembered and best-loved moments in the Passover *seder* (especially for children) takes place when someone (usually a child) is asked to open the door for Elijah. This is the biblical prophet who, according to tradition, will return to announce the coming of the Messiah or messianic age, which brings freedom, peace, justice, and redemption to the world.

There is always an aura of excitement when the door is opened for Elijah, and it creates a kind of mystical moment when all our hopes for the future of the world are drawn together in the symbol of this ancient prophet. We set out a special glass of wine (the Cup of Elijah) that sits in the center of our table untouched throughout the *seder*, waiting for Elijah to enter and drink.

Since Passover is a holiday that celebrates the liberation of our past and the freedom we dream for the future, Elijah and his messianic message is a perfect symbol of our hopes and desires for the world. There is a lovely custom of filling Elijah's cup by having everyone at the table pour a little wine from their glasses to symbolize that the messianic age will come only if we all contribute to make it happen.

Living Our Values

Passover is a holiday of values and ideals, of hopes for the future and memories of the past. For example, when we retell the story of the ten plagues in Egypt, it's a tradition to remove a drop of wine from our cups at the mention of each plague. This is a reminder that the freedom of our ancestors meant Egyptians had to suffer too, and since they were created in God's image, our joy should be diminished. One of the most important ideas that Passover represents is that *we* are not free as long as *any* man or woman is not free. We can hardly rejoice fully in the defeat of our enemies as long as others are oppressed, suffering, or being sold into slavery.

Passover teaches us that oppression and slavery take many forms in our lives. We are slaves when we feel trapped in jobs that rob us of our sense of self-worth and fill our days with unsatisfying drudgery. We are slaves when we stay in abusive or self-destructive relationships or marriages. We are slaves when we fall prey to addictions of all kinds, whether drugs, alcohol, gambling, or any other self-destructive impulse that we allow to control our lives.

Oppression is found as well in the poverty and hunger that plague the lives of millions throughout the world. As long as people live each day in the pursuit of the most elemental needs of life—shelter, food, and clothing—they are slaves. To live in a world in which tens of millions of men, women, and children go to bed each night without adequate health care is to support a system that keeps people from experiencing the fullness of their liberty.

Personalize Your Passover

You can personalize Passover in hundreds of ways. The entire family can be involved in creating Passover decorations, *seder* plates, cups for wine, the *Haggadah*, or even creative place cards for the table. Family members, no matter how old or young they might be, can help prepare the meal or the special Passover ritual foods.

Children can help make *charoset* by peeling (or eating!) apples, sprinkling in cinnamon, or breaking up walnuts. They can set the table or help serve the meal (one custom is not to serve yourself during Passover, since having another serve you is a sign of freedom).

An excellent way of involving the entire family in discovering the meaning of Passover is to hold up each item on the *seder* plate one at a time and ask each member of the family to think of their own personal associations or meanings for every symbol.

1. For *maror*, ask, "What is bitter in the world today, in your own life, or in the lives of family or friends?"
2. For the shankbone, ask, "What are you willing to sacrifice in order to solve some of the world's problems? Also, what is something in your life that is worth sacrificing for?"
3. Hold up the parsley or the egg (symbols of renewal, spring, and rebirth) and ask, "What has been an experience of renewal or rebirth for you (or us) this year? What areas of our lives are in need of hope and what can we do about them?"
4. Hold up the *charoset* and ask, "What do we use today as our building blocks for the future? What holds our personal relationships or family together that is important to each of us?"
5. Point to the salt water and have each person declare anything in their lives or the world that is worth shedding tears over. Ask, "How can we make it better, fix the world around us, help to repair torn friendships?"

Simple activities such as these can be done verbally as you sit at the table or written by everyone beforehand and shared as part of the *seder* experience. These are merely a few examples of the many different ways that you can personalize your Passover experience to make it more meaningful and relevant to your family.

THE "TEN-MINUTE" HOLIDAY

For many people, the idea of celebrating a holiday they haven't grown up with is extremely intimidating. They stress over all the history, rituals, customs, foods, blessings, and unfamiliar rites they would have to learn well to celebrate the holiday the "right way."

The most important element is your willingness to try something new, to take it one step at a time, according to the pace and level of involvement that fit your lifestyle. Holidays do not have to be elaborate events, filled with religious details and traditional customs. They don't have to last three hours, either. They can be simple, tailor-made activities that you share with your family to mark these special occasions during the year as significant Jewish moments.

That is why we believe that nearly every celebration can be a "ten-minute" holiday if you want it to be. Chanukah can be celebrated as simply as lighting candles in the menorah and reciting the appropriate blessings. You can write the blessings in advance on individual pieces of paper (or on one large sheet that hangs on the wall) so that everyone can easily read them at the appropriate time. This simple ritual can take no more than ten minutes each time you do it.

If having your own Passover *seder* is too intimidating at first, you could simply have a dinner that includes one *seder* plate in the middle of the table. If you do nothing more than hold up each item on the plate and repeat what we have written in this chapter about each one, or ask your family to share their own associations of what the items symbolize, you will have acknowledged Passover in a "ten-minute" holiday.

This rule can also lend itself to every *Shabbat*. Lighting candles, blessing the wine and challah, and saying "*Shabbat shalom*" and, presto, you have a weekly "ten-minute" holiday.

CHAI NOTES

- Judaism comes to life through its customs, holidays, and traditions that fill the Jewish year.
- A challenge you face as a new Jew is your ability to integrate Jewish holidays into your family life.
- The only way you'll know when holidays occur is to consult a Jewish calendar.
- Jewish holy days kick off each year in the fall with Rosh Hashanah.
- Five days after Rosh Hashanah and Yom Kippur comes yet another holiday: *Sukkot*.
- *Simchat Torah* is the day we celebrate by reading the end of Deuteronomy and follow with the first lines of Genesis to demonstrate that the annual cycle of reading the Torah never ends.
- *Tu B'shvat* reminds us to plant trees in Israel and our own communities.
- Purim is known for its costumes and carnivals (and sticks, if you're lucky) and celebrates the Jewish victory in ancient Persia over the villain Haman.
- Passover celebrates the Jewish exodus from slavery in Egypt.

- Shavuot marks the giving of the Torah to Moses and the Jews at Mount Sinai.
- *Tisha B'av* commemorates the destruction of both the First and Second Temples in Jerusalem, and the anniversary of the edict to expel all the Jews from Spain.
- *Yom Hashoah* is Holocaust Remembrance Day and occurs before Israel Independence Day.
- *Yom Ha-atzmaut* marks the anniversary of the declaration of Jewish statehood.
- Chanukah commemorates the first recorded fight for religious freedom in 165 BCE.

8

Facing the *Bet Din*

ח

Most people feel tense when they hear they have to take a test. Now combine that with the fact that three members of a religious court, or *bet din*, have the power to decide whether you officially become Jewish. It's a little intimidating to say the least. But don't despair. If you have fulfilled all the requirements of your particular synagogue, showed a genuine interest in becoming Jewish, and your conversion rabbi has recommended you to appear before a *bet din*, he is confident that you are ready. Conversion rabbis only order *batei din* (the plural of *bet din*) for converts that have gone to great lengths to demonstrate they are ready to become Jewish.

BEHIND THE *BET DIN*

We know facing the *bet din* can feel a little like meeting the man behind the curtain in the *Wizard of Oz*, but we promise that's not the intent. Sometimes the best way to reduce preconversion jitters is to get familiar with the people that have the clout to bring you into the fold. A *bet din* is comprised of at least one rabbi and two others who are either observant or educated laypeople. Often rabbis handpick knowledgeable and supportive members of their synagogue to serve on *batei din* to involve them in important matters of the synagogue, and because convening three rabbis simultaneously might very well limit the number of conversions.

In the Conservative, Reconstructionist, and Reform movements, you will likely know one or more of your *bet din* members, but not always. Typically, you don't meet them in their official *bet din* capacity until your conversion (sponsoring) rabbi has convened a *bet din* on your behalf. In the Orthodox movement, your sponsoring rabbi will ask you to meet with your state's rabbinical council, which assigns a *bet din* outside of your sponsoring rabbi. Unlike the other three movements, as an Orthodox convert, you meet with your *bet din* early and periodically throughout the next two years until your sponsoring rabbi feels you're living the life (Torah observant, *shomer Shabbos, kashrut,* etc.) and he (there are no female rabbis in the Orthodox movement) convenes your conversion date.

Batei din witness and sanction conversion, divorce, and even communal religious matters such as *kashrut.* Historically, *batei din* decide matters of civil law and enforce ritual compliance within the Jewish community. Jews have presided over their own affairs from ancient times until around the twentieth century. *Batei din* even preside over business matters and disputes when requested by synagogue congregants. Jewish communities recognize letters from *batei din* as binding according to Jewish religious law. Some members of modern Jewish movements use *batei din* instead of civil courts to handle financial and personal matters. This allows members to avoid hefty legal fees or overburdening court dockets and offers them the ability to resolve their transgressions based on Jewish values versus legal statutes.

Traditionally, the Orthodox movement only allows men to serve on *batei din,* but the other three movements allow women on *batei din* equally with men. Some Conservative synagogues are slower to allow women to serve on *batei din* than others, but the movement permits it nonetheless. The chances of your *bet din* convening after hours or on a day of Jewish significance are nonexistent because *batei din* only convene during daylight hours, with the exception of *Shabbat* and other major holidays or festivals.

USE "WE" TERMS

It's rare for a *bet din* to turn you away if you've made a commitment to live a Jewish life, shown that you're converting out of personal choice, and talk in "we" terms when speaking about the Jewish People. Saying "we" shows that you consider yourself part of the tribe, whereas using "they" indicates that you're having difficulty embracing the Jewish People. Rabbis treat conversion seriously and will provide you the tools needed to complete your course and convert with ease. Many times, you can prepare yourself simply by taking an active role in class.

Taking time to answer life-changing questions not only helps you pave the right religious/spiritual path but also helps you transition into your Jewish identity that much quicker. Your rabbi wants to see you articulate your desire to be Jewish and what you envision so she can help you achieve your goal. She will also want to know that you have mastered your terms list because, unlike other Judeo-Christian religions, there are plenty of terms that Jews use in Hebrew and Yiddish.

It's likely your conversion rabbi will tell you not to worry; however, that doesn't mean you won't. Many converts can't help agonizing over what the *bet din* might ask. There is no getting around the fact that whether your class is eighteen weeks, twelve months, or twenty-four months, you have no control over the *bet din*. Just the idea of being "judged" over such a broad range of information can make anyone squeamish. The flip side is that the notion of not knowing encourages converts to learn quite a lot. Let's face it: if you knew the exact questions your *bet din* would ask, then you would only need to study those. The idea is that you cover as much as possible; the questions are more about your dedication and intent rather than your volumes of Jewish knowledge.

Chances are your conversion rabbi will arrange a *bet din* once you've shown a sincere interest, attended classes, asked insightful questions, and completed assignments (e.g., essay questions or defining Jewish vocabulary words). The chance of a *bet din* turning any convert away is rare. There was a case where a *bet din* member asked a convert who Jesus was and the convert responded, "Jesus was a prophet." That comment concerned the *bet din* and resulted in more questions. Many more questions later, the *bet din* vetted the convert, but the lesson is that the Jewish People consider Jesus a rabbi (teacher) and *not* a prophet. It's doubtful that your *bet din* will ask this question, but be prepared just in case. We won't say passing the *bet din* is a given, but you would really have to botch it for your *bet din* to bypass you.

Your *bet din* is looking for a sense of commitment, familiarity with customs, identification with values, indications that you're part of the tribe, and readiness to take that next step. They're not trying to set you up to fail. Conversion rabbis are confident their students will succeed once they recommend them to go be-fore a *bet din*. Even so, Jewish law mandates that converts must go through this process (as rigorous as it may seem). The good news? Time is not an issue if it's something you desire. Not even the twenty-four-month conversion process has stopped those that truly want to convert and become Orthodox.

DON'T SWEAT IT

Let us save you some hand-wringing here. Enjoy your free time. There is no need to cram for what your *bet din* might ask. Don't let the thought of going in front of three judges get to you. All three are there to help you convert, not put you on the hot seat. Jennifer made the mistake of cramming an entire day on Labor Day weekend. Her family rented a beach house and she ended up skimming twelve months' worth of class work, including eleven pages of vo-cabulary words, in a portable tent while her family boogie-boarded nearby.

In some ways, it brought Jennifer back to her college years on spring break. Yet instead of surfboards vying for her attention, it was volumes of Jewish his-tory, a spiral notebook, and a welter of vocabulary words. She now refers to her family's aquamarine and yellow tent as her "bent on becoming a Jew" tent. She sacrificed a day of family fun just so she could ace whatever zingers her *bet din* tossed her way. But guess what? Not one of the three asked her a single question or vocabulary word she so fervently inhaled that day. The questions they asked were high level and only assessed whether her heart and head were in the right place. While she knew that her *bet din* would determine whether her Jewish knowledge was up to par, she didn't know the questions would be so broad. To Jennifer's surprise, they asked questions she could have answered without cracking a book or ogling a vocabulary list, questions like the following:

- Why do you want to be a Jew?
- What does the Sabbath mean to you?
- Tell me about your belief in God.
- How will you raise your children?

She honestly thought she had to be prepared because one of the three might lob a trick question at her. This was not her experience or that of others who have come before a *bet din*. Your *bet din* isn't there to trip you up. They *want* you to succeed. While it's natural to be a little nervous, don't let it ruin your weekend. The questions are to gauge your sincerity and to make sure you're converting of your own free will. Most questions they softball you are asked to assess your commitment to Judaism, to measure your ability to put aside the religion of your youth, and to prevent you from embracing a faith that conflicts with your ideology. The bottom line is that your *bet din* wants to confirm that you're making this leap of faith because you absolutely want to, *not* because you're trying to please someone, prove a point, hold a splintered relationship together, or for any other reason but your own desire.

Still, you may worry about what to say in the off chance a *bet din* member asks you something you don't know. Like April suggests, be honest:

> If my *bet din* asked a question that I didn't know the answer to, I was going to say that I've grown up with Jewish people practically my whole life, and they don't necessarily know all the answers either, and I don't think that makes someone not Jewish. It just means that you don't have as good of a memory for history as the next guy. Sure, I was worried that I would be put on the spot and that I wouldn't know something huge that I should know, but I had just been in the class, so it was all still pretty fresh. (April, thirty-three, attorney)

ASSESSING YOUR INTENT

Other questions your *bet din* might ask include the following:

- What rituals/aspects of Judaism have you incorporated into your life?
- Tell me about your last Passover *seder.*
- Do you have any regrets about putting your former religion aside?
- Does subjecting your family to the growing trend of global antisemitism bother you?
- Do you have any doubts about being Jewish?
- Is your family on board with your decision?

Your *bet din* might also dig into your basic Jewish vocabulary list. For converts, knowing Jewish vocabulary is just as important as the list of acronyms that new hires of high-tech companies have to inhale. Getting the lingo down is vital for both to succeed. So don't be surprised if your *bet din* asks questions like these:

- How are you making *tikkun olam* part of your life?
- What contribution of *tzedakah* will you make this year?
- How do you observe *Shabbat* as a family?
- How can visitors tell your home is Jewish?

The last question is easier than it looks. Some items that make homes Jewish include *mezuzot, hamsas,* a *ketubah* (Jewish marriage license), challah plate and cover, *Shabbat* candles and candlestick holders, a menorah, a dreidel, and even Chanukah stuffed animals. Jennifer had all of these items except the *ketubah* by the time she converted. There is no hard-and-fast rule on how much decor you need to have for a Jewish home, but the main idea is that the conversion changed your life in such a way that you're living a Jewish life and your home reflects it. This is no different than Christians who decorate their home with crosses, seasonal decorations, and even artwork that represent their faith.

> It was a little nerve-racking, but on the other hand I knew that, just like a good martial arts studio, you don't put people up for testing if you're going to flunk them. Instead, you would tell them they're not ready to test. The rabbi that's working with you knows if you're ready. (Laura, fifty-three, financial consultant)

Remember to be yourself and answer honestly when meeting your *bet din.* Even if a *bet din* member asks something that you haven't covered yet, it's quite all right to say, "I don't know that yet but I'm eager to learn about it. Can you fill me in?" This shows your interest and gives the *bet din* member the ability to share some of her vast Jewish knowledge, which is also a *mitzvah.* Remember, the *bet din* is on your side. You would have to present a deep conflict for them to have reservations about rubberstamping your conversion, like wearing a *kaffiyah,* crossing yourself, or whipping out a BLT.

Once your *bet din* is satisfied with your answers, your sponsoring rabbi gives you a special blessing, then shows you to the *mikvah.* There is a little wiggle room here depending on your denomination. If you're becoming Conservative or Orthodox, then your movement requires both men and women to undergo this spiritual cleansing when converting. But if you're becoming Reconstructionist or Reform, then your movement strongly encourages you to participate in all conversion rituals, including the *mikvah,* but does not necessarily require them. Participating in all aspects is wise, especially if you ever wind up moving and attending either an Orthodox or a Conservative synagogue. Most rabbis see these rituals as a pivotal moment where Jews recognize and embrace their Jewishness.

CRAMMING SOLD SEPARATELY

It's natural to be anxious about any process that you don't have control over, and going before a court of any kind is bound to make you uneasy. Understanding the process will help you know that your *bet din* is there to help. This rabbinical court is different than other courts in the respect that a judge in a civil court is supposed to be completely neutral, but a rabbi on a *bet din* is actually rooting for you. That's not to say they wouldn't tell you to take a hike if you blurted out that you're still planning to celebrate Christmas, but their main purpose is to see that you're fully committed and converting for the right reasons.

You can breathe easier knowing that you can enjoy time with your loved ones and there's no need to cram for your "Jewish final." It's also comforting to know that once your rabbi convenes a *bet din* on your behalf, you're well on your way to becoming Jewish. Still, no one expects you to memorize everything you learned and regurgitate it for the *bet din*. Most college graduates can't even remember what was on their last political science exam, much less four thousand years of history. What's important is where your heart and head are and how you plan to continue living a Jewish life.

CHAI NOTES

- Your rabbi is confident you're ready once he's convened a *bet din* for you.
- A *bet din* is composed of at least one rabbi and two others who may be observant laypeople.
- Saying "we" shows that you consider yourself part of the tribe, whereas "they" doesn't.
- *Bet din* questions are more about your dedication and intent than your volume of Jewish knowledge.
- Your conversion rabbi will arrange a *bet din* once you've shown a sincere interest.
- Relax! There is no need to cram for what your *bet din* might ask.
- Knowing basic Jewish vocabulary is important.
- Jews have a tendency to have some decor that reflects a belief in Judaism.
- If a *bet din* member asks you something you don't know, be honest.

9

Mikvah and More

ט

Few days besides your graduation or wedding can prepare you for your conversion. All three signify endings and beginnings. Graduation represents the end of years of study and the beginning of putting that reservoir of knowledge to work. Likewise, your wedding represents the end of barhopping with buddies (for many of us) and the beginning of a lifelong bond (for not nearly enough of us). Converting to Judaism means walking across a threshold rich with many things Jewish, yet being okay with leaving childhood religious beliefs and customs on the other side. It's a day of rejoicing and renewal as well as a day of saying farewell to familiar beliefs that may have once held significance.

THE *MIKVAH*

Going to the *mikvah* is something to celebrate. You may have heard of a *mikvah* in passing, but we will attempt to remove any mystery that might still linger. A *mikvah* is a natural body of water or, in most cases, a warm pool that has a connection to natural water. Anyone entering a *mikvah* does so for immersion according to rules and customs of Jewish law. Immersion is a biblical commandment of the highest order, equated only with *mitzvot* like *kashrut* and *Shabbat*.

Most *mikvot* (plural of *mikvah*) contain about two hundred gallons of water. Since water is the primary source of all living things (and the human body is more than 50 percent water), the thought is that immersion in the *mikvah* can purify, restore, and replenish your life. All *mikvot* contain "living water" from a source that has never been dormant such as fresh spring water, rainwater, or melted snow.

There are plenty of purposes for full immersion. Here are some of the more popular ones:

- Immersion prior to a wedding ceremony
- Marking men's, women's, and children's conversions to Judaism
- Honoring personal milestones such as graduations, birthdays, anniversaries, and *b'nai mitzvah*
- Beginning anew by marking the end of *shivah* (Yiddish for seven days of mourning), divorce, rape, abuse, or recovery after illness
- Marking the end of a woman's monthly menstrual cycle or honoring *taharat hamishpachah* (family purity)
- Noting the onset of key life-cycle events in women such as menstruation, miscarriage, infertility, pregnancy, birth of a child, or menopause
- Preparing for something that takes great mental or physical concentration or effort
- Just because (no one said you had to have a reason)

The reason most baptisms and conversions involve water is because we often think of water as containing healing and spiritually cleansing properties. In many ways, it's not that different from an adult baptism in a Christian faith, but instead of having a preacher dunk you while fully clothed in front of an entire congregation, this is in private in the buff. Yes, naked. No worries though, as the rabbi or the person witnessing will obviously be the same gender as you and you will be reciting prayers with your head above water, not frolicking through the water like the opening scenes of *Baywatch*.

Here are some tips to get the most out of your *mikvah* experience:

- Tour your *mikvah* in advance to get acquainted with the surroundings.
- Fees for *mikvah* use help to defray operating costs and are either per visit or via annual membership. Most pay through conversion class but ask your rabbi if in doubt.

- Invite family, classmates, or friends to accompany you (same-sex guests can be present during your immersion).
- Bring a towel and appropriate reading material that puts you at ease (in case you're early).
- Put your hair up in advance if it's long, but plan on getting soaked head to toe.
- Take time before you immerse to reflect, meditate, or pray to prepare for your big occasion.
- Trim your nails, shave (or wax) your legs (if you're female), and remove any nail polish before your visit (polish is not permitted).
- Take the rest of the day off and have some "me" time or "family" time to reflect on your new life direction. Celebrate with a family meal or outing to mark the occasion.
- Entering the *mikvah* waters is as blessed and meaningful as you make it. Having the right *kavvanah* (intention) means you can make it that much more meaningful.

Typically, you invite a friend of the same sex from your synagogue to accompany you. Your *mikvah* attendant serves as a witness (and as a support system) who is familiar with the prayers and can assist you as needed. Most Jewish friends are flattered to get an invitation to welcome you into the fold. Don't hesitate when asking a congregant you know well, for most consider witnessing a conversion an honor. Sometimes you might even find a package deal. For instance, Jennifer asked her Hebrew teacher/cantor, who was very receptive. Interesting enough, just as it was a family affair for her family (her husband and twins were in tow), it was also one for the witness since her husband happened to be Jennifer's conversion rabbi.

If you're a male convert, no need to recruit a witness, as you will likely have one or two already built in: your *bet din*. It might sound less personal, but look at it this way: one is likely your rabbi, and it's less work for you because they're already there. Usually, only one takes on the task of ensuring you have fully immersed yourself and recited prayers while the other two are likely hanging around the doorway so they don't overwhelm you.

Prepare to recite the blessing for *mikvah* immersion, followed by the *Shehecheyanu* (which you'll say every time you do something new in Judaism). Once you are immersed chest high, you recite the following prayer.

בָּרוּךְ אַתָּה יְיָ אֱלוֹהֵינוּ מֶלֶךְ הָעוֹלָם
אֲשֶׁר קִדְּשָׁנוּ בְּמִצְוֹתָיו וְצִוָּנוּ עַל הַטְּבִילָה.

Baruch atah Adonai Eloheinu melech ha'olam,
asher kid'shanu b'mitzvotav v'tzivanu al ha-t'vila.

"Blessed are You, Lord, our God, Ruler of the universe, who has sanctified
us with Your commandments and commanded us concerning immersion."

Then there is the *Shehecheyanu*:

בָּרוּךְ אַתָּה יְיָ אֱלוֹהֵינוּ מֶלֶךְ הָעוֹלָם
שֶׁהֶחֱיָנוּ וְקִיְּמָנוּ וְהִגִּיעָנוּ לַזְּמַן הַזֶּה.

Baruch atah Adonai Eloheinu melech ha'olam
she'hecheyanu v'ki'y'manu v'higiyanu lazman ha'zeh.

"Blessed are You, Lord, our God, Ruler of the Universe, who has granted
us life, sustained us, and enabled us to reach this occasion."

For some, saying prayers naked in front of a witness is not exactly what you
had in mind when you chose to become Jewish. If this describes you, there are
many ways to feel more comfortable in the *mikvah*. For instance, your witness
can respect your privacy by turning around while you're getting into the water
and face you once you're immersed chest deep. The same goes when you're
finished with the prayers and exiting the water. It's a good idea for your witness to turn around out of respect for your privacy. Feel free to discuss it beforehand, as this might be a new experience for both of you. Another tip is to
discuss how much help you need during prayers.

If you have young children who are converting with you, they go to the
mikvah also. Those of the same sex go with you and immerse after you. Children of the opposite sex go with an appointed family member or assigned
rabbinical staff for immersion.

Saying your blessing in the *mikvah* is not that much different than reciting standard wedding vows after the clergy repeats the line first. In many
ways, your actual conversion is a lot like marrying the Jewish People. It's
wise to ask your witness to speak a phrase or two of each prayer at a time
so you can repeat it. Having someone say the phrase first ensures that you
don't draw a blank, and ensures your *mikvah* experience is meaningful and
memorable.

I know now, having completed my conversion, that I must do the work to really feel Jewish, to learn the rituals of *Shabbat* dinner, to be able to recite the prayers that every born Jew has grown up with, to fully grasp the history of the Jewish People, to feel at home at services. I experienced the ritual of immersing myself in the waters of the *mikvah*. I will forever cherish that memory as the moment I officially became Jewish. The women at the *mikvah* embraced me with such sincerity that I felt as if I was truly coming home and being reunited with a family I had been estranged from for all these years. I recognize, however, that I cannot just immerse myself in the water and really feel complete as a Jewish woman, for it is a process with a continual journey that has no marked destination. In fact, the moment I held the Torah in my arms at my naming ceremony, I proclaimed my dedication to Judaism. It was an emotional moment for me, walking with the Torah in my arms as members of the congregation touched it and blessed and welcomed me. I have found my spiritual home. (Renee, thirty-five, real-estate agent)

MODESTY TAKES A BACKSEAT

While the nude part sounds risqué, it's not. (It's also super safe and anyone who might be wigged out at the thought of hot tubs as *mikvot* should know *mikvot* follow strict hygienic guidelines that include daily cleaning and chlorination.) It's about the same as when actors report that their scene in the buff had zero sex appeal. Actors repeat lines while converts recite prayers. There is not much sexiness to either but unlike creating the illusion of seduction for a movie-going audience to advance a plot, the requirement of being nude in the *mikvah* is to cleanse impurities of the past and start with a new slate. Since you're repeating two prayers chest deep along with the person leading the ceremony, there is no time to consider the fact that you're nude. Jennifer's three-year-old daughters, on the other hand, thought it was the best indoor pool they had experienced and asked if they could return later that day to swim.

> The *mikvah* was a very special experience. It was almost emotional for me. My close Jewish friend acted as my witness. I had read the *Shema* aloud while my fiancé, in-laws, and others waited outside. I was very nervous that day, very anxious. Looking back, even more so than the day I got married or had my son! (April, thirty-three, attorney)

Entering the waters of the *mikvah* allows you to experience a tradition well over three thousand years old. The *mikvah* is so essential to Jewish life that the

Talmud requires Jewish communities to build a *mikvah* before constructing schools and synagogues. Why is the *mikvah* so important? Mainly because Jewish family purity laws call for women to cleanse themselves following menstrual periods. Brides also use it to purify themselves prior to weddings, and both men and women enter it (separately, of course) prior to High Holy Days like Passover and Yom Kippur. Many consider it a kind of renewal or rebirth that allows them to wash away any ill feelings, baggage, or frustrations in a desire to start over, regenerate, or improve.

> Once my daughter got in the *mikvah*, she didn't want to get out. I think she thought it was more like a big bathtub. She wanted to swim around. It was very meaningful, especially going under. My witness had never seen a conversion like this, and I gathered from her response that it was very special. (Laura, fifty-three, financial consultant)

CONVERSION CEREMONY

Upon leaving the *mikvah* (and dressing), your witness will accompany you to your conversion ceremony. This part is typically brief but is also the part friends and family can attend. Think of it like graduation. Once your ceremony ends, you are officially Jewish. Often your rabbi will ask you to recite an oath of allegiance to the Jewish People while you touch or hold the Torah and recite a prayer. You may be wondering how many you can invite to your conversion ceremony. There is really no magic number. Most tend to invite either their spouse or significant other and a friend or two. Sometimes converts include a mix of friends from their past religion and from their synagogue. Others have supportive family members present. Still others treat it as a midsize wedding, and that's OK too. Here is one person that didn't let a number define how she celebrated her new faith:

> It was very public for me. Converting was making a statement. Some people just have two or three friends. Mine was atypical. I probably had forty or fifty people. My daughter had one friend there that was her age and I had one as my witness—my best friend. At one point, the rabbi said that he didn't know if everyone would fit in the room. It turned out it was packed, but everyone fit, barely. (Laura, fifty-three, financial consultant)

CIRCUMCISION

Women, this section is going to make you glad you don't have a penis. Men, this section will make you glad you do. *Brit milah* or *hatafat dam brit* are processes that bring boys (and men) into the covenant of Israel. Trained *mohelim* perform both according to observed tradition that dates back nearly four thousand years to the time of Abraham. While some view this practice as medieval and even irrelevant, most understand that it represents a bond between God and every male Jew. The fact that this bond focuses on the male reproductive organ—the penis—infers that every boy (or man) entering into a covenant with God promises to produce Jewish offspring.

The Midrash indicates that Abraham circumcised himself in order to know God better, but waited until the advanced age of ninety-nine. While that probably won't work for you, especially if your movement requires it, you do live in a time when analgesics can alleviate pain and practices are typically safe and antiseptic. Luckily, most males in North America receive in-hospital circumcision days after birth. For those, the choice for accepting the covenant of Israel is easy: *hatafat dam brit*. If you were born outside of North America and have not undergone circumcision, then your conversion rabbi will likely recommend circumcision. In fact, if you're joining the Orthodox or Conservative movement, you have no choice, as circumcision for uncircumcised males (or *hatafat dam brit* for males already circumcised) is required. Reform and Reconstructionist movements recommend that male converts undergo all conversion rituals but may give you leeway since some consider this ritual less about Jewishness and more about tradition. Some consider it medieval or even barbaric. Talk with your rabbi to know where your movement and synagogue stands on this.

Years ago, another reason *mohelim* performed circumcisions was to prevent the spread of disease. Luckily, this is not a concern unless the convert is in developing countries where AIDS is rampant. Today, the practice is more about welcoming you into the House of Israel. It's more about connecting you to God and entering you into the long line of Jews that have come before you.

HATAFAT DAM BRIT

Historically, about 70 percent of newborn boys in the United States undergo circumcision either for religious or social reasons. Interestingly enough, about 30 percent of the world population makes circumcision mandatory. This means men converting stateside who had circumcisions at birth, or those among the 30 percent born outside of the United States who have, can gladly skip the information on *brit milah* and focus solely on the *hatafat dam brit*.

During this ritual, it's customary for converts to receive their chosen Hebrew name and to recite prayers in Hebrew or in English. Today, the Orthodox or Conservative movements require converts to undergo *brit milah* (circumcision) if they have yet to undergo circumcision or *hatafat dam brit* if they have, while Reconstructionist and Reform movements encourage converts to participate in all conversion rituals, but it's not required. The *hatafat dam brit* is a ritual reenactment of circumcision where a *mohel* recites a blessing while removing a drop of blood from beneath the head of the penis (the glans). This area is symbolic as it represents where the foreskin previously attached. Most *mohelim* who perform *hatafat dam brit* (or those men who have received it) will tell you it's quick and relatively painless. Some report it feels the same as plucking a stray hair.

Most male converts learning about this ritual probably never wanted to know their rabbi or a trained *mohel* this well. Luckily, you can feel a tad more comfortable knowing that your *mohel* will likely cover your penis in gauze, and many *mohelim* use surgical gloves so as not to make direct contact. Most *mohelim* will give you helpful hints like pulling on the base of the penis toward your body to ensure the skin near the head of the penis is taut.

Next, the *mohel* will swab the area under the head of the penis with alcohol. Think of the rest as occurring fast and only feeling a slight poke of a needle. Once the skin is broken, the *mohel* or rabbi says an appropriate blessing and you say your portion. For young boys, either the *mohel* or the attending rabbi recites the blessing. Ceremonies for *hatafat dam brit* vary slightly between synagogues and even movements. Some prayers like the *Shehecheyanu* have staying power and are nearly always required.

Honestly, compared to getting your back waxed or giving birth, the *hatafat dam brit* doesn't even come close. Most men report that the circumcision ritual was over before they knew it. Some have compared it to a daughter that has her ears pierced at a relatively young age, except unlike ears there is only one *bulbul* (penis) to consider (and the needle doesn't go through). While it might be a tad uncomfortable, it's fast and less painful than when a person opts for a piercing in their nether regions (and we have yet to hear of any studs or rings remaining as a result).

Cases where a *bet din* might waive a *brit milah* or the *hatafat dam brit* include situations where the ritual could cause physical harm as in the case of hemophilia (uncontrollable bleeding) or where it may cause extreme psychological distress (don't get your hopes up for the latter, as these cases are rare). Each *bet din* evaluates situations like these on a case-by-case basis, so holding out for a waiver might not be your best bet.

While there is no commandment in the Torah requiring circumcision or even immersion, the Talmud contains the initiation rites that all movements follow. Orthodox and Conservative movements require either circumcision or *hatafat dam brit*. Orthodox *batei din* don't accept *hatafat dam brit* performed by Conservative *mohelim* and require a second.

Look at Yisrael Campbell, the stand-up comic who underwent three circumcisions (one at birth and two *hatafat dam brit*, one when he converted to Reform and another when he became Orthodox). Campbell's Broadway comedy show—*Circumcise Me*—probably would have never made it to the stage if the pain outweighed the benefit. Even though we know the opposite is true, it still makes for good comedy. Some might wonder what happens if you convert from one movement to another. Here is what this stand-up comic (or serial circumciser) had to say about it: "I converted to Reform then Conservative and then, Orthodox. Three circumcisions is not a religious covenant, it's a fetish!"

BRIT MILAH

There's no denying that male converts going under the knife *really* want to be Jewish. Simply put, adult circumcision isn't exactly bringing male converts in by the droves. After all, a surgical procedure seems a lot to ask of any convert. Comparing it to gifts Christians score during the holidays just seems masochistic. Yet even this ancient requirement hasn't stopped male converts from becoming Jewish.

Unlike Abraham, who circumcised himself without the benefit of pain relievers, converts these days undergo *brit milah* in day surgery. A qualified surgeon who either is a *mohel* or accompanied by a *mohel* is your best option. Trained *mohelim* are easy to find through your rabbi, synagogue, or movement (see Resources).

Surgeons use surgical adhesive (invisible stitches) for sutures. Talk with your surgeon to find out which technique is right for you. There are a few options to relieve pain, including anti-anxiety medications as well as topical numbing creams, which a nurse would apply thirty to sixty minutes before the procedure. The surgeon/*mohel* you choose will likely recommend injecting a local anesthetic. This may sting a bit (the numbing cream will reduce the pain), but it prevents pain during the step when he carefully snips away the foreskin. Like most surgeries, this procedure occurs in an operating room under the supervision of doctors and nurses. Some doctors/*mohelim* retain only male nurses to assist with this procedure, so ask your doctor if this is a concern.

Luckily, the recovery time is brief. Your doctor will prescribe antibiotics, analgesics, and sometimes even anti-nausea medications and will ask you to schedule follow-up appointments to monitor your progress. Most people return to work after a day or two and report residual pain for a few days to a week. Scheduling surgery on Thursday or Friday works well as it gives you the weekend to recover. Typically, swelling, discoloration, and postoperative pain are normal but subside. Resuming sexual activity depends on how fast you heal. Most surgeons recommend taking a break from sex for at least two to four weeks since arousal, erection, and ejaculation will be uncomfortable.

Months later, the *brit milah* will be like any other surgical procedure—a distant memory. Many Jewish converts that wish to have kids often inquire about *brit milah* requirements for newborns. The main requirement is to leave your calendar open eight days after your son is born.

BRIT MILAH FOR NEWBORNS

Timing is the most important factor when scheduling a *brit milah* for baby sons. Jewish parents traditionally hold a *brit milah*, or *bris*, eight days after their son is born. While the American Academy of Pediatrics has identified several medical reasons to perform a circumcision, the reason Jews perform this ritual is purely religious. The Torah mentions the covenant between God and Abraham twice. In Genesis 17:1–14, circumcision is the act that joins Abraham and all Jewish descendants in a covenant with God:

> Abram was ninety-nine years old. God appeared to him and said, "I am God Almighty. Walk before Me and be perfect. I will make a covenant between Me and you, and I will increase your numbers very much. . . . This is My covenant between Me, and between you and your offspring that you must keep: You must circumcise

every male. You shall be circumcised through the flesh of your foreskin. This shall
be the mark of the covenant between Me and you. Throughout all generations,
every male shall be circumcised when he is eight days old. [This shall include]
those born in your house, as well as [slaves] bought with cash from an outsider,
who is not your descendant. [All slaves] both houseborn and purchased with your
money must be circumcised. This shall be My covenant in your flesh, an eternal
covenant. The uncircumcised male whose foreskin has not been circumcised,
shall have his soul cut off from his people; he has broken My covenant."

Circumcision also arises in Leviticus 12:3:

On the eighth day, [the child's] foreskin shall be circumcised.

Many Jews consider *brit milah* sacred since the Torah gives Jews the ability to
circumcise even when the eighth day falls on *Shabbat*. Parents just need to
inform their rabbi and *mohel* ahead of time so the *mohel* can bring the items
needed to perform the *brit milah* a day earlier to avoid carrying items on
Shabbat.

CALMING CONVERSION JITTERS

Just as graduation and wedding day comes to pass, so does your conversion
day. Your big day is an hour or so out of your entire life that will pass before
you know it. It might be worthwhile to exercise, have breakfast with those
you care about, or simply read something enjoyable before you meet your
bet din. For some, Manischewitz or Slivovitz will do the trick. Seriously,
there is no need for this, as everything you need to know you have already
learned from your conversion classes. There is little to prep for before your
actual conversion.

As for any student, those seeing you through your big day are there to
support you, so allow them to do so. Your rabbi has faith in your abilities or
she would not have given you the green light to proceed. So take a deep
breath and try not to take this ritual or yourself too seriously. Remember
that you're becoming a Jew. You're not campaigning for the Oval Office.
Most would tell you this is a good thing, since we haven't had any Jews hold
the highest office yet. But don't let becoming a Jew deter you if you're po-
litically motivated. This is America, after all. Why not be the first convert to
Judaism to sit in the White House?

CHAI NOTES

- Anyone entering a *mikvah* does so for immersion according to Jewish law.
- Insert the word *meaningful* for *modesty* when entering the *mikvah*.
- *Mikvot* adhere to strict hygienic guidelines that result in daily cleaning and chlorination.
- Trained *mohelim* perform both *brit milah* and *hatafat dam brit* according to a tradition that dates back to Abraham some four thousand years ago.
- Orthodox and Conservative movements require adult circumcision or *hatafat dam brit*, whereas Reform and Reconstructionist movements encourage (but may not require) converts to undergo all conversion rituals.
- Ceremonies for *hatafat dam brit* vary slightly between synagogues and movements.
- Unlike Abraham, who circumcised himself without pain relievers, converts these days enjoy the benefits of antibiotics, analgesics, and sterile operating rooms.
- Many Jews consider *brit milah* sacred since the Torah gives Jews the ability to circumcise even when the eighth day falls on *Shabbat*.
- It might be worthwhile to exercise, have breakfast with those you care about, or simply read something enjoyable before your conversion starts.
- Take a deep breath and try not to take this ritual (or yourself) too seriously.

10

Tradition

׳

Not much in life can prepare you for the Jewish traditions you are about to embrace when you convert. From learning an ancient language to recognizing nuances in Torah to experiencing religious and cultural firsts, becoming a Jew is anything but quick and easy. Consider what hoops your rabbi might ask you to face before joining the tribe:

- Learn basic Hebrew with a little Yiddish thrown in for good measure
- Have your penis poked by a *mohel* or go under the knife via a surgeon (guys only, of course)
- Take a nude bath where you recite prayers in Hebrew in front of a witness
- Appear before a court in the hopes of getting a verdict of *mazel tov!*
- Recite a prayer in Hebrew while touching a sacred handwritten parchment

Before that, you'll learn about holidays where you blow into a hollowed-out ram's horn. Then you'll spend a week outside in a see-through shack and shake an oversized lemon and some branches. Next you'll wear a costume and make a ruckus every time someone mentions the bad guy's name. Soon you'll spin a top to memorialize war and light a bunch of candles while reciting prayers in Hebrew. Later you'll eat a bland cracker and a funky-tasting fish while reflecting on how our people were slaves in Egypt. Finally, you'll develop love for a country that you've never set foot in, and much more.

It's true your movement may not require you to fulfill all these traditions. But they will in time be the same ones that tug at your heartstrings the hardest, make you feel part of a tight-knit community, and even prompt you to laugh, cry, or at times roll your eyes. But in the end, tradition works about the same as quirks in your own family. It plays a starring role in your life and is the same reason the cult classic *My Big Fat Greek Wedding* became such a hit in 2002. After watching this romantic comedy, Windex takes on a whole new meaning.

WHY TRADITION MATTERS

Yet there is another poignant example that oozes tradition. When the musical *Fiddler on the Roof* first hit the Broadway stage in 1964, no one could have predicted that it would become one of the most performed musicals of all time. It became the first musical in history to surpass three thousand performances. After all, here was a play about an obscure little Jewish *shtetl* in tsarist Russia in 1904, and the struggles of a poor Jewish milkman named Tevye. We see Tevye's attempts to keep the traditions of his family alive while his five daughters inevitably desire to assert their independence and leave their deeply rooted traditions behind.

The poignancy of the story, plus the universal message of family, love, and the tensions between clashing generations and cultures, has touched the hearts of millions ever since. Through it all, the theme that has resonated with so many over the decades is reflected in the powerful opening number of the show, when Tevye and the entire town of Anatevka gather to sing the powerful anthem "Tradition."

Tradition pulls on the heartstrings of everyone who ever grew up with rituals and customs that have passed down from previous generations, regardless of the faith or culture involved. We seem to have a fundamental need to create symbols and rituals that link us from one generation to the next and provide a concrete way of passing on the values that offer meaning and purpose to our lives.

Judaism is the evolving religious civilization of the Jewish People. Throughout its four-thousand-year-plus history, Jewish customs, rituals and traditions, and even communities have ebbed and flowed, flourished or languished, on continent after continent. The need for the Jewish People to create meaning and purpose in their lives has created life-cycle rituals and rich traditions that mark significant moments in Jewish history.

MORE THAN A NURSERY

Adding on to your family often brings up the need to reassess whether or not your car (and often your home) is big enough for your new arrival. But as a Jew, you have other traditional ceremonies to consider, such as a Hebrew naming ceremony and potentially a *bris* if you have a son. Luckily, Jewish tradition is clear but also reassures you that the very first *mitzvah* in the Torah—*pru urevu* ("be fruitful and multiply")—is one of the greatest *mitzvot* of all.

BRIT MILAH

When a Jewish boy is born, the expectation is that his family follows a tradition that goes back to Abraham, the first Jew. In Genesis 17:10–14, God commands Abraham to circumcise every male in his household at eight days old as a sign of the covenant between God and the Jewish People. This ceremony, known in Hebrew as *brit milah*, is binding and practiced by all Jews today throughout the world. It involves a religious ceremony with blessings that reference Genesis and welcome the baby boy into the covenant of the Jewish People via circumcision and a Hebrew name.

Most *brit milah* ceremonies take place in the home of the family on the eighth day of the boy's life. Some parents choose to have their son circumcised in the hospital and then follow with a naming ceremony either in the home or a synagogue on the eighth day. Typically, friends and family gather at these *brit milah* ceremonies, casually called a *bris* or a *brit* (see page 114).

Girls are welcomed into the covenant of the Jewish People by the giving of a Hebrew name in a ceremony similar to the *brit milah*, minus the circumcision, of course. This ceremony also takes place either in the home or in a synagogue and fulfills the same function of formally welcoming the child into the family of the Jewish People via a Hebrew name that connects the daughter to her family's past. Names are chosen in many ways. Some give their newborn the same Hebrew name of a deceased relative to honor a loved one's memory (the Ashkenazic custom), while others honor a living relative (the Sephardic custom). Either one is authentically Jewish.

COMING-OF-AGE

Bar mitzvah for a boy and *bat mitzvah* for a girl are both rites of passage that occur at thirteen for boys and twelve or thirteen for girls, depending on the Jewish community. Either way, the *bar* or *bat mitzvah* ceremony is a way to recognize that a child is assuming the religious responsibilities of Jewish adulthood (e.g., being counted as part of a *minyan*, fasting on Yom Kippur, and being honored with an *aliyah*).

In contemporary Jewish tradition, a coming-of-age ceremony such as this symbolizes that the child is worthy of increasing responsibility and can make more adult choices about life paths. The central moment of the *bar* or *bat mitzvah* is when the ark is opened, the Torah scroll is taken out, and then passed from generation to generation, from parents to child. When the child takes the Torah in his or her hands, it is as if an inner voice is saying, "Yes, this is now my story too, and not merely the story of my parents, grandparents, and so on."

TYING THE KNOT

Jewish weddings are famous throughout the world for pomp and circumstance. This includes tasteful decor, music, singing, and dancing while the newlyweds and their parents are paraded through the crowd on chairs. Most can bet on an overabundance of food, drink, and joy, along with a *chuppah* (wedding canopy), a *ketubah*, the breaking of a glass, and so much more. In fact, we devote chapter 12 to weddings because there is so much more to tell.

R.I.P.

Death is not a popular topic for obvious reasons. Not many use it as a conversation starter, a calling card, or, heaven forbid, a pickup line. But Judaism goes out of its way to mark significant life-cycle moments with rituals and customs that span crib to crypt. Judaism approaches death as a natural part of life and recognizes that life and death are in God's hands, not ours. It also understands life is a divine gift.

In the Jewish tradition, when someone dies the body is treated with sacred respect. Traditionally, the burial occurs within a day (or two) of death. Family members see to it that the body is washed and prepared for interment, and someone recites prayers and watches over it until it reaches its final resting place. Before the cemetery, the body enters a closed casket, as an open casket implies the body is on display. Jewish tradition understands our loved one is no longer present, and to put the vessel that carried that person on display is seen as turning our loved one into an object. This is where your memories, stories, videos, and photo albums come in handy.

Sometimes deceased loved ones have special requests. Jennifer's mother-in-law, Leda, had a soft spot for chocolate. She asked that family members have plenty around when she passed away, so besides putting dirt on the casket (see below), all the attendees dropped Hershey's Kisses in too.

Some traditions of Jewish burial include the following:

- Placing a shovelful of dirt on the casket at the end of the ceremony to fulfill the *mitzvah* of physically seeing to the dignified burial of those we love.
- Tearing a black ribbon (or, in Orthodox tradition, part of the mourner's clothing) near the heart (*kri'a*) to symbolize the emptiness that death creates.
- Sitting *shiva*: staying home for seven days without working while family, friends, and neighbors visit and bring food to help those mourning.
- Holding a daily *minyan* of *shiva* for a brief service that includes reciting the *Kaddish*, the traditional memorial prayer.
- Avoiding joyous celebrations for thirty days to complete the mourning and grieving period.

For the next year, whenever *Kaddish* is said in synagogue, family members have the opportunity to rise for this prayer of mourning. A year later, the *Kaddish* memorial prayer is recited at the gravesite, and an unveiling occurs where a simple marker is placed according to Jewish tradition. Close family and friends usually pay their respects and leave small rocks as a sign they were there since flowers die.

On every anniversary (*yahrtzeit*), the *Kaddish* is again recited in synagogue and many buy *yahrtzeit* candles for deceased loved ones at either a synagogue gift shop or a grocery store that has a kosher section. The key here is to check the death date on the Hebrew calendar, as it's always different than the Gregorian calendar (see page 78). *Yahrtzeit* candles burn for twenty-four hours.

SACRED RITUALS AND CUSTOMS
Kashrut

You hear the word *kosher* often, and you see food labels with the *U* or *K* inside a circle at the supermarket (if you look at labels, that is), but what does it really mean? The word *kosher* in Hebrew literally means "fit," and traditionally refers to which foods are designated as "fit" to eat. The Torah outlines permitted and forbidden foods that were intended in biblical times to keep Israelites as a distinct people and help prevent the possibility that they might easily disappear into larger, surrounding cultures. Throughout history Jewish dietary laws have continued to function as a way of reinforcing a sense of uniqueness and belonging as part of the Jewish community. In fact, many believe keeping kosher is one of the most important things you can do as a Jew.

Jewish dietary laws have also been a way for Jews to approach one of the most everyday and ordinary acts of life—eating—as a sacred act. For those who keep kosher, eating becomes more than merely a method of physical sustenance, but rather a way to create a spiritual consciousness about food. It allows us to transform what might otherwise be mundane into something sacred and profound. Keeping kosher can remind us that the spiritual quality of our lives is a direct result of the personal choices we make every day.

Who is required to keep kosher? Actually, anyone; think of it as being vegetarian with a few extra rules attached. But honestly, the Orthodox movement is the only movement that expects members to keep kosher. The other major movements in North America (Reform, Conservative, and Reconstructionist) do not require members to adhere to kosher dietary laws, though nearly all follow them in synagogue kitchens.

Interested in what the laws entail? Here are a few rules to give you a taste:

1. Foods forbidden: animals without cloven hooves (e.g., camels, rock badgers, hares, pigs, etc.) and *all* shellfish.
2. Foods permitted: animals with cloven hooves, those with scales, and fish like tuna, carp, salmon, and herring.
3. Birds and mammals must be killed in a humane way according to Jewish law.
4. All blood must be drained prior to eating.
5. Certain parts of permitted animals may not be eaten.
6. Fruits and vegetables are permitted but must be bug-free (thank goodness!).

7. Meat from birds and mammals is not permitted with dairy (some wait thirty minutes to several hours before consuming either on the same day). Fish, eggs, fruits, vegetables, and grains can be eaten with either meat or dairy. (Some believe that fish cannot be eaten with meat for the same reason.)

8. Utensils (including pots and pans and other cooking surfaces) that have come into contact with meat may not be used with dairy and vice versa. Many kosher kitchens have dual refrigerators, utensils, plates, and dish-washers—one for meat and one for dairy.

Kosher laws and restrictions are extensive. One such restriction absent from the Torah is that wine or grape juice (virtually all products derived from grapes) must be kosher, as ancient rituals relied on wine to practice idolatry. This restriction is still practiced today by those who keep kosher.

There is also a contemporary movement called "Eco-*Kashrut*" where choices regarding food consumption and money spent are evaluated to help encourage a more environmentally sustainable sustenance for our planet. An eco-kosher decision might be to abstain from eating food that is grown in factory farms that offer inadequate health care for workers, those that employ children oversees, or those that violate the ecology of the planet.

Mezuzah

You may have noticed an ornamental ceramic, metal, or glass amulet hanging on the doorpost of a Jewish home. This is a *mezuzah*. In the Torah, we are commanded "to write them on the doorposts of your house and upon your gates." In fact, Deuteronomy 6:9 is an essential prayer in daily and *Shabbat* services that Jews have recited for the past two thousand years. The physical manifestation of this takes the form of a *mezuzah* (doorpost), a small cylinder into which a piece of parchment is inserted with the words of the *Shema* and the *V'ahavta* (the prayer that asserts the oneness of God).

It's a *mitzvah* to honor God by affixing a *mezuzah* to the doorpost of your home. Some Jews put a *mezuzah* only on the front door of their homes, some on front and back, and some on every door of the home except the bathrooms. There is a brief ceremony for affixing the *mezuzah* that includes a traditional prayer to affix the *mezuzah* and the *Shehecheyanu* prayer, which gives thanks that we are alive, sustained, and allowed to reach this particular moment in life. Having a *mezuzah* on your door is both a way to make a statement of belonging to the Jewish People and community, and a daily reminder that your home is a small sanctuary (*mikdash me'at*) and true spiritual center of your life.

Tefillin

Don't get alarmed if you attend a morning service at a traditional synagogue any day except *Shabbat* and see most men wearing small leather boxes strapped to their foreheads and arms. Yes, it might seem unusual, and no, it really isn't. What you are seeing is *tefillin*. These boxes contain the four verses from the Torah that make mention of the *mitzvah* of binding the laws of the Torah as a sign on our arms and before our eyes. Strapping these on is seen as another way to fulfill the *mitzvah* expressed in the Torah in Deuteronomy 6:8, where it says, "You will bind them as a sign upon your hand, and they shall be for frontlets before your eyes." Wearing *tefillin* fulfills the words of the Torah and reminds us that if our thoughts are directed toward doing *mitzvot* and bringing more holiness into the world, our hands will follow.

Magen David

One of the most recognizable Jewish symbols is the *Magen David*, or Star of David (or even Shield of David). There is no specific mention of it in either in the Torah or biblical literature. It appears to have emerged from around the eleventh century as a Jewish amulet with two opposing triangles that form a hexagram. Many believe that the symbol was meant to bring spiritual protection from King David, the most powerful Jewish ruler of all time. What Jew could go wrong having a great warrior/writer/poet and author of the psalms as their guardian?

Regardless of its unknown origins, the *Magen David* has become an almost universally recognizable symbol of Judaism and is found in synagogues and Jewish art and jewelry throughout the world. Perhaps even more widely recognizable today is its prominence on the Israeli flag. Unlike fifty-seven-plus countries that claim to be Islamic, there is only one Jewish country in the world: Israel.

Chai

Another popular Jewish symbol is anything that contains the Hebrew letters *chet* and *yud* to spell the word *chai* (life). Much artwork and jewelry integrates the *chai* symbol for good luck to those who wear it. Since each of the twenty-two letters of the Hebrew alphabet has an equivalent numerical value—i.e., *alef* = 1, *bet* = 2, *gimel* = 3, to the end of the alphabet—the number 18 is considered equivalent to *chai* since *chet* = 8 and *yud* = 10.

That is why in Jewish tradition people often make contributions to charitable causes in multiples of eighteen, or give gifts for special occasions in similar amounts. To give a gift in a multiple of eighteen is to say, "I wish you a healthy and joyful life." It is a simple yet meaningful Jewish tradition that anyone can easily adopt.

KNOWING WHAT'S IMPORTANT

Judaism is, above all else, a way of life that promotes ethical choices in our everyday lives (see chapter 17). Thousands of years ago, its practice gave the world the idea now called "ethical monotheism." This means that there is only one God who is the same for all people regardless of how they see, describe, or understand God. Perhaps even more important than simply teaching all people were created by the same God is that God actually cares how we treat each other.

It's this idea, that God is not only the source of creation but also the revealer of ethics and morals, of good and evil, of right and wrong, that is perhaps Judaism's most significant spiritual gift to the world. When we read in Genesis about the creation of humanity, one of the first things it teaches us is human beings are created *b'tzelem elohim*, or in "the image of God."

Here are more significant spiritual and ethical values that Jewish civilization has introduced to the world that have become an integral part of what we now understand as Jewish tradition:

Torah, *Avodah*, and *G'milut Chasadim*

One of the best-known sayings from the Talmud is that the world is sustained by three things: Torah (learning), *Avodah* (sacred service or worship), and *G'milut Chasadim* (acts of loving-kindness). These are the three pillars of Jewish life that have sustained Judaism spiritually from Talmudic times until today in every country where Jewish life has flourished.

Torah

The Torah represents the ancient story of our physical beginnings with Abraham and Sarah inheriting the Land of Israel, and our spiritual heritage. It represents the Jewish People's encounter with God and the lessons learned from hundreds of years of slavery in Egypt, the giving of the Ten Commandments at Mount Sinai, and the notion that God cares about all of us. It also represents the most important spiritual values of Judaism, outlines each major holiday and festival, commands the observance of *Shabbat*, introduces *kashrut*, and is the basis of all future Jewish law and ethics.

Avodah

Originally, *Avodah* referred to priests that officiated at the Temple of Jerusalem. After the Romans destroyed the Temple in 70 CE and synagogues emerged with rabbis as teachers serving as the spiritual leaders of the Jewish community, *Avodah* took on other meanings. Ever since that time, *Avodah* has referred more to prayer and worship and the acts that give expression to the spiritual longings of the Jewish People. Nurturing a healthy spiritual life as part of the Jewish community has become one of the important pillars of Jewish life.

G'milut Chasadim

Acts of loving-kindness, or *G'milut Chasadim*, are the large and small things we do that deliver more joy to the world. Whether you're caring for a family member, helping those less fortunate, or simply being there for a friend in need, *G'milut Chasadim* are necessary building blocks of a considerate society. Judaism teaches that for society to thrive, we need not only personal spiritual discipline but commitment to learning and making society a better place.

That is why these three are seen as the cornerstones upon which the entire world is built: Torah, *Avodah*, *G'milut Chasadim*. Their power lies in the fact that every person has the capacity to study Torah, participate in daily acts of spiritual discipline, and distribute greater doses of loving-kindness to the world.

Tzedakah

Many think of charity upon hearing the word *tzedakah*, but the term means so much more. *Tzedakah* comes from the root *tzedek*, which means "justice" or "righteousness." Ever since Talmudic times, *tzedakah* has referred to the act of giving of one's resources, funds, and otherwise to help those that are in need. It's not only one of the most important ethical values of Jewish life; it is understood to be a fundamental obligation of what it means to be a *mensch* (good person) and fulfill the *mitzvah* of being a good Jew.

Giving *tzedakah* is taught to children in many ways in the Jewish community. As one of the weekly rituals of Jewish life, parents put money into a *tzedakah* box on *Shabbat* and give money for their children to contribute as well. This is the same when children attend Sunday school. Many synagogues consider it so important that the box is placed outside classrooms so it's the first thing a child sees when approaching. Once they have collected it, the students give the *tzedakah* to a local nonprofit organization or to Israel. Many times, families repeat this at home (see page 75).

In the Jewish tradition, one gives to others not out of "charity," whose root comes from a Latin word for "love," but out of "justice" and "obligation." You don't give because you're in a good mood or you *feel* like it; you give because it is expected of you.

Shalom Bayit

Family is the most important foundation of Jewish life. We began as a family in biblical times and have continued to embrace the value of family ever since. Most Jewish holidays and festivals are celebrated at home with our family. We gather around the dinner table before Rosh Hashanah to bring in the New Year, and we break the fast at the end of Yom Kippur hoping to be written in the Book of Life another year with our families. We light the Chanukah candles for eight nights as a family, giving gifts and singing songs of the brave Maccabees. We sit with our families for hours at our Passover *seder* tables retelling the story of our enslavement in Egypt and the tradition of how God freed us with a strong hand and an outstretched arm to bring us to Mount Sinai and give us the Torah.

Practically everything we do in Jewish life happens as a family. This is why the idea of *shalom bayit* ("peace in the home") is such a powerful theme in Jewish tradition. The rabbis even tell stories in the Talmud of how God spends time mending broken relationships between husbands and wives because peace in the home is such a high spiritual priority. We are taught that God even tells a white lie to Abraham to retain *shalom bayit* when Sarah laughs at the prospect of aging Abraham fathering a child with her. From this example, rabbis teach that we should mirror God's footsteps and preserve family harmony in our own lives.

"If I Forget You, O Jerusalem"

Jerusalem has remained the center of Jewish civilization ever since King David established it as the Jewish capital around the year 1000 BCE. That means for three thousand years Jews throughout the world have prayed for the peace of Jerusalem. They have made pilgrimages to Jerusalem three times a year as they celebrated the biblical festivals of *Sukkot*, *Pesach*, and Shavuot. They have written poems, songs, and prayers about Jerusalem and lived in it continuously for all those millennia.

Jerusalem (*Yerushalayim*) means "City of Peace." Unfortunately, throughout its long history, there have been many periods of time when peace was the furthest thing imaginable. Yet the fact that you can stand in the middle of the old city of Jerusalem today and see holy sites from all three major religions is amazing. It's the city where Christians believe Jesus taught and died. The same city where Muslims believe Mohammed ascended to heaven. And the same city where Jews believe the Temple of Solomon stood adjacent to the remaining Western Wall. Jerusalem is unique in that it plays a pivotal role for the majority of religious people on the planet.

"If I forget You, O Jerusalem, may my right hand lose its power" (Psalm 137). This poetic gesture emphasizes the central role Jerusalem plays in the religious and communal life of the Jewish People. Jewish civilization cherishes Jerusalem as the birthplace of the Kingdom of David, whose rule and that of his descendants lasted over one thousand years. From the Roman destruction of the Temple in 70 CE to the dispersion of the Jewish People throughout the world to today, Jews have quoted this poignant psalm to declare the importance of Jerusalem to the Jewish People.

Pikuach Nefesh

The Talmud teaches us that *pikuach nefesh* (saving of life) is the most important *mitzvah* in the Torah. Yes, another one. Various rabbis in the Talmud and throughout Jewish history have continually pointed to one or another as "the most important" *mitzvah*. That's why ultimately it is up to you to decide on which *mitzvah* is the "most important." Each creates a deeply complex ethical code of conduct that has inspired each generation anew to emulate godliness by bringing holiness into the world.

CORNERSTONES OF JUDAISM
Torah

When we mention Torah, we are generally referring to what is contained within the Torah scrolls that sit in every ark in every synagogue in the world. They begin with the creation of the universe and continue with the beginning history and foundational stories of Judaism and the Jewish People itself. They tell of the patriarchs and matriarchs—Abraham, Isaac, Jacob, Sarah, Rebecca, Rachel, and Leah—and the covenant between God and our ancestors with its promise of Israel as the perpetual homeland of the Jewish People. They continue through our enslavement and ultimate liberation from Egyptian bondage by God through Moses and the revelation of the Ten Commandments and Torah itself at Mount Sinai. They conclude with the subsequent forty years of wandering in the desert on the way to redeeming the Promised Land. These five books, which specifically constitute the Torah, also serve as the first five books of the Hebrew Bible, or *Tanakh*.

Tanakh

The Hebrew Bible is composed of thirty-nine books in three distinct sections, called the Torah, *Nevi'im* (or "Prophets"), and *Ketuvim* (or "Writings"), which together form the acronym T.N.K.—simply referred to as *Tanakh*. Also referred to as the Hebrew Scriptures, the *Tanakh* was completed and "canonized" (fixed as sacred) around 400 BCE and has served as the foundation of Jewish ethics, values, and way of life ever since. *Nevi'im* consists of twenty-one books of prophets, who one by one criticize the Jewish People for straying from God's commandments and practicing idolatry by worshipping other gods in various ways. *Ketuvim* are sacred writings that include such books as Ezra, Nehemiah, Daniel, Ruth, Chronicles, and Esther, which are written as if they are biblical history. They also include wisdom literature such as Proverbs, Psalms, Ecclesiastes, Job, Lamentations, and others in which the biblical authors share insights about life and death, good and evil, and the challenges of living in accordance with God's will.

Mishnah, Gemara, and Talmud

All religions have laws and ethics that instruct followers on what is and isn't permissible. In many ways, morality and religion go hand in hand. This is where *Mishnah, Gemara,* and the Talmud come into play. First, let's start with *Mishnah* to give you an idea of how laws and opinions influence Judaism today.

Mishnah

Maybe you've heard about the oral Torah? Well, the *Mishnah* is the first written recording of the oral Torah. It contains sixty-three tractates arranged in six
sedarim (orders) that ancient rabbis developed in their ongoing interpretation
of Torah from the time it was codified until around the year 200 CE. This is
when Judah Ha-Nasi (also known as Judah the Prince and Rabbi) undertook
the monumental task of creating a comprehensive book of *halachah*, the *Mishnah*. It's a collection of legal rulings and opinions about agriculture, holidays,
civil and criminal matters, ritual purity, and so forth.

Gemara

Anyone who has ever studied for a final is familiar with the meaning of the
Aramaic word this section is about. *Gemara* means "to study," and it refers to
the collected conversations, discussions, arguments, and commentaries that
the rabbis in their academies in both Israel and Babylonia conducted based on
their study of the *Mishnah*. The twenty-volume collected works of the *Mishnah* and *Gemara* together make up the Talmud. The celebrated religious
scholar Rav Ashi edited the Talmud around 500 CE. The Talmud forms the
basis of all traditional Jewish law.

Midrash

Do you like meaningful stories that have real ethical reach? Then one day you
might want to study Midrash at your synagogue. Midrash refers to the stories
and anecdotes written by rabbis over the past several thousand years to illus-
trate lessons derived from the Torah or as a form of commentary to a biblical
text. Midrash is a very broad category of writing that includes any rabbinic
commentaries. It does not claim to be explanations of specific Jewish laws but
rather illustrates moral and ethical lessons through memorable stories. There
are numerous collections of Midrash written in different geographical locations throughout the world at different periods of time from several thousand
years ago up to today.

Siddur and Machzor

Every religion has a book to follow at services. Judaism is no different. Ours is
the *siddur*. It means "order" and refers to the arrangement of prayers that
various rabbinic authorities have compiled throughout history after the de-

struction of the Temple. After this time, synagogues as houses of worship replaced the Temple as the central site of ritual sacrifices. Rabbis created orders of prayers that they then led the community in reciting as the religion evolved.

Machzor is the prayer book that is used only on the High Holy Days of Rosh Hashanah and Yom Kippur. It contains the prayers of the regular *siddur* plus special prayers that reflect the themes of repentance, forgiveness, and the recitation of communal sins and transgressions of the past year that specifically reflect the spiritual themes of this sacred season called the "Days of Awe."

Hebrew

Hebrew is the language of the Jewish People. Ancient Hebrew (biblical Hebrew) is the language of the Torah and the *Mishnah*, while modern Hebrew is the rebirth of Hebrew and the national language of the state of Israel. Hebrew communicates many fundamental Jewish values such as *tzedakah, shalom, shalom bayit, Shabbat, Yom Tov,* and *G'milut Chasadim.* These terms are unique and hard to translate adequately into any other language. Not only is Hebrew the language of Jewish ethics and values, but it also carries with it the history of Jewish civilization that remains central to our way of life (see chapter 5).

Yiddish

Most everyone has heard Yiddish music, jokes, and slang. But guess what? *Yiddish* means "Jewish" and it's the language of Jews who grew up in Eastern Europe in the Middle Ages. It uses the Hebrew alphabet and vocabulary similar to German with many unique borrowings from Hebrew.

Jews in Poland and Russia spoke Yiddish, and many of its expressions have come into common usage in modern English, like *shlepping, meshuggah, mensch, bagel,* and *maven.* It is no longer used by most Jews in the world, although it is still spoken by certain *Hasidic* Jewish sects and there is a national center for the study of Yiddish in the United States that is dedicated to keeping the language alive.

Ladino

Ladino is another unique language of the Jewish People. It was the language of the Sephardic Jewish culture spoken throughout the Spanish empire, Turkey, North Africa, and to some extent, France and Greece. It's a form of Judeo-

Spanish, and other languages heavily influenced it, such as Hebrew, Aramaic, Turkish, and Greek. It's being kept alive somewhat by Jewish communities that continue to use it in music in the Sephardic communities of Israel and Latin America.

MAKING IT WORK

Simply put, there is no one "right way" to be Jewish. This is your opportunity as a convert to acquaint yourself with the rich customs, rituals, and practices that Judaism has to offer and decide which ones you feel strongly about to incorporate into the minds and hearts of your family.

CHAI NOTES

- Not much in life can prepare you for the Jewish traditions you are about to embrace.
- Newborns require a Hebrew naming ceremony and traditionally a *bris* if a boy.
- *Bar* and *bat mitzvah* are both rites of passage that recognize entering Jewish adulthood.
- Couples that have Jewish weddings are symbolically connected to all Jewish couples that have wed throughout time.
- *Kaddish* is a prayer of mourning recited to honor loved ones who have passed away.
- It's a *mitzvah* to honor God by affixing *mezuzot* to the doorposts of your home.
- The *Magen David* has become a universal sign of Judaism and is on the flag of Israel.
- Only Orthodox Jews are required to keep kosher but any Jew can.
- *Chai* is a popular symbol that means "life" and has a numerical value of eighteen.
- Jerusalem has remained the capital of Jewish civilization since 1000 BCE.
- *Pikuach nefesh* (saving life) is the most important *mitzvah* in the Torah.
- Hebrew is the Jewish language and the official language of Israel.
- *Yiddish* gave us words like *shlepping, meshuggah, mensch, bagel*, and *maven*.

11

Living Single

יא

One of the most often expressed complaints about Jewish life is that it's tough to be Jewish and single and feel at home in the Jewish community. Almost everything about Jewish tradition and communal life practically shouts "family." Nearly all Jews celebrate every holiday primarily at home. Most people join synagogues because they want to give their children a Jewish education and identity. There are also a significant number of *mitzvot* that revolve around the roles of mothers and fathers and presume that everyone has a family that's celebrating, sharing ritual moments, or creating *shalom bayit*, the traditional idea of "peace in the home."

When we ask people to imagine a *Shabbat* table on Friday night, most conjure up images of parents facing a decorative table with women lighting candles and reciting the blessing and, moments later, men holding up the *kiddush* cup to bless wine. Soon many hands tear challah and all recite the *Hamotzi* prayer. Finally, parents place their hands on the heads of their children as a gesture of loving-kindness and recite blessings for them. Almost no one will imagine a single person, reciting blessings at an otherwise empty table, celebrating holidays and festivals alone.

And yet there are approximately 1.7 million adult Jews of all ages who are single. For many, learning to feel whole about Judaism without a partner or a larger immediate family is one of the most important emotional and spiritual challenges of everyday life. It's almost as if the Jewish deck were stacked against their success. Who can imagine a Passover *seder* alone? Who can imagine building a *sukkah* in which to recite blessings, shake the *lulav* and *etrog*, and sit down to eat and celebrate *Sukkot* alone? Who can imagine lighting the Chanukah candles for eight nights, singing the blessings, and opening presents alone?

The first thing to accept is that your Judaism is yours, and your Jewish identity belongs to you and you alone, regardless of whether you are single, married, in a committed relationship, a parent, or anything else. When someone decides to become Jewish, it is always an intensely personal choice.

So how can a single individual, a man or a woman, who wants to live a full Jewish life ever feel fully part of the Jewish community without a larger family with whom to share the rituals and celebrations of Jewish life? Ask Renee:

> The catalyst for my conversion was my recent divorce—becoming a single mother, longing to be the best example I could possibly be to my daughter, to raise her with a sense of spiritual grounding that I was not afforded up until this point in my life. As I find myself challenged by the emotional rollercoaster of divorce, I have found such a sense of peace immersing myself in Judaism. The best analogy I can use is to equate it with the feeling of falling in love; it cannot be explained so easily, yet you are almost powerless to deny the affect it has over your entire being. It just feels natural and right. As I reflect on my childhood, I realize that this has been the natural progression for me all along. (Renee, thirty-five, real-estate agent)

THE MANY MEANINGS OF "FAMILY"

The first thing to realize about the word *family* is its definition is much broader than relating to biology, genetics or numbers, and certainly not by the presence or absence of children. The author Richard Bach once wrote, "The bond that links your true family is not one of blood, but of respect and joy in each other's life. Rarely do members of one family grow up under the same roof."

As Bach so poignantly put it, parents, siblings, or children do not define family; rather, family is the loving connection that one person feels for another. That's why we believe the Jewish community offers many opportunities for single Jews of any age to forge loving, nurturing bonds and still feel complete. The broader our understanding and definition of family becomes, the easier it is for us to recognize the many opportunities that exist for creating extended "family ties" in our daily lives.

> I was scared at first that I would stand out and everyone would stare at me if I went to a synagogue to attend Friday-night services as a single woman. In fact, I had to go "*shul* shopping" for a while to find just the right fit, but when I walked into one synagogue and several people immediately welcomed me at the *Oneg Shabbat* after the service, I instantly felt as if I finally belonged. (Alexis, thirty-two, account executive)

Sometimes it's a challenge to find the right synagogue fit, but if you live in a large urban or suburban community, you have the luxury of trying out several synagogues until you find one that feels like home. "Feels like home" is key because when your synagogue becomes an extension of your home, you'll find people with whom to celebrate holidays and *Shabbat*, and a community to share the highs and lows with. We encourage you to start by meeting with the clergy of any synagogue in which you're potentially interested and sharing your personal story and the fact that you are searching for a spiritual home. Every synagogue is eager to welcome new members; some are just better at it than others. When the rabbi or cantor knows you from a personal meeting, and knows that you are looking to make a connection with the community, he or she is much more likely to facilitate that connection with others that are just as welcoming.

Some synagogues have special programs for inviting members to share *Shabbat* meals, holiday celebrations, or Passover *seders* with existing families. Other synagogues have active singles groups or adult education classes where members or nonmembers can attend lectures, presentations, or functions that make it comfortable to come as a single and where "couple" status is irrelevant.

We are social animals, and it usually feels better to share the holidays, *Shabbat*, or other special occasions with family or friends. Of course, there is nothing wrong with celebrating *Shabbat* or any holiday or ritual on your own. Enjoying your own meal, lighting the candles, blessing the bread, saying the *kiddush* over wine, and even singing a *Shabbat* song can bring a great sense of peace, wholeness, and fulfillment without any other person in the room. To be fully Jewish and to celebrate any holiday in no way requires you to share it with other people. In fact, the Talmud specifically teaches that although it's a tradition for women to light *Shabbat* candles, if you are a single man or a man alone, then it's just as much your *mitzvah* to light them yourself. The rule then follows that essentially any gender can fulfill any tradition, and individuals are encouraged to look for opportunities to celebrate Jewish life and ritual and fulfill any *mitzvah* in the Torah.

You'll find the same principle in the *Haggadah* and in Jewish traditions surrounding Passover. Even if you hold a Passover *seder* alone, and even if you're a scholar, you are still supposed to fulfill the *mitzvah* of telling the story of the Exodus of Egypt, the miracle of our liberation, and to thank God for the blessing of freedom.

Of course, Passover is also a perfect example of how one can easily find others with whom to celebrate. Most synagogues hold Passover *seders* that you can make a reservation to join. Jewish communities sometimes hold them compliments of the Jewish Federation. Some synagogues match congregants who have no family with other congregants or families willing to open their homes to celebrate holidays like Passover.

Many times this is a perfect opportunity for groups of singles to gather together to celebrate, as they often do in Jewish communities that create singles holiday groups for Chanukah, *Sukkot*, Passover, or the weekly celebration of *Shabbat*. Again, this is often done by the Jewish Federation or JCC, depending on the community in question and how they approach the opportunity to put singles together either with each other or with larger family groups. You can often find these resources by contacting your local Jewish Federation office, local JCC, or the closest synagogue and simply asking them for help (see Resources). Naturally, searching the Internet can open up a world of possibilities for anyone looking to make connections with other Jews.

Most Jewish institutions, including individual synagogues, now have Facebook pages that advertise communal activities, services, celebrations, and opportunities for anyone who wishes to find details on when and where these activities will take place. Jewish social networks are growing, and JDate has become one of the more popular ways for Jewish singles to meet. Age is not a concern. Consider that Jennifer's father-in-law met his bride on JDate after losing his wife of forty-five years and reaching the young age of seventy.

Making a concerted effort to meet up with other singles will guarantee no downtime in the friend department. Look on the Internet for "Jewcrew," "koolanu," "myjworld," "jmix," and other communities that keep popping up every day, and you'll find ways of connecting with Jews from across the street or around the world. This is one additional way to feel connected to the larger Jewish world and a part of the Jewish community regardless of whether or not you're affiliated with a specific synagogue or participate in a local Jewish singles group.

There are many opportunities to connect with other Jews and to not let your status as a single person get in the way of feeling a full and accepted part of the Jewish community. Many who are recently Jewish feel slightly intimidated by the thought of jumping into a group of Jewish strangers and find it easier to start with one other Jew or one Jewish family with whom to share a *Shabbat* meal or celebrate a holiday. Often a local rabbi or cantor can make that connection for you too.

If you share the holidays with one other person, you will begin to feel more competent in your Jewish identity and more comfortable reaching out to try other Jewish opportunities in your community. Sometimes it is simply easier to show up at your synagogue or Jewish function if you have someone that can accompany you. This is often the case for attending any event. Most people just don't feel comfortable going solo.

The best advice is to find another Jewish single to join you, and chances are you will help each other along the way. Often you can find another person who is in the same situation as you from the local conversion class (perhaps the one you took yourself), or by asking your rabbi for names of other recent converts who have recently gone on the same spiritual journey you have taken.

Another way of approaching the challenge of being single is to see if your local synagogue has a *chavurah* they can recommend for you to join. Some synagogues have groups specifically for singles. Others have groups that contain mixes of single people and those with partners, and some synagogues have *chavurot* specifically designed as book clubs, holiday celebration groups, or purely social groups. This can often be a wonderful way to feel a part of a smaller Jewish community that allows you to celebrate holidays, study with friends, or learn with others, or just have positive social experiences with other Jews.

Remember, if you chose Judaism as an adult, it means that you are self-motivated enough to risk giving up what is comfortable to gain meaning and purpose in your life. That means that if your synagogue or Jewish Federation lacks the kind of group that you're seeking, you're probably the perfect person to start one. Every Jewish communal leader, member of the clergy, and active Jewish communal worker would just love to have someone like you to help them create a group that provides meaningful connections to other Jews like you. If it doesn't exist, don't let that stop you. Take the initiative yourself and have faith that you'll find professionals within the Jewish community and local synagogues who will gladly partner with you in making your dreams a reality.

Often the best ideas come out of frustration and adversity. The old adage that necessity is the mother of invention is undoubtedly true, and if you can think of a meaningful group that you would love to see in your community, you can make it happen.

Living single can be a blessing or a curse, an opportunity or a disadvantage, all depending on your attitude and point of view. The most powerful tool you have at your disposal and the one that inevitably determines your success in life is your attitude. Simply put, attitude is everything. If you are single, the best attitude to take is to accept your singleness and then figure out what various implications of that singleness might be.

In what ways is being single an advantage? For example, not worrying about someone else's needs, making independent decisions without consulting another, showing up at the last minute to a performance and scoring a great seat rather than a mediocre pair, spending less money, or potentially banking some.

How is being single a liability? Perhaps in being invited to events with couples or larger families, having to eat alone much of the time, craving more human interaction, or feeling uncomfortable participating in activities where you're the only single. List the pros and cons, and then create positive responses to overcome the disadvantages to help you fully immerse yourself in the Jewish community.

Being single means different things to different people. For you, it may mean that you have to summon a greater degree of courage to face the sometimes-intimidating situations where most people in the room have a partner. See your singleness as an opportunity to stretch your own inner spirit, to strengthen your sense of personal self-worth so that it clearly doesn't depend on the acceptance of others or whether or not you're with a companion. Know that you're perfect the way you are, that you have created the life you are living, and that you have the capacity to continually reinvent yourself in ways that most people cannot. The fact that you have chosen your own spiritual path proves you have a stronger sense of self than most, and the resolve and commitment you demonstrated shows you can do whatever it takes to create a meaningful life.

FINDING YOUR OWN "JEWISH MOTHER"

Everyone needs their own Jewish mother (minus the guilt part, of course). Since you are a convert, we're betting your mother isn't Jewish. Interestingly enough, that is an area we can remedy. No, we're not talking about replacing your own mother or creating one in a lab. Yet there is a huge benefit to tapping into years of experience that can only come from a Jewish mother. After all, think of all the generations of advice that could potentially help you along the way. Of course, you can always be your own "inner parent" and simply impart all the wisdom you would imagine a Jewish mother might say, but just like every professional seeks their own mentor, we feel every convert needs their own Jewish mother.

First, many synagogues have programs for seniors (Steven's congregation calls them "Sages" and Jennifer's synagogue calls them "*Chai* Society"), and these programs make a fabulous hunting ground for locating your own personal Jewish mother. Most people have complicated relationships with their parents, so it's often easier to find a sweet, loving, nurturing relationship with someone else's parent (or child, for that matter) than it is to do the same with your own. Seek out a place where older Jews live or gather and literally show up to one of their programs and ask for a volunteer Jewish mother. You'll be surprised how many people will jump at the chance to be your volunteer Jewish mother. On the other hand, if you feel personalities are key, and you pride yourself on matchmaking, then scope out that perfect Jewish mother and ask her in confidence. This is also preferable if finding your Jewish mother is something that you feel is personal and you don't want to broadcast it.

Depending on where you live in America, you can find potential volunteer Jewish mothers by looking up organizations like Hadassah, National Council of Jewish Women, Women of Reform Judaism, and Na'amat USA. Just go to one of their local meetings and let people know you're newly Jewish and looking for someone to take the role of a volunteer Jewish mother. Volunteering for any of these Jewish women's organizations gives you numerous connections to others that will help build a spiritual and social Jewish network of support (see Resources). Volunteering is also one of the best ways to experience a sense of gratitude for life's gifts (i.e., love, great friends, or companionship) and to feel a greater sense of overall meaning and purpose.

Sometimes the best source of a volunteer Jewish mother is to borrow the mother of a friend. If you know someone who is Jewish, tell them (or their mother) that you don't feel complete without a Jewish mother and would like their help to make it happen. Many people are happy to share their mothers and will treat your request as a reason to invite you to celebrate holidays, festivals, *Shabbat*, or even Jewish life-cycle events. Think of what you can learn by spending Passover with a family. Perhaps you'll be invited to a Jewish wedding, a *bar mitzvah*, or even a trip to Israel. Experiencing these events or learning about your history helps you see the world from their eyes.

If you live in a large metropolitan area, there will likely be Jewish communal institutions that welcome your participation. Some cities have Jewish museums, holocaust memorials, or communal celebrations and commemorations that are open to anyone. These may provide you with places to go to be Jewish, activities to participate in, and people with whom to share the experience. There are even special vacation opportunities for Jewish singles of all ages. All it takes is a few keystrokes on the Internet to find Jewish activities from cruises to community dances to parties. If you're coming up short, contact . . . you guessed it, your synagogue, the Jewish Federation, or the JCC, and ask for a list of upcoming events and activities.

Mazel tov in advance once you locate your Jewish mother. But why stop there? If you're feeling the urge, try finding a Jewish father the same way (except focus on men's organizations instead of women's), or even consider finding a Jewish family to serve as your symbolic Jewish family.

DON'T AMPUTATE YOUR PAST

One of the conversion challenges people often overlook is how to cope with the tremendous sense of loss that comes from no longer feeling it's appropriate to celebrate non-Jewish holidays and rituals that were positive memories of your past. People ask, "Is it OK to visit my family on Christmas now that I'm Jewish?" "What do I do when my family invites me to participate in the holidays or celebrations or rituals that I grew up with now that I have become Jewish? Isn't it an act of disloyalty to the Jewish people if I remain part of my previous family and am with them during holiday seasons?"

Becoming Jewish doesn't mean amputating your past. You're always the person you grew up to become, with memories, relatives, and life experiences that ultimately led you to the spiritual path you have taken. It's one thing to embrace a new religious civilization and become part of the Jewish People, and it's another to expect you to deny relationships that have been an integral part of making you who you are.

Becoming Jewish doesn't mean running away from your family or your past. It's especially important when you're single and rely on your own family for support and emotional connections that are important during holiday seasons when people tend to feel most isolated and alone. Yes, it's true that as a Jew it is no longer appropriate to take communion at a Christian religious service, or kneel in church and affirm a statement of faith or belief in Jesus. But Steven and his wife Didi attend several Christmas Eve services in their community every year and feel perfectly comfortable sharing the experience with their Christian friends. Your presence in a church, mosque, Hindu temple, or any other sacred site of another religion does not imply you're unfaithful to your new Jewish identity or religion. You can be secure enough in your own Jewish identity to experience sacred, moving moments that other religious traditions evoke.

If you were ever away at college and lived in a dorm, you might recall the experience of discovering for the first time that other people celebrate different holidays, worship in a different manner, or observe different religious rituals than the ones you grew up with in your own home. There is certainly nothing wrong with college roommates sharing in each other's religious traditions, learning from one another, and appreciating the beauty of spiritual traditions that are new and different. The same is true for you as an adult if you choose to convert to a religion that is different from the one of your youth. Our advice is for you to enjoy and celebrate differences regardless of where you might find them.

This is definitely a case in which you *can* go home again, and if you want to share your parents' holiday or any other relative's celebration, feel free. It's one thing to celebrate a holiday as your own and another to join family in their celebration. It's easy to let family know that, while your parents celebrate Christmas, you celebrate Chanukah. Most parents understand given the right support and encouragement, and if they don't now, they usually do in time. For a single person, "going home for the holidays" is often the best solution to feeling lonely during what can be a stressful time of year. The trick is simply to look at your visit as a family reunion experience and not as an expression of religious belief or commitment.

Celebrate your Judaism and be single-minded (pun intended) in your commitment to create a loving, nurturing, inspiring Jewish life for yourself. Know that just as Judaism is an evolving religious civilization, so is your Jewish life. Don't despair if you ever have moments where you feel like a third wheel or that you're not up to par in your practice. All of that will change with time, and there is no substitute for life experience. The more you show up to synagogue, Jewish activities, events, experiences, and celebrations, the more comfortable and at home you'll feel. The more you participate in Jewish communal life, the more connected you will become, the more people you will meet, and the more rich and rewarding your Jewish life will be.

CHAI NOTES

- There are 1.7 million adult Jews of all ages who are single.
- Feeling whole about Judaism without a partner and an immediate family is often the most important emotional and spiritual challenge of everyday life.
- Your Jewish identity needs to depend solely on your own inner sense of belonging to a Jewish community.
- Family is defined not by parents, siblings, or children but rather by the loving connections that one person feels for another.
- Jewish community offers many opportunities for single Jews of any age to forge loving, nurturing bonds and still feel complete.
- Some synagogues match congregants that have no family with other congregants or families willing to open their homes to celebrate holidays like Passover.
- Another way of approaching the challenge of being single is to see if your local synagogue has a *chavurah* they can recommend for you to join.
- There is a huge benefit to tapping into years of experience that can only come from a Jewish mother, father, or family.
- Becoming Jewish doesn't mean running away from your family or past.
- You can be secure enough in your own Jewish identity to experience sacred, moving moments that other religious traditions evoke.
- Find singles groups, and if you can't find them, start them.

12

All This for a Wedding?

יב

Every couple anticipates their wedding day. Will it be indoors or outdoors? Will it seat two hundred or twenty-five? Will it be formal or informal? Will it lead to a sugary beach or medieval architecture? Ahh, everyone loves a wedding. But Jewish weddings add an extra layer of structure, custom, and ritual of their own. From signing the *ketubah* to anticipating the *bedeken*, to standing under the *chuppah*, to circling seven times and smashing a ceremonial glass, Jewish weddings are steeped in tradition.

TURNING TWO INTO ONE

Jewish tradition traces the concept of marriage to the first couple mentioned in the Torah, Adam and Eve. In Genesis 2:18, God says, "It is not good that man should be alone. I will make a help mate for him." And when God created woman to be the life partner with man, Genesis 2:24 adds, "Therefore shall a man leave his father and his mother, and shall cleave unto his wife, and they shall be one flesh."

Today these words sound quaintly hetero-central since they only express one form of a loving relationship. But it still conveys the fundamental notion that people are social by nature and are expected to "be one flesh" with another. These verses mark the beginning of the entire institution of marriage. Whether it's between a man and a woman, two men, or two women, the idea is for a couple to make a lifetime commitment to each other. Essentially, all the customs, traditions, and rituals surrounding weddings have emerged from God's fundamental words that *life is to be shared*.

The basic form of Jewish weddings is fairly simple. It's really a combination of two separate ceremonies: the *erusin* (betrothal ceremony) and the *nisuin* (marriage ceremony). Long ago, these ceremonies occurred about a year apart. A family would hold a simple betrothal ceremony where the bride and groom were legally pledged to one another in the presence of witnesses who would sign a *ketubah*. Then the families of the bride and groom would have about a year to prepare for the wedding. This gave the bride's family time to calculate her dowry or the "bride price" that the groom and his family would pay. At the same time, this period gave the groom's family time to gather the dowry and wherewithal to begin their married life together.

The wedding ceremony that exists today still has traces of those days. This is the technical reason why there are traditionally two blessings over wine during the wedding—one to symbolize the betrothal and the other to celebrate the marriage.

In many traditional weddings, brides and grooms spend an entire week apart prior to nuptials. Today, there are fewer couples observing this tradition fully and most stay apart only a few days. This is also because more couples are living together prior to saying, "I do." Still, some observe the tradition by staying in different locations the night before their wedding. Doing so creates a special sense of newness and anticipation once they reunite under the *chuppah*, when they sign the *ketubah*, or during the *bedeken*.

Mikvah

Another beautiful custom that many Jews practice prior to the wedding ceremony involves brides and grooms visiting the *mikvah* for ritual purification. Today the *mikvah* has become a creative source of spiritual transformation Jews use as a powerful symbol of transition at special, spiritual moments in life. Some immerse in the *mikvah* prior to the High Holy Days each year as a way of starting each New Year with a sense of renewal. Some use the *mikvah* as a symbol of renewal and transformation after experiencing personal crises, trauma, or even after their menstrual cycles.

When it comes to preparing for a wedding, it has long been a custom for a bride to invite her bridesmaids and any other women in her party to join her at the *mikvah* for a prewedding ritual celebration. You might call it a Jewish bachelorette party. Some bring food and drink and create a true atmosphere of celebration so that when the bride emerges from the water, there is a spiritual recognition that she is leaving one stage of life for the next (see chapter 9).

Tish

One of the most meaningful parts of the wedding rituals takes place before the wedding even begins. It's the "pre-ceremony ceremony" in which the bride and groom are surrounded by immediate family and sometimes the wedding party to sign the secular and spiritual documents of the wedding. In some traditional weddings, the groom and his entourage sit at a *tish* (separate groom's table), where they drink shots of alcohol and sing Hebrew songs. During the same time, the bride and her entourage gather in another room so they can pay special attention to her bridal dress, flowers, and makeup. At one point, the groom might then lead his attendants (singing all the way) in a procession to where the bride sits waiting, and all gather together for the *bedeken*.

Bedeken

Simply put, the *bedeken* is a way for the groom to make sure he's marrying the right girl. Jewish legend traces the *bedeken* back to the biblical story of the patriarch Jacob who fell in love and worked for seven years for the right to marry Rachel. When the moment came, Jacob lifted the veil to kiss his lovely Rachel only to see that her older sister Leah was there instead. Their father Laban switched the two sisters under the *chuppah* prior to the ceremony. While Jacob married Rachel soon after (polygamy was common then), the idea behind the *bedeken* is so the groom can unveil his bride to make sure that no one pulls a "Laban."

MORE THAN ART

At the same time as the *bedeken*, both bride and groom take part in signing the *ketubah*. A *ketubah* is a legal document in the Jewish faith designed to protect a woman's rights. In Talmudic times, a woman did not enjoy the same rights as she does today. Using a *ketubah* stretches back over two thousand years when a famous rabbi named Meir wrote what became the first prenuptial agreement between a groom and the bride's father for his daughter's hand in marriage. Rabbi Meir shook things up when he prepared a legal document that stated the bride was entitled to two hundred *zuzim* (the currency of the time) if the husband divorced her after the wedding.

Today the *ketubah* is no longer strictly a legal document, since according to Jewish law it's the legal system of the country in which Jews live that takes precedence over Jewish law. As a result, there are probably hundreds of different versions of texts that are used from one *ketubah* to the next. Instead of seeing it as an official document, most view their *ketubah* as a spiritual reminder that their union is more than simply a legal agreement. It becomes a physical reminder that their marriage is primarily a spiritual partnership between the bride and groom. Many are beautiful, artistic, and end up framed and displayed as artwork for all to see.

The *ketubah* usually has a place for two witnesses to sign along with the bride, groom, and the rabbi (or officiant). There is a lovely custom among Persian Jews that once the bride, groom, and witnesses have signed the front of the *ketubah*, everyone in the wedding party signs the back. This continues until the back of the document is filled with witnesses of the couple's commitment to one another.

In many weddings, it's also customary to read some or all of the *ketubah* during the wedding ceremony. Traditional Jews read the entire *ketubah*, which may be written in its original form in Aramaic. More liberal and contemporary rabbis and couples may read part of their *ketubah* text in English, especially because so many are written in such beautiful, poetic language and often express the hopes, dreams, and spiritual commitment of the couple.

Many engaged couples purchase their *ketubah* online or find a local artist through their synagogue. The benefit of commissioning an artist is that you can have a one-of-a-kind piece made that no other couple will ever own. The benefit of purchasing online is that you can shop as long as you want and never leave the comfort of your own computer. Many sites categorize *ketuvot* (plural of *ketubah*) by Jewish movements to help narrow your options.

There are many different ways to conduct a wedding and to celebrate the joining of two people's lives in marriage. Of course, all the traditions and customs covered apply equally to gay or lesbian couples. In those circumstances, couples can still opt for a personalized "commitment ceremony." Many rabbis and cantors consider such ceremonies to carry the same sense of reverence and holiness (*kedusha*) as heterosexual marriages. As a result, there are now various versions of traditional Jewish wedding ceremonies to celebrate and consecrate such spiritual unions.

It's helpful to remember that there is no one "right" way to celebrate a wedding. Of course, there are customs and traditions that have emerged over thousands of years of Jewish civilization that are common to many Jewish weddings. At the same time, every couple is unique, and every rabbi or cantor has the opportunity to be creative and personal and design a ceremony that is meaningful for that specific couple.

That is why we always encourage couples first to understand the elements that go into a traditional Jewish wedding, and then to make their ceremony as intimate, personal, and meaningful as they can.

FOUR POLES AND SOME FABRIC

Most Jewish weddings take place under a *chuppah*, or "wedding canopy." The canopy can be constructed of almost anything. The *chuppah* is traditionally a symbol of the new home that the couple is creating through the wedding ceremony. Often it's simply four poles and a covering (often a *tallit* in traditional weddings). A *chuppah* can be as simple or as ornate as you desire, whether made out of roses, wooden poles, or simply an overhanging tree.

There is also a beautiful custom with its origin among Spanish Jewry for the *chuppah* to simply be a prayer shawl that is wrapped around the shoulders of the bride and groom, creating a sacred space of closeness between them. Steven always uses a *tallit* in this manner to wrap around a couple at their wedding to symbolize that the home they're creating together has nothing whatsoever to do with physical structures, but rather with what's inside. It's a reminder that wherever they are on earth from that moment on, whether in the finest of structures or under the stars, as long as they're together, wherever they are is home.

WALKING IN CIRCLES

There is an ancient custom steeped in Jewish mystical tradition where the bride approaches the groom then circles him either three or seven times. Both three and seven are mystical numbers in Judaism and many other religious traditions.

Three is a number that appears often in biblical literature. The sun, moon, and stars; the three patriarchs Abraham, Isaac, and Jacob; the three angels whom God sends to announce Sarah is expecting from ninety-nine-year-old Abraham; and the three days of darkness in the ninth plague of Egypt. Three is also a traditional Jewish number that signifies legal intentionality. It's the number of rabbis in a *bet din*, and when traditional Jewish law indicates that someone has accepted a legal document from another, the court asks the person to hold the document and walk three steps.

Seven is a number that signifies another kind of spiritual symbol. It's a symbol of completion and creation, as in the seven days of the week, and is a traditional symbol of perfection. The oldest symbol of Judaism and Jewish civilization is the seven-branched menorah that stood in the ancient Temple in Jerusalem. It was a reminder of the words written in the book of Proverbs 20:27, which taught, "The light of God is the soul of the human being." Thus, by circling the groom seven times, the bride implies that their marriage will be the central source of divinity, holiness, and light in their lives.

Of course, having the bride circle the groom was also a symbol of the bride leaving her father's home for her husband's, and as such is fundamentally a sexist, male-centered symbol. That is why many modern couples have adapted this custom in a more egalitarian way by having the bride circle the groom three times, then the groom circles the bride three times, and then each circles the other the final time. Some believe the entire circling process wards off evil spirits.

GETTING TO "I DO"

Upon entering under the *chuppah*, the first blessing usually recited is one of welcome. The traditional version begins with a quotation from Psalm 118:26 that states, "Blessed is one who comes in the name of God, we all bless you out of the house of God." This traditional Hebrew blessing of welcome is simply a way of indicating that two lives are about to be joined as one in marriage. In fact, the very name *kiddushin* (marriage or betrothal) comes from the root word *kadosh*, which means "holy." Judaism understands joining two lives together in a loving bond is an expression of holiness in its purest form. The person who officiates the wedding (whether rabbi, cantor, or other officiant) is *mesader kidushin* (one who arranges holiness), because we recognize that marriage is one of the ultimate expressions of what it means to create a sacred relationship.

The next prayer, *Mi Adir*, is sung to welcome the groom and the bride under the *chuppah* with words that invoke God's blessings upon them: "The One who is mighty above all, the One who is blessed above all, the One who is great above all, the One who is distinguished above all, may the One bless the groom and the bride."

SHEVA BERACHOT (SEVEN BLESSINGS)

The core of a Jewish wedding involves seven blessings. As we have mentioned, seven is a mystical number that signifies both completion and creation. The blessings refer to Adam and Eve as a symbol of the universality of marriage and the value of not living alone but finding a spiritual partner to share your life. They speak of God, who created all people in the Divine image and likeness. They also make reference to Zion (Israel) and to rejoicing in the joy of brides and grooms who find love with each other as Adam and Eve did. God is acknowledged as the source of gladness and joy, song, harmony, celebration, peace, companionship, and love. There is even a reference to the city of Jerusalem celebrating with the bride and groom and filling with the sounds of music, song, and joy in the weddings of its children.

Then bride and groom usually exchange wedding rings. Next, the groom puts a ring on the finger of his beloved and recites the key phrase that binds them together in marriage according to traditional Jewish law:

הֲרֵי אַתְּ מְקֻדֶּשֶׁת לִי, בְּטַבַּעַת זוֹ, כְּדַת מֹשֶׁה וְיִשְׂרָאֵל.

Harei at/ata mekudeshet/mekudash li b'ta-ba-at zo k'dat moshe v'yisrael.
"Be sanctified unto me as my wife/husband, according to the laws of
Moses and the Jewish People."

Once finished, his bride places the ring on her beloved and recites the same phrase.

It's always helpful to remember that there is no one right, magical way to perform almost any ritual. Rituals, customs, and traditions have emerged organically out of everyday experiences and the needs of people who use them. In this case, these rites are designed to enhance the spiritual and emotional power of those at the altar. For that reason, Steven's basic rule is "Whatever works, works," and he encourages couples to find rituals that best reflect the joining of their lives together in sacred unions. If it works and adds a sense of meaning and purpose to the ceremony, then it's worth including it, regardless of whether or not its origins lie within traditional Jewish custom.

In Jewish tradition, wine is a symbol of joy, and joy gets multiplied by two, as there are traditionally two blessings over wine during the wedding ceremony. The first is at the beginning and not only represents the sweetness and joy of the wedding but, as we mentioned earlier, also stands as a symbol of the betrothal ceremony. The second blessing over wine comes as part of the Seven Blessings and is both a way to symbolize the equality of the relationship and also to represent the sweetness and joy of the marriage ceremony.

THE PLAIN GOLD BAND

Many have heard about the traditional custom for plain gold wedding bands and often question its origin. According to Jewish tradition, when two individuals entered into a legal agreement like a marriage, they would exchange something of agreed-upon value to serve as a binder. The rabbis of old were concerned that if the bride's ring was later discovered to be undervalued due to a worthless stone, the binder would be null and void.

To prevent marriages from becoming invalidated, rabbis decreed that the groom only provide a plain gold band. This way the value is evident to all. Today, since the ring itself is not specifically seen as a legally binding entity but rather serves as a symbolic expression of love, it's acceptable in some movements to use any ring, but not in others. The Orthodox and Conservative movements still require a plain gold band. Reconstructionist and Reform movements allow any ring the couple selects. Check with your rabbi to see exactly what your synagogue requires. There are couples who wear a higher-value ring after the ceremony as jewelry and keep their plain bands as keepsakes.

THE GROOM WORE STEEL-TOED SHOES

The ultimate symbol of a Jewish wedding occurs at the end of the ceremony when someone, usually the groom, stomps on a glass. There are many different reasons offered over the centuries as to why we break a glass. The most often shared is that even in times of great joy the Jewish People have wanted to remember the destruction of the Temple in Jerusalem, and that while outside the state of Israel, they were still in exile.

When officiating a wedding, Steven shares how in life there are often circumstances, experiences, and relationships that create a wedge between newlyweds. In fact, there may even be times when those external influences appear like they're determining the quality of the couple's relationship. Yet, when looked at from another vantage point, such external influences are really as fragile as glass.

When the couple smashes the glass at the end of the ceremony, it's as if they're demonstrating their mastery over all those external forces and symbolizing that the strength, growth, love, and commitment in their lives depends totally upon the two of them and what they create in their daily lives.

Obviously, there could be any number of explanations, rationales, and reasons that someone might attach to the breaking of the glass. We encourage you to come up with your own explanation that will give the most meaning and purpose to your wedding as possible.

The wedding ends with the pronouncement that the couple has officially joined each other's lives in marriage, and they kiss and exit the ceremony thrilled to start their new lives together. Some couples like to practice another Jewish tradition called *yihud* (separation). This is where the couple exits the *chuppah* and immediately goes into isolation to enjoy their new status as a married couple.

In ancient times, this isolation was actually used as an opportunity to consummate the marriage and demonstrate that the bride was a virgin (if that was the expectation). Today it's simply a beautiful opportunity for the couple to gather their emotions and focus together in private with one another and then emerge from their privacy to greet guests and family for the first time as a married couple.

GETTING A *GET*

Just as joining a couple is considered a spiritual act in Jewish tradition, so is the decision to end a marriage in divorce. And just as there is a *ketubah* to initiate the marriage, there is one to end it called a *get*. In traditional Jewish communities, a *get* is given by the groom to the bride, and in egalitarian, contemporary Jewish life, either partner can give it to the other.

The process of Jewish divorce is as formal a ritual as the wedding ceremony or rituals of conversion. In Orthodox tradition, a Jewish divorce proceeding can only be initiated by the husband. Both husband and wife come before a *bet din* and declare that they no longer want to remain married. The *bet din* asks a series of formal questions to ensure that this undertaking is voluntary, and then a scribe writes the *get* for the husband to give to the wife in the presence of the *bet din*. In accordance with Jewish law, once a wife holds the document (the husband drops it into her cupped hands) and walks three steps away from her husband to signify she accepts, the *bet din* pronounces their divorce.

Since outside of Israel our country's laws take precedence over Jewish law, a *bet din* only presides over a Jewish divorce proceeding after the couple is legally divorced.

In nontraditional Jewish communities in North America, either the husband or wife can initiate a Jewish divorce. In many liberal communities, a rabbi can pass on the paperwork of the *get* to either ex-spouse whether or not the other is present or interested in receiving it. In such cases, the rabbi simply sends a copy of the *get* to the ex-spouse as a matter of courtesy and to ensure the proper notification should the ex-spouse care to wed again in the future. Getting a *get* is key, as many rabbis will not officiate a wedding of two Jews who previously married Jews unless they have a *get*.

When all is said and done, Judaism views every person as sacred, every relationship as a gift from God, and every wedding as the joining of two lives created in the image of God. Jewish tradition even goes as far as to say that there are always three who participate in every wedding: the couple getting married and God. The sentiment may or may not be spiritually compelling, but the idea is to communicate that every decision of every couple to join their lives in marriage is an act of faith in themselves, in the future, and in the sacredness of life.

CHAI NOTES

- A Jewish wedding is *kiddushin*, which means "holiness."
- Some brides and grooms visit the *mikvah* for ritual purification prior to their wedding.
- The bride and groom sign a *ketubah* prior to the wedding.
- Grooms unveil brides in a ceremony called a *bedeken* to ensure the right person is present.
- Marriage occurs under a *chuppah*, which can be as simple as four poles and a *tallit*.
- Traditionally, wedding rings are plain gold bands so their value is clear to all.
- Breaking a glass at the end of the ceremony has many different interpretations.
- Just as there is a *ketubah* for marriage, there is a *get* for divorce.

13

Raising Jewish Kids

יג

Think you're having a hard time grasping the ins and outs of Judaism? How about your children? You're making a conscious choice to convert, yet your children, depending on their age, just might be getting dragged along with you. So how can you effectively impart over four thousand years of wisdom, culture, and traditions when you're learning it from the ground up? This is a key concern for converts that have children or stepchildren, and even those that are planning to have children in the near term.

We can all agree that our role as parents is to raise kids who are independent and secure in their values and convictions. So what can you do to assimilate your brood into an ethically challenging environment? How can you create a warm and loving Jewish home life while encouraging them to fulfill their own personal life goals and dreams? Successfully raising Jewish children involves being part of a larger Jewish community. It means connecting with a local synagogue so that your children reap the benefits of a formal Jewish education. It also entails connecting them to a larger community of Jews to celebrate holidays and festivals and mark powerful life-cycle moments. In short, passing on important lessons starts with you paving the way by setting an example of what it means to live a Jewish life.

HANG ON! HELP IS ON ITS WAY

As a rabbi and author of several counseling books on interfaith relationships, Steven has addressed a number of specific child-raising issues that many converts wrestle with when raising children Jewish. Here are some of the most common questions people ask about raising Jewish children:

Q & A

Q: Will my child lose his religious identity in public school?

A: Not necessarily. Yet it also doesn't mean your child will gain much in this department except perhaps tolerance for kids of various religions. Public schools try hard to recognize religious holidays like Chanukah and Eid, but overall most plan activities associated with Christian holidays. In fact, most public school teachers will go out of their way to assure Jewish, Muslim, Sikh, or Buddhist parents that *their* class is "secular." But in December an army of Santas and Christmas trees are taped to the walls with a dreidel or two hanging topsy-turvy. Holiday parties are typically a replacement for Christmas parties, and spring egg hunts are code for Easter egg hunts. Kids love the fun activities all the same.

Unless you plan to spring for private secular schools or Jewish day schools (both of which are pricey), then you need to be flexible and get involved. Create an open dialogue to discuss what's happening in class so you can fill in the Jewish voids and volunteer in your child's class to explain Chanukah, Passover, or any other holiday, tradition, or custom. For even more help filling in the gap, enroll your child in religious education at a local synagogue and get involved in a local Jewish community center to continue promoting a healthy Jewish identity.

Q: How can I help my sixth grader feel Jewish if he converted to Judaism but was raised Christian until now?

A: Helping your child feel Jewish is a function of involving him in Jewish activities, experiences, special moments, and celebrations. Feeling "Jewish" grows primarily out of doing, so the more you expose him to positive, enjoyable, nurturing Jewish experiences, the more he will develop a positive Jewish self-image.

Q: We live in a community where there are no other Jews and the nearest synagogue is fifty miles away. How can we help our children feel Jewish out here "in the country"?

A: Obviously, you are in a do-it-yourself Judaism situation. Don't despair. Judaism has always been primarily home-centered anyway, so you can create a rich, nourishing, active Jewish life anywhere, as long as you search for ways to bring Jewish culture, tradition, ritual, and customs into your home.

The rabbis of Jewish tradition used to refer to the home as a *mikdash me'at*, a "small sanctuary." They felt that every family could bring holiness, sanctity, and specialness into their home through the rituals they perform, the celebrations they share, books they read, and attitudes they teach. Your job is to find resources that will help you to teach your children the fundamentals of Jewish ethics, and to bring as many rituals and holiday celebrations into your home as you are comfortable with.

Another suggestion is to identify Jewish personalities in news, film, recordings, or television whenever you find them, to build a sense of positive Jewish pride of association with your children. One of Jennifer's favorite ways to do this is to play Adam Sandler's Chanukah songs for her twins. Captain Kirk and Mr. Spock are both Jewish—who knew?!

Q: I was horrified the other day when my daughter came home from school and confided that a classmate told her Jews weren't nice people because they killed Jesus. How do I handle this?

A: Assuming your child is of elementary-school age, your first response should be to comfort and reassure and emphasize that the classmate is wrong and that Jews are as nice and wonderful as any other group. You might hold her and say, "That was a mean thing to say. I'll bet it hurt your feelings."

It's appropriate to let your child know that she hasn't done anything wrong, that the other child is at fault for saying something hurtful. You might also say that if the classmate's parents knew, you are sure they would be disappointed and ask where such a mean and untrue idea came from.

If your child is curious about Jesus, you might simply tell her that Jesus himself was Jewish, and a wonderful teacher a very long time ago, and of course Jews didn't kill him. If it were one of our children, we would actually let her classmate's mother and father know in a friendly, nonintimidating way. It's okay to let the parent know that his child picked up some undesirable and inaccurate information about Jews and Jesus, and we are sure they wouldn't want such hurtful statements repeated to other children.

Q: Last week my children and I were in the mall and they wanted to visit Santa's house, sit on his knee, and tell him what they want for Christmas. I told them no because we are Jewish and we don't believe in Santa. They were devastated. I felt that I didn't handle this well. What do you think?

A: Well, Steven remembers that he used to visit Santa in the department stores when he was a child, sit on his knee, and tell him that he was Jewish so he wanted things for Chanukah and not Christmas. Most of the time, Santa seemed to be Jewish too! Of course, Steven turned out to be a rabbi, so maybe you should watch out . . .

Anyway, we don't think it's a big deal to enjoy Christmas lights, visit Santa's house, or help friends and neighbors (or even relatives) trim their trees. That is not the same as "celebrating" Christmas in our eyes, and we think it's easy to make the distinction clear to your children. Very few children really think that the white-bearded man in the mall is going to magically bring them whatever they want anyway. If anything, the mall Santa is just a cheery reminder of what they want from *you*.

Q: My sixteen-year-old son has announced his plans to live on a *kibbutz* in Israel this summer. I have mixed feelings about this. On the one hand, I'm proud and happy, but on the other, I'm frightened for his safety. Should I let him go?

A: Your concern is understandable given all the publicity that Israel gets in the news, and the fact that she is still officially at war with her Arab neighbors. However, Steven lived in Israel for two years and sends teenagers from his own congregation there every year to participate in a variety of outstanding programs. It never fails to be one of the most important and moving experiences of their lives, not to mention an excellent process of maturation.

We strongly recommend that you let your son experience Israel. It is an invaluable lesson in self-reliance and connection to the greater world of Jewish community, and the physical dangers are far less than walking down a street in most urban centers in America. Second tip: Don't believe everything you see in CNN's Situation Room. Israel proper is a very safe place to be. Compared to American standards, Israelis are experts when it comes to physical safety.

Q: Although my husband is Jewish (I was raised Lutheran), he was not raised with a sense of his own background. I would like our children to have a greater understanding of their background, but without my husband's help, I literally don't know where to start. What do you suggest?

A: This book is a good place to start, of course, and there are other books and materials on basic Judaism. There are also introduction to Judaism courses given in nearly every city in North America, and most local synagogues have classes on raising Jewish children or celebrating Jewish holidays as well.

The best thing you can do is take a class on Judaism together with your husband. This would not only give you a common vocabulary to share when raising children with a positive Jewish identity but also undoubtedly help strengthen your relationship in the process. In the end, of course, it is obviously much better to have the involvement and support of your husband in your child-raising efforts, as children learn from both parents, not just one.

Q: My son came home crying today. Another kid called him a "kike" on the playground. How can I make it better?

A: This issue is similar to any instance when someone calls your child names. The most important thing to point out is that, unfortunately, throughout life we meet up with people of all ages who say mean and insensitive remarks to others. Sometimes kids like to hurt other kids' feelings, just because it makes them feel better or superior to put down someone else.

Name-calling is a very hurtful thing, and it's appropriate for your child to sob or feel sad because of it. The word *kike* really doesn't have any meaning to either your child or the child who said it, except to stand for something cruel and unconstructive. Perhaps you can use this as an opportunity to hold your child in your arms and tell him that too often people are foolish and hurtful toward others. Thinking about how awful it feels is a way of reminding ourselves of how important it is to treat others in ways that we would like to be treated.

Q: There are so many negative stereotypes about Jews and Jewish behavior. How can I prepare my child to deal with them?

A: There are negative stereotypes concerning just about every ethnic group that exists on our planet. Most of the negative Jewish stereotypes won't affect your child until he or she is a preteen or teen, at which time it is possible to teach a little of the history of antisemitism and where these stereotypes came from. We have found that a brief history lesson on the realities of medieval Europe and persecution of Jews by the Church and European governments provides an excellent basis for youths to understand and respond to negative stereotypes that remain today.

Q: We are expecting our first child soon, and my Catholic mother says she cannot sleep at night knowing that her grandchild will not receive a Christian baptism. She is convinced that our baby will be condemned to purgatory. Help!

A: There are two ways to approach this issue. First, you can decide that since the baptism is so important to your mother, and meaningless to you and your husband (e.g., the ceremony doesn't make your child Catholic or prede-termine future child-raising choices), you will oblige and baptize your child. Steven knows many interfaith couples who have chosen this option and raised their children Jewish, celebrated their *bar* and *bat mitzvahs*, and managed to placate the strong feelings of everyone to some degree.

Second, you can simply tell your mother that you don't believe your child will be condemned to purgatory for foregoing baptism. You can let her know that you still love her just as much, but as an adult, you have chosen not to baptize your child.

Jennifer told her Catholic father she had no plans to baptize her twin daughters, for she saw no honor in undergoing a ceremony that was important to her father, yet meaningless to her and her husband. Imagine having this discussion with your father in his hospital room only weeks before he died. It was a tough bedside discussion, but it was important for Jennifer to hold her ground.

What you need to consider is this: if you bend on this issue to make your mother happy, what else will you have to bend on in the future? Your child has numerous milestones ahead where your mother may want to insist on what she wants. Then what? The bottom line is that this is your child, not your mother's, and you need to feel that you're living it your way, not hers.

Q: The High Holidays are approaching, and I would like my son to accom-pany me to synagogue. "Ah, Mom," my son said, "who cares about that old stuff?" How can I combat my son's sense of apathy?

A: The best thing to do is to create a positive, nurturing, happy Jewish en-vironment within your home year-round by incorporating Jewish customs, rituals, holidays, and ethics. In that way, your children come to value being Jewish for all it adds to their lives, and getting them to participate in the High Holidays or any other Jewish activity is not so difficult.

Of course, Jews of all ages get bored with High Holidays—the many hours of sitting in prayer-filled services and listening to long sermons and even lon-ger chants in Hebrew. The trick is to see the High Holidays as an opportunity to get in touch with the values that are most important to you and use it to move your life forward toward your personal spiritual goals.

Making sure that you aren't just a "holiday-only" Jew will set a pattern of behavior and identification that encourages participation in all Jewish holi-days. It is also valuable to point out that ideas, themes, and thoughts that form the center of the High Holiday experience are just as relevant and powerful today as when they first occurred. All of us need some time each year to reexamine who we are and where we are going, what we stand for, and who we want to become. This is the primary purpose of the High Holidays.

Q: My son did not undergo circumcision at birth. He is now twelve and is asking about *bar mitzvah*. Must he undergo circumcision beforehand?

A: No, not unless he wants to have a *bar mitzvah* in a traditional synagogue. Being circumcised, although one of the most distinguishing marks of Judaism for the past four thousand years, does not make a boy a Jew. Nor does it make someone not Jewish if he isn't circumcised.

Synagogues don't generally ask boys if they are circumcised, or ask them to publicly "whip it out." But chances are if he's ever gone to the restroom at the synagogue . . . it's likely not a secret. That said, most rabbis are more concerned with the choices you make year in and year out that distinguish your life as Jewish than anything else. Circumcision, although practiced by the vast majority of Jews, is still a private decision for the family and the son (if he is old enough) to make. There are many other more public and more important ways to demonstrate Jewish identity and a connection to the Jewish People (including celebrating special life-cycle events such as a *bar mitzvah*), and that is what is really important.

Q: Every December my children get upset when they see the neighbors' Christmas festivities (parties, trees, lights, presents, etc.). How do I explain that Christmas is for Christians and Chanukah is for Jews? How do I overcome their jealousy for their friends' celebration when we don't celebrate it anymore?

A: You do it exactly as you think. You say, "Christmas is a holiday for Christians to celebrate the birthday of Jesus. It isn't our holiday, so we don't celebrate it in our own home, but we can celebrate with our friends in their homes since it's their holiday. We celebrate Chanukah for eight nights instead, and perhaps we can invite some of our Christian friends over to celebrate Chanukah with us."

If your child becomes upset over how many presents his friends receive at Christmas, you can tell him what you would if he went to a birthday party and then got jealous because the birthday boy got all the presents. Children need to recognize that all people are not exactly the same, that each of us has times when we get presents and attention, but now is not one of those times.

It's best not to deprive your child of a wonderful experience, as long as it's clear that this isn't *your* Christmas celebration. Allow your child to share Christmas with his Christian friends or relatives, or perhaps volunteer at a local hospital to allow Christian workers time off with their families. This would be the best "Christmas present" you could possibly give your child.

This is also your cue to make Chanukah as interesting as you can. You don't have to break the bank, but you can certainly mix things up by designating some nights for gifts and do other meaningful activities in between so that Chanukah is rich and memorable. We know Christmas is a hard act to follow, but that doesn't mean Santa has a monopoly on fun or that Chanukah can't compete. Remember, Christmas is only one day. You have seven more to show just how fun Chanukah can be. Done right, it can be less commercial and much more meaningful.

Consider dedicating a night to *tzedakah* or to another value that you hold dear. You can show your children what it means to be charitable by taking gifts to an orphanage, arranging a performance at a senior citizens' home, or volunteering at a local soup kitchen. Another night you can raise your family's awareness of the arts and take your brood to a play, a Jewish museum, or whatever suits your fancy. The idea is that there are so many ways to show your children that Chanukah is much more than light parades and gift giving. If these efforts go over well, you can consider making them part of your Chanukah traditions.

LIVE IT YOURSELF

Raising Jewish children is both a challenge and an opportunity. That is why ultimately one of the aspects of Jewish culture and tradition that holds the highest priority for many parents is the question of how they can successfully pass on an understanding of Jewish ethics and values to their children. We have found that the most important way to teach Jewish ethics to your children is simply to live them yourself. That is why the most important child-raising advice we can impart is to be the kind of adult you want your children to become. Fill your life with Jewish rituals, traditions, and holidays so that your children grow up with a rich experience of what living a Jewish life is all about. There is a reason that a famous rabbinic saying is that a community is too heavy for anyone to carry alone.

Being Jewish is a communal enterprise, not a solo venture. Use the resources that are available within the larger Jewish community in which you live. Join a synagogue, frequent a JCC, and seek out programs offered by your local Jewish Federation and other local Jewish organizations. Doing so helps you expose your children to a wide range of Jewish activities and life experiences.

As we have said throughout this book, Judaism is about *belonging* more than *believing*. That is why one of the keys to raising Jewish children is to consistently look for opportunities for them to feel that they belong to a community beyond themselves and their own family. Find a *chavurah* (group of friends) at your synagogue, or ask your congregation to help place you in one. Most synagogues pride themselves on placing families in groups with other like-minded families so their kids can have immediate friends and the parents can have some adult chat time. Many synagogues are fairly good at this and have *chavurot* that have enjoyed each other's company for over twenty years.

Becoming Jewish is a lifelong process whether you choose Judaism as an adult or grow up Jewish from birth. Teach your children the values you cherish, the Jewish life that gives you the greatest sense of fulfillment, and you will be doing the best you can possibly do to successfully raise Jewish children in today's highly mobile world.

CHAI NOTES

- Helping your children feel Jewish is a function of involving them in Jewish activities, experiences, special moments, and celebrations.
- How your kids live is dependent upon you and the model you set through your actions.
- Going to Israel is one of the most important and moving experiences for teenagers, not to mention an excellent process of maturation.
- The trick is to see the High Holidays as an opportunity to get in touch with the values that are most important to you and your personal spiritual goals.
- Making sure that you aren't just a "holiday-only" Jew will set a pattern of behavior and identification that will encourage participation in all Jewish holidays.
- Christmas is a hard act to follow, but that doesn't mean Santa has a monopoly on fun.
- Becoming Jewish is a lifelong process whether you choose Judaism as an adult or grow up Jewish from birth.

14

Adult *B'nai Mitzvah* and Beyond

יד

Having a *bat mitzvah* or *bar mitzvah* sounds strange to anyone over the age of twelve or thirteen. Yet plenty of adult Jews enroll in this course every single year. What draws adult Jews to achieve this rite of passage typically meant for preadolescents? Plenty. A former Orthodox Jew told us she never had a *bat mitzvah* as Orthodoxy reserves this public right of passage exclusively for boys. Another classmate who grew up Muslim wanted to set a good example for her Jewish children following her conversion. There were other Jews by birth who mentioned that their secular parents never really considered this coming-of-age ceremony that significant for their kids.

The reasons seemed to multiply. A classmate who grew up in a Reform temple told us her parents thought it was important for her brother but not for her. Yet another classmate from Israel was raised by a non-Jewish family and later yearned to embrace his Jewish heritage. In other words, the stories are endless. And who can blame them? Besides fulfilling a lifelong dream, students who complete the class become more familiar with Hebrew prayers, have an *aliyah*, and typically read from both the Torah and the *Haftarah*.

RITE OF PASSAGE

The *bar* or *bat mitzvah* journey is markedly different depending on whether you're a youth or an adult. For youths, this rite of passage is a life-cycle event that entails coming to grips with reaching Jewish adulthood. For adults, it marks reaching a new religious milestone that further defines them as a Jew. Adults, much like young teens, co-lead their *b'nai mitzvah* service. No need to panic. You won't have to do anything that a twelve-year-old girl or thirteen-year-old boy hasn't already done. Hebrew can be tricky if your movement requires it, but consider this an opportunity to learn the language of the Torah and an experience that is solely Jewish. And as you'll see from Jennifer's *bat mitzvah* story a bit later, it's also a chance to say to the world that you're proud to be a Jew.

Most courses you'll encounter cover all or some of Jewish history, Jewish thought, Torah and its interpretation, and Hebrew. Course lengths vary between movements and even synagogues. Check with your synagogue to see what it takes to achieve your *bar* or *bat mitzvah*. The synagogue Jennifer converted through offered an eighteen-month conversion/*b'nai* (many achieve it together) *mitzvah* program spread over two calendar years. This meant any convert who took the adult *b'nai mitzvah* course immediately following conversion only had to undergo a two-year course as opposed to three years if they waited a year or longer. The idea behind the skipped year is that, if you take the courses back-to-back (each course is one year), your Hebrew is still fresh. Those that wait a year or longer before enrolling in the *b'nai mitzvah* risk losing a great deal of recall and memorization that can easily require another year to bring back up to speed.

Synagogues usually celebrate *b'nai mitzvah* immediately after the ceremony. Ask your rabbi about this, and if you have the time and patience, volunteer to coordinate one or more activities. Usually rabbis could use help communicating information to the class, arranging a group photo, planning the ceremony structure, preparing and printing the program, scheduling rehearsals with the cantors, and even collecting money to honor the *b'nai mitzvah* candidates with a luncheon. It's also a fast way to make new friends at your synagogue.

FACING YOUR FEARS

Jennifer learned in graduate school that it took a certain kind of person to deliver an awe-inspiring public speech and that she preferred to work behind the scenes (Steven prefers the *bimah*). Fast forward to Jennifer's *b'nai mitzvah* class. She must have taken a deep sigh upon learning that part of achieving *bat mitzvah* meant reading from the Torah in front of hundreds. For her, public speaking came hard; then multiply that by chanting it in a foreign language—Hebrew—and it's enough to make those on the fence reconsider. But her resolve was strong, and in situations like this, a strong resolve will give you the strength to do just about anything.

Have someone you love capture the moment with a photo of you with your rabbi and classmates before your adult *b'nai mitzvah* service. Your synagogue will likely publish a program of your big day too. Hang on to it. Jennifer's class even had a video available for a small purchase. Hint: Skip the video. It's a great keepsake if you think you'll show your kids or grandkids. But unless you're the type of person who cozies up to wedding or graduation reruns each year, chances are your adult *b'nai mitzvah* video (as meaningful as it is) will end up as a dust catcher.

WHAT CAN YOU EXPECT?

Just like every conversion program varies, so does every adult *b'nai mitzvah* class. Your rabbi will likely emphasize the areas of Judaism that your movement holds dear, with some of his own interests thrown in for grins. He might talk more about *tzedakah* or *tikkun olam*, or if he's a history buff, it might be the Second Temple or the Maccabees. It really just depends.

We can't stress enough to hang on to your class syllabus. In fact, make a copy for home and one that travels with you so you can stay current on your assignments. Jennifer traveled every week while in her *b'nai mitzvah* class, so it was helpful to have one with her at all times. Here is a sample of the syllabus that Jennifer used to give you a bird's-eye view into potential topics that your rabbi might cover.

ADULT *B'NAI MITZVAH* SYLLABUS—CONSERVATIVE

First Term
1. Oct. 19   God: An Introduction
2. Oct. 26   God in the Hebrew Bible
3. Nov. 2   God in the Talmud
4. Nov. 9   God in *Halakhah*

5. Nov. 16	God in Kabbalah
6. Nov. 23	God in *Hassidut*
7. Dec. 7	God in Modern Jewish Thought
8. Dec. 14	God and Us
9. Dec. 21	Conclusions: My God

Second Term

10. Jan. 11	Social Justice: An Introduction
11. Jan. 18	The Prophets and Social Justice
12. Jan. 25	The Ethical Impulse in Rabbinic Judaism
13. Feb. 1	How Kosher Is Kosher?
14. Feb. 8	Am I My Sibling's Keeper If My Sibling Lives Halfway Around the World?
Feb. 15	No Class: *Yom Limmud*—Community-wide day of study
15. Feb. 22	Opening the Gates of Torah: Including People with Disabilities in the Jewish Community
16. Mar. 1	A Torah of Justice: A View from the Right?
Mar. 8	No Class: Purim Carnival
17. Mar. 15	Social Justice and the World of Business
18. Mar. 22	A Torah of Justice: A View from the Left?
19. Mar. 29	Environment
20. Apr. 19	Creating Covenantal Communities: Building Relationships, Developing Leaders, Taking Action

Passover break and final preparations: There will be extra times set to meet with cantors in final preparations for the adult *b'nai mitzvah*.

Saturday, April 25—Adult *B'nai Mitzvah*

Texts:
Walking with God, The Ziegler School of Rabbinic Studies
Walking with Justice, The Ziegler School of Rabbinic Studies
Source: Congregation Beth Yeshurun

As you can see, Jennifer had an interesting yet challenging year. She wrote the following about what she learned and how the class impacted her:

I learned so much during my *b'nai mitzvah* class that it not only strengthened my resolve as a Jew but it also prepared me for reading what months before seemed impossible: the Torah. This was no small feat because I wasn't just at the *bimah* reading Hebrew to a few but to a few hundred. The nice part was that my teacher prepared me so well that the word *nervous* wasn't even part of my repertoire. Once I knew Hebrew well enough, I disowned every word equivalent to that and replaced it with one word: *chutzpah*. This word became my guiding light of how I would live my life—although *mensch* is a good one to work toward too. One thing that stood out throughout my class is that unlike Christianity, where Jesus hogs center stage, in Judaism God is the main character.

WHAT ELSE CAN YOU LEARN?

Most synagogues offer many classes on topics other than conversion and adult *b'nai mitzvah*. Some offer coffee and commentary that covers next week's Torah portion so you, too, can learn why many rabbis claim the Torah has seventy faces. Weekly study is part of Jewish life, so classes like this often help Jews in searching their soul for meaning, doing *mitzvot*, and learning to be a *mensch*. Often, you can enroll in a nuts-and-bolts class that covers Jewish beliefs, holidays, and life-cycle events. A class like this serves to enrich your understanding of living a Jewish life, and in some synagogues doubles as a requirement of your adult *b'nai mitzvah* program. Introductory Hebrew and often a second year of Hebrew is available for adults interested in leading prayers for *Shabbat* morning service and reading Torah and *Haftarah* portions (typically filled with adult *b'nai mitzvah* students).

You'll find classes that introduce adults to the Talmud. Topics could include Jewish history and culture that covers everything from antisemitism to Zionism. Many synagogues have classes that feature selected psalms to help Jews understand the beauty and wisdom of our people's earliest prayers to God. Some classes help Jews understand how our tradition attempts to understand God by surveying sources in the Torah, Talmud, Midrash, Kabbalah, and more.

Besides classes, you'll also find plenty of workshops, seminars, committees, and clubs to participate in. Some synagogues have meditation and yoga workshops, while others have a brotherhood for men and a sisterhood for women, and even book clubs. Some have groups that meet about Israel and the Jewish state's security and to plan trips to the Jewish homeland yearly. Others hold family camps, charity drives, and support groups to help congregants achieve balance and overcome crises. Some synagogues have all this and more.

Some will also have interfaith workshops for members with spouses that are unwilling to give up their prior religion and convert. Traditionally, couples that fall into an interfaith category will likely be in one of three movements: Conservative, Reconstructionist, or Reform. Here is an excerpt of a Yom Kippur speech that a Conservative convert gave detailing her journey to Judaism and the amazing support she received from her non-Jewish husband:

> In my case, my husband is not Jewish. However, he is 100 percent supportive and behind our commitment to have a Jewish life and home. There came a point in my exploration of Judaism that I realized that, unlike with Christianity, it would be difficult for me to be solely and independently Jewish in our household. Being Jewish involves your entire daily life with family as a focus of that life. So my husband and I had quite a number of conversations over time regarding our agreement to have a solely Jewish home.
>
> I had thought about converting to Judaism for a long time. When I was about twenty years old, I discovered Judaism, and it was as if I dropped into a whole new world. I was in amazement about it, and astounded that it was there the whole time and somehow I didn't see it. At that time, I experienced intense feelings that overwhelmed me, but my reaction to this new and unknown world was to run away. I essentially ran from it and back to what was familiar to me.
>
> As a consequence of not converting then, I buried my spirituality. Once I realized this a few years ago, I decided to explore Judaism both religiously and as a way of life without committing myself to conversion. It was a way for me to get my feet wet without feeling like I was drowning. Initially, I read many books, and I analyzed the differences between Judaism and Christianity, becoming intensely aware of all the assumptions and beliefs that I had blindly bought into in my youth as "the" truth.
>
> In my opinion, the conversion of our home to a Jewish one is a gift for all three of us. I can say that stepping out of the mainstream culture as we have and learning a new language, faith, and way of life has taken courage on all of our parts. But I especially want to acknowledge the courage and strength of my husband and daughter, who have been willing to look at falling in love with Judaism as I have. (Laura, fifty-three, financial consultant)

VIRTUAL LEARNING

By now you know Judaism has a rich culture, and congregating with fellow Jews is a big part of it. But if you can't find a classroom course that piques your interest, there are oodles of online classes that make it easier than ever to satisfy your thirst for Jewish knowledge in the comfort of your own pajamas.

Depending on the sites you browse, you can find courses that focus on one of Judaism's greatest compendia of wisdom—the Talmud. You can study texts that relate to family, marriage, child rearing, and the like—teachings that help you walk away with a better understanding of Jewish wisdom as it pertains to your own worldview. Or maybe your interest lies in the Dead Sea Scrolls. There are courses that help you deepen your understanding into early Judaism using these scrolls as lenses to the past. You'll also find courses on how to live as a Jew, learn more about Judaism, and pass on beliefs and customs to your children. Some programs even offer courses on secular Judaism so you can understand why some Jews embrace traits of their culture while sidestepping those that relate to religion.

Luckily, there are plenty of nonacademic courses for you to take as well. Besides Jewish history, you can take interactive e-learning courses that even allow you to communicate live with teachers from Israel. Courses like this help you learn to speak, read, and write in modern Hebrew. Some online providers also offer courses to deepen your knowledge of biblical Hebrew (see Resources).

Most would agree that becoming an adult *b'nai mitzvah* requires lots of study, preparation, and an extra helping of *chutzpah*. Yet all would agree that co-leading a service with your classmates ranks right up there with your graduation, wedding, or even the birth of your child. Why? The effort you put into it is as long as carrying a baby full term. Soon, you'll be able to read, speak, understand, and chant Hebrew and have a greater understanding of your Jewish heritage and its rituals and traditions. Just think, before your big day, you'll learn how to sing prayers you may have never known the tunes to, read from the Torah, and develop a greater understanding of what it means to be a Jew. Plus, the service is deeply moving because of the amount of wisdom imparted, gained, and shared along the way. The more you study, the more your appreciation of Judaism and its values enrich your life.

Attending services, studying Torah, and learning prayers creates an opportunity for your entire family to explore your own spiritual paths, deepen your own relationship with your synagogue, and grow closer to God and to Torah. *B'nai mitzvah* is a great goal to work toward, but there are plenty of courses you can take before or after it. Consider Judaism as an exciting new world to explore, and enrich your knowledge by learning something meaningful every year. Whether you're picking up a new book on your Jewish roots, participating in a *minyan*, taking an online Hebrew course, making a trip to Israel, or even making *aliyah*, there is always more to learn about your lifelong relationship with Judaism.

CHAI NOTES

- Plenty of adult Jews enroll in adult *b'nai mitzvah* courses each year.
- Adults, much like young teens, co-lead their *b'nai mitzvah* service.
- Check with your synagogue regarding course lengths as they vary between movements and even synagogues.
- Most adult *b'nai mitzvah* courses you'll encounter cover all or some of Jewish history, Jewish thought, Torah and its interpretation, and Hebrew.
- Your rabbi emphasizes the areas of Judaism that your movement holds.
- Hang on to your syllabus and make a copy to travel with so you stay current.
- Your class strengthens your resolve and prepares you for reading the Torah.
- Consider volunteering to help prepare for your *b'nai mitzvah* ceremony or celebration.
- Some online courses include studying the Talmud, Hebrew, or the Dead Sea Scrolls.
- The *b'nai mitzvah* service is deeply moving because of the amount of wisdom imparted, gained, and shared along the way.
- Soon you'll recite, chant, and sing Hebrew even though it seemed impossible at first glance.
- You'll find there is always more to learn about your lifelong relationship with Judaism.

15

Is Madonna Jewish?

שו

If you grew up Catholic, as Jennifer did, you learned about heaven and hell and even purgatory—that strange in-between place where lost souls go. You likely believed that God had a son and his mortal mother was a virgin who, interestingly enough (ahem), got knocked up by God. Yet by the time you complete your conversion, you'll equate those beliefs with the same disbelief adults have toward the Easter Bunny, Santa Claus, and the Man in the Moon. Religiously liberated is probably the best way to describe it. No middlemen between you and God (your rabbi is your teacher, not an intermediary). You'll also never again have to see someone else's depiction of what God looks like in man's image. Except for fleeting descriptions of God in the Torah and Talmud, the idea of what God looks like or even what God is never gets much attention.

For Judaism, what is most important is life in the here and now, not what happens after we die. But there *is* a mystical side to Judaism, just one not often discussed until recently. It's Kabbalah. Yes, that "in religion" sweeping through Hollywood. With followers like Madonna, Demi Moore, Ashton Kutcher, Roseanne Barr, Rosie O'Donnell, Zac Efron, Britney Spears, and even socialite (if that's the right name for what she does) Paris Hilton, Kabbalah seems more like a cult than a religion.

That's mainly because Kabbalah *isn't* a religion. It also isn't (in its pure form) a cult. Judaism, Islam, Christianity, Hinduism, and Buddhism are religions. Some would even go so far as to claim paganism is a religion. But that's a topic for another book altogether. In all fairness, if Judaism is a tree, Kabbalah is a branch.

UNDERSTANDING THE ROOTS

Let's start with a story. See how it sits with you:

It is about two thousand years ago. The Roman Empire occupies what is now the Land of Israel. Not only are they heavily taxing their "citizens" but they are also imposing their will on their subjects. Fear rules the streets. Jews must practice their religion in secret, or face death. As the Roman grip on the throat of Judaism tightens, one man rises above the fray. A great rabbi emerges, a true leader of the Jews, who is teaching his followers how to look inward, how to understand the soul and its relationship to God, how to achieve a near oneness with the Creator himself. He even has his own disciples, who share the task of teaching his beliefs.

Incensed at the increasing stories they hear about this "Father of the World," the Roman leaders in Jerusalem sentence him to death. Thousands line the streets of Jerusalem to watch his agonizing torture with whips and flails and, ultimately, his slow, excruciating death. But because of his mastery of all things physical and spiritual, his pain is fleeting, and he dies with nothing but joy, love, and forgiveness in his heart.

His name is well known. He was, of course, Rabbi Akiva.

Surprised? Don't be. At that time, there were *many* Jewish leaders the Romans despised, arrested, and crucified . . . not just the one we've all heard stories about. But Akiva really *was* special, and his top disciple, Rabbi Shimon Bar Yochai, was perhaps even greater. The Romans thought so too, because they put Yochai on their hit list. He and his son hid themselves in a cave for thirteen years. Each day, Yochai literally buried himself to his neck and meditated on God, man, and the universe. Seems extreme, but what else is there to do in a cave with no TV?

Once freed, Yochai tapped one of *his* disciples, Rabbi Abba, to document all the knowledge both Akiva and Yochai had amassed. Abba did as asked, writing in parable and metaphor to protect the secrets of his great teachers from those not ready to learn them. The result was a very large set of Aramaic writings called the *Zohar*, or "radiance."

Unfortunately, as Jews were sent into the Diaspora, study (and copies) of the *Zohar* slowly disappeared. But in pre-Inquisition Spain of the thirteenth century, where Judaism and mysticism were both blossoming, a Jewish writer named Moses de Leon published the *Zohar* as a set of multiple volumes, having "discovered" a copy of it in a cave in Israel. True study of Kabbalah began. What rabbis initially spread orally from generation to generation—hence the name *Kabbalah*, which means "receiving"—now had a set of documents to work from.

WHAT IS KABBALAH?

And what a story they told. Scholars have often said there are four primary differences between studying Torah and studying Kabbalah (see figure 15.1).

Where the Torah deals with the history of the Jewish People and the laws God gave us, it does not deal with *why* things happened. Why did God create us to begin with? Why did he free us from slavery? Why us? Kabbalah helps address these questions.

And while the Torah is firmly rooted on the ground, starting with the creation of Adam from dirt, Kabbalah delves into the mysteries of the soul. Who are we really? Does our soul survive? Can a body exist without a soul? What is the foundation of evil? How do we commune with God?

You may be surprised to learn that, according to Kabbalists, the soul has three primary components: *nefesh, ruach,* and *neshamah.* The *nefesh* is the basest part of our soul. It enters us at birth, and every human has it. *Nefesh* is linked to our "animal" instincts and relates to emotions like anger or sadness, cravings like food or thirst, or desires like lust or greed. We develop this part over time. *Ruach* literally means "spirit." This is the part of the soul that defines our morality and allows us to know right from wrong. Finally, *neshamah* is the higher soul, and it is found in those who are enlightened and developed.

Figure 15.1

Torah	Kabbalah
How	Why
Body	Soul
Code	Secret
Physical	Spiritual

This is what truly makes us unique from everything else on earth. It allows us to be aware of God's existence and presence, and is the part of us that exists in the afterlife.

There are even additional components of the soul that not everyone has. One, *neshamah kedoshah*, or the "holy higher soul," is a piece of the soul we receive when we have a *bar* or *bat mitzvah*. Another, the *neshamah yeseira*, is a special "extra" soul we obtain on *Shabbat*.

You may recall a book published in the mid-1990s titled *The Bible Code*. In it, researchers demonstrated how they could extract true prophecies and occurrences from the letters of the Torah using mathematical analysis. They claimed to foretell the assassination of Israeli Prime Minister Yitzhak Rabin and showed how *The Bible Code* had prophesized the JFK assassination, World War II, and more. Following its publication, claims rose that *The Bible Code* had also predicted the World Trade Center attack and even an alien crash landing at Roswell, New Mexico.

Whether true or not, *The Bible Code* is a fundamental belief of Kabbalah. Early Jewish sages claimed the Torah was actually a coded letter from God, and that if we knew how to decipher it, we would have access to God's greatest secrets. Kabbalists have applied thousands of methods to decode the Torah, but few know if they've succeeded because Kabbalah remains shrouded in secrecy.

Hopefully you've seen *Raiders of the Lost Ark* because, if not, we're about to ruin it for you. Historically, Kabbalah has remained a secret for much the same reason Indiana Jones fought to keep the Ark of the Covenant out of the hands of the Nazis. Not only was it immensely powerful, but in the wrong hands it also runs the risk of cataclysmic consequences. In the final scenes, of course, the Ark delivers God's wrath on the unworthy. The same is thought to be the case with Kabbalah.

An offshoot of Kabbalah is *gematria*, or Jewish numerology. This takes the code further by revealing that the twenty-two Hebrew letters have corresponding numbers. Remember discussing in chapter 10 how the same Hebrew letters that represent the number eighteen also spell the word *chai*? That's probably the most common example of *gematria*. Kabbalists use *gematria* to discern all the names of God (there are, by the way, seventy-two of them), compare the value of words and Torah sections, and even validate the truthfulness of biblical stories.

The final difference between the Torah and Kabbalah is one of physicality versus spirituality. While the Torah discusses God's (and man's) actions in the physical realm—with the occasional miracle or angel dropping in to make things more interesting—Kabbalah focuses on the spiritual. What *is* God? How do we fit in God's plan? What is the Universe? How can we become closer to God? What happens when we die?

This is where Kabbalah naturally becomes very deep and introspective. Because of this, we will give you an overview of some of the key beliefs of Kabbalah. But neither of your authors are Kabbalah experts. Our goal is to explain Kabbalah and how it fits into Judaism. If Kabbalah interests you, talk to your rabbi. Find out where you can learn more with a proper Kabbalah teacher. Frankly, there are very few in the world.

THE FIVE LAYERS

Kabbalists discuss five layers of God's emanation, using an image much like an archery target. At the center is *Ein Sof*—infinity. From there, Kabbalists believe God's presence emanates outward in levels. Using light as a metaphor for each of God's emanations, Kabbalists work to capture as much light as possible. They believe in a sort of Jewish karma: do good, get light; do bad, lose light. When you gain light, you're closer to God. Good things happen to you. When you lose light, you move closer to the base human. Things don't happen the way you want them to. You have less control of your environment.

Deeper than the emanation of God are the ten attributes God uses to keep the universe running. They are labeled the *Sefirot*, or "the counting." Listed in descending order they are as follows:

1. *Keter*—The Crown
2. *Chochmah*—Thought
3. *Binah*—Understanding
4. *Da'at*—Intellect
5. *Chesed*—Loving-kindness
6. *Gevurah*—Justice
7. *Tiferet*—Mercy
8. *Netzach*—Eternity
9. *Hod*—Glory

10. *Yesod*—Foundation

11. *Malchut*—Kingdom

Yes, we said ten, but there are eleven in the list. The *Da'at* is considered the "Tree of Life" and is the location where all *Sefirot* are connected. Many depict it as an empty slot for this reason and for reasons that become more obvious in the next paragraph.

Let's look a bit deeper now. *Keter* literally means "crown" but really refers to that which is above human comprehension. In the *Zohar*, *Keter* is called "the most hidden of all hidden things." Since human intellect (*Da'at*) is conscious knowledge, and *Keter* is unconscious knowledge, they are considered two aspects of the same thing, and thus there are ten *Sefirot*. An easy way to understand this is to consider the right side of your brain, which is where imagination and creativity come from, and the left side of your brain, which is where recall and analysis come from. They are two sides to the same brain. *Da'at* and *Keter* are similar in that regard.

Kabbalists divined connections between these *Sefirot*, much as we just combined *Keter* and *Da'at* (or even between the two parts of your brain). For simplicity, many depict the entire set of *Sefirot* and their connections in a tree diagram (see figure 15.2). And since this is Kabbalah we're talking about, there are twenty-two connections—one for each letter in the Hebrew alphabet. This is not an accident, but *gematria* in practice.

The basic underpinning of Kabbalah is the belief that God's will pours through the primary *Sefirot* of intellect, creating a world where each event and interaction consists of a larger, logical pattern. Think of events and actions like a giant quilt or puzzle.

A foundation for the concept of *Sefirot* is that God has both male and female components. This comes from Genesis 1:27: "God created man in His own image, in the image of God He created him, male and female He created them." Kabbalists believe that doing *mitzvot* is a way to combine the male and female attributes of God to bring harmony to the world.

KABBALAH IS JEWISH

Depending on the branch of Judaism you're in, you will have more or less contact with Kabbalah. For *Haredi* Orthodox Jews, Kabbalah is an integral part of belief and prayer. It's weaved into much of what *Haredim* believe and

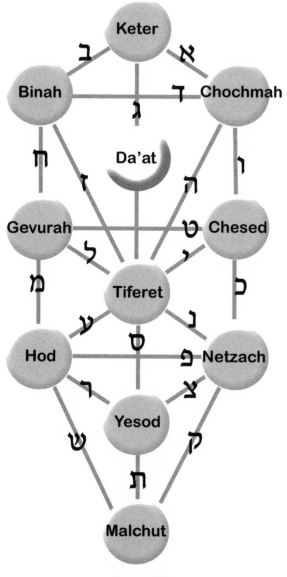

Figure 15.2

follow. If you are not *Haredi*, chances are your connection to Kabbalah is much fainter. Aspects of it remain in the liturgy of all branches of Judaism, but the study and practice of Kabbalah is more or less gone. Most that want to study true Kabbalah, which we define as an integral part of Judaism, are asked to master the Torah and the Talmud first. Once they have grasped both, then and only then are they ready to study Kabbalah. This is because without having a vast knowledge base of Judaism, Kabbalah by itself is like trying to grow a branch without the tree.

Even so, Kabbalah is a Jewish practice. As you've seen, it is a two-thousand-year-old extension of our belief system that attempts to answer questions the Torah seemingly doesn't (except in code). It's an integral part of our history and liturgy. It was created by Jews, nurtured and protected by Jews, passed from generation to generation of Jews, and ultimately is studied and practiced by Jews.

KABBALAH IS *NOT* JUDAISM

Even with this brief explanation of Kabbalah, it's clear that you must be Jewish to truly understand and internalize its teachings and practice. Without understanding the roots that sustain the tree, which in turn creates the branch, you really can't get the essence of the branch. Similarly, you can't be a surgeon without knowing how the body works. Those that try invariably end up with lots of malpractice suits.

So when big names tout their following of Kabbalah, but they have not converted to Judaism, are they Jewish? We say they aren't. *You* are going through Jewish conversion. You are working with an ordained rabbi, proceeding through a structured program designed to teach you from the ground up about what it means to be a Jew. You are learning Hebrew, practicing prayers, studying Torah, and integrating Judaism into your being. When you go through your conversion ritual, you will swear off any other religion. You will be a Jew and *only* a Jew.

"Pop" Kabbalah does have a basis in true Kabbalah, but it is more of a philosophy than anything else. It's not a religion. According to those who lead the pop Kabbalah movement, one can be Buddhist, Christian, Muslim, Jewish, or even agnostic and still follow Kabbalah. They are essentially adopting useful beliefs and practices from Kabbalah and discarding what doesn't work for them. While this might be catchy for someone interested in "spirituality" but bored with organized religion, it veers drastically away from any practice that we call real Judaism.

Now some would say that this is exactly how multiple branches of Judaism were created. Movements saw a need to modernize, so they left some criteria out to suit their needs. But there's a significant difference here. Perhaps Jennifer's experience will help you see it.

TRYING POP KABBALAH

Years before converting, when my husband and I practiced zero-tolerance religion (I mean we decorated a tree and hung lights, but it was out of habit rather than any religious significance), I became interested in Kabbalah. It was the hip thing in Hollywood, and I thought it might be a religious practice Adam and I could share. We had just moved to Southern California, and as luck would have it, the Kabbalah Center gained our email address and quickly offered us a complimentary book and tape. But there's more.

This was not like going to a church or synagogue. It was more like buying from Amazon.com. Once we received our items, we started getting catalogs, offers, and ultimately a call from Yakov, our "teacher." He had a heavy accent and a pushy approach. And since he was a Kabbalah "teacher," he must be a rabbi, right? Wrong. His job was to "assist" us in development of our Kabbalah knowledge. But first, we needed to purchase the twenty-two-volume set of the *Zohar* for a truly ungodly amount. Strike 1.

Now even though Adam could read Aramaic—the letters are the same as in Hebrew—the *Zohar* they offered us had no translation. Adam could pronounce the words but didn't know the meaning, and I couldn't pronounce or understand the words. In essence, we would be lost in translation after emptying a huge chunk of our bank account for a text that neither of us could read. The answer from the teacher was simple. "You don't need to study it. All you have to do is *look* at the pages. The power is in the letters themselves." Strike 2.

Next we asked about more advanced courses than the ones we had purchased. We learned about all sorts of ways to become closer to God, improve our luck, become better people, and so forth. Some required us to purchase and wear red strings from Rachel's tomb until they fell off to keep away the evil eye. All cost oodles of money. Now we all know that your synagogue needs money to operate, but it does not charge you every time you walk into a service. Strike 3.

"Pop" Kabbalah is a business, plain and simple. It's an entity designed to help people feel better about themselves using Jewish mysticism as its offering. But it's definitely *not* Judaism. It's not even a religion. It's simply a leaf that has fallen from the branch.

So is Madonna Jewish? Who knows? Perhaps she has worked with a rabbi and undergone a conversion process much like the one you are going through now. Perhaps she has been to the *mikvah* and immersed herself while saying the appropriate prayers. Perhaps she has even sworn off all other religions. But we doubt it. Just going by the often-reported Hebrew name Esther and using Hebrew letters and *tefillin* in her videos doesn't make her Jewish. Maybe more interesting, multifaceted, and much more marketable (and unforgettable), but certainly not Jewish. And if she hasn't converted, then she is simply a nonpracticing Catholic following a feel-good philosophy based on two-thousand-year-old Jewish mysticism.

IS KABBALAH FOR YOU?

Deciding to study Kabbalah is a quest that only you can decide. It's one that requires loads of commitment and discipline, and frankly, years of study, if you're interested in studying the real Kabbalah and not pop Kabbalah. But we can help. If you are thinking about pop Kabbalah, then you can probably guess our perspective. There's no difference between wearing a red string, blue string, or bleu cheese on your wrist except that the latter keeps people, not the evil eye, away. On the other hand, building a strong foundation in Judaism is the only way to enter the world of Kabbalah. Otherwise, you're paying for a feel-good snake oil that bears no resemblance to the true Kabbalah.

And when we say "world," it truly is a world unto itself. The practice remains shrouded in mystery, waiting to have the next generation of expert Kabbalists demystify its code. Prepare to dedicate years of study to embrace it and even more to understand it. Scholars in Judaism study for decades before they truly grasp the meanings of Kabbalah. If Kabbalah interests you, we strongly encourage you to seek out reputable Jewish Kabbalah groups with whom you can study, question, and learn.

CHAI NOTES

- What is most important in Judaism is life in the here and now, not what happens after we die.
- If Judaism is a tree, Kabbalah is a branch.
- Moses de Leon "discovered" a copy of the *Zohar* in a cave in Israel.
- According to Kabbalists, the soul has three primary components: *nefesh*, *ruach*, and *neshamah*.
- Kabbalists discuss five layers of God's emanation, using an image much like an archery target.

- There are ten *Sefirot*. Kabbalah considers *Da'at* and *Keter* as two aspects of the same thing.
- Kabbalists believe that doing *mitzvot* combines the male and female attributes of God and brings harmony to the world.
- Pop Kabbalah is designed to help people feel better about themselves using Jewish mysticism as its offering.
- Scholars in Judaism study for decades before they truly grasp the meanings of Kabbalah.
- Find reputable Jewish Kabbalah groups to study with if Kabbalah interests you.

16

Do They Hate You Too?

שׂנא

It's a sad fact. Some people hate Jews. We don't have to dig to find violent or hateful examples. Few can forget the eighty-eight-year-old antisemite who fatally shot a security guard inside the Holocaust Museum on June 11, 2009. Others cringe at the jaw-dropping comments from eighty-nine-year-old former White House correspondent Helen Thomas, who told a reporter in June 2010 that Jews should "Get the hell out of Palestine," and that they should return to Germany, Poland, America, "or wherever they came from."

Gee, come to think of it, Jennifer's paternal grandfather came from Minturno, Italy, and her paternal grandmother came from Sicily. In fact, her husband's paternal grandfather came from Lithuania, and his paternal grandmother came from China. Would that mean that one quarter of Jennifer needs to go to Minturno and one quarter to Sicily, while one quarter of Adam needs to return to China and one quarter to Lithuania? Hmm. Helen Thomas is Lebanese. Does that mean that she needs a one-way ticket to Beirut? Seriously, no Americans would remain stateside if we followed Thomas's logic. No wonder she announced her "retirement" soon after her career-ending comments.

Still others are dumbfounded over the campaign that Minister Louis Farrakhan launched in July 2010 to vilify Jews everywhere. But could that blind hatred find itself fixed on you? Chances are unlikely, but let's examine what we know.

CENTURIES OF JEW HATING

Antisemitism has deep roots that date back millennia. In modern times, antisemitism raised its ugly head in the 1920s, decades before the Holocaust. Once the Holocaust ended in 1945, many European countries made concerted efforts to curtail antisemitism. As a result, there are more than sixty Holocaust museums worldwide to educate generations on the monumental tragedy that affected six million Jews and five million non-Jews alongside them.

Visit any of these and you'll be amazed at the number of countries that have tried to eradicate Jews. It's an eye-opener and an education that all people need to experience—one that can make even the most cynical rethink their position. Take Quanell X, for example. He's the leader of the New Black Panther Party in Houston, Texas. After touring the Houston Holocaust Museum, Quanell X became enlightened and apologized for his past statements on Jews. Those who can stomach a tour and exit without a heavy heart indeed need theirs checked. It's a tear-jerking exercise to learn that any group has had to endure millennia of hatred and near extinction from so many civilizations.

EYES WIDE OPEN

This doesn't mean that you'll personally experience Jew hatred. Nor does it mean everything will be blue and white. Typically, you have to be in the wrong place at the wrong time. Even so, the chances of experiencing antisemitism are small. But you should prepare yourself in case you run across it—or it finds you. Many times, it will be subtle but hair-raising. For example, in July 2010, Jennifer was in Santa Monica with her family, an Israeli friend, and his daughter. A shirtless man a few feet ahead of them sported a large swastika tattooed on his back. Very different from the numbered tattoos that Nazis forcibly branded on Jews' arms. It's gut-wrenching to see a person consciously wearing a symbol that represents the genocide of your ancestors. But it's still happening.

Was it out of ignorance, a lame attempt to be cool, or something sacred to this person's belief structure? Or was he just an idiot? It's hard to know. But we can tell you that along with conversion comes a set of Jewish eyes that allows you to see the world from a whole new vantage point. This is where getting informed is important, but you can easily see why ignorance is bliss. Jennifer's not sure how she would have reacted to the swastika tattoo pre-Jewish, but she's sure it wouldn't have felt as if she were suffocating despite the sea breeze.

There were other occasions where Jennifer unknowingly opened herself up to Helen Thomas–types that advocate our demise. One incident occurred at work, while the others were on Twitter. The work incident was by far the most alarming because it involved a colleague whom Jennifer considered a "work friend." As she says:

> At the time, I was a writer at a Fortune 500 company, and I had invited some colleagues to my vow renewal. My husband and I planned it two years after I converted and exactly twenty-four hours after my adult *bat mitzvah*. We were so excited about finally exchanging vows at a synagogue that we had such great memories at along with rabbis, friends, and family we loved. Our wedding was only weeks away.
>
> I was in the hallway when this particular colleague approached me to chat about a project we were working on. As we were about to go our separate ways, he looked into my eyes and said, "You know, I like to control the information just like Hitler did."
>
> My pulse dropped, and instantly I knew what Jews entering the gas chamber felt. In a word: violated. My colleague raped me with his words. I was a contractor at the time and relayed the incident to my in-house manager, who later hired me but laughed off the incident. I was shocked, as it clearly violated the company's HR policy, but at the same time I was thankful that I got a closer look at my colleague's character and at the formation of my Jewish identity. I knew at that moment that I was a Jew first and a professional second. No intimidation tactics at work or elsewhere would ever change that.

SHOULD YOU BE CONCERNED?

There is an undeniable upswing in antisemitism in the United States and around the globe. Vocal antisemites like Farrakhan, political commentator Pat Buchanan, Venezuelan President Hugo Chavez, Iranian President Mahmoud Ahmadinejad, those involved in the Free Gaza Movement, and many member countries of the United Nations continue their anti-Jew and anti-Israel rhetoric.

> Before becoming a Jew, I never noticed the Israeli Consulate even though I drove past it daily going to and from work. It was only at that time that my world opened up. I noticed the Palestinian protestors that were dogging Israel on the bridge. I interacted with my community differently and developed a greater awareness of global topics concerning Jews, like the territorial dispute between

Israel and Palestinian Arabs and the move for a Palestinian state. I even realized what it was like to be a minority, as our son is one of only two Jews in his elementary school. And I was more in tune to word choices. I couldn't help but notice when a friend casually used the phrase "Jewing a person down" when purchasing a car. As he was talking, I casually pulled out my Star of David and let it hang down on my chest while I watched his face freeze. I don't believe he meant any harm, but it was my way of offering a subtle lesson in religious tolerance. (Chris, thirty-five, IT director)

The number of antisemitic events around the world more than doubled from 2008 to 2009, according to a Tel Aviv University study. The report, released in April 2010 by the university's Stephen Roth Institute for the Study of Contemporary Antisemitism and Racism, showed there were 1,129 recorded incidents in 2009 versus 559 in 2008. The Anti-Defamation League website shows that antisemitism is pervasive in all corners of the world.

Even in July 2010, the Arab world was publishing deeply offensive and hateful caricatures of Israelis and Jews in their criticism of Israel in the Gaza flotilla aftermath. Two months prior, Polish police detained five fans of Resovia Rzeszow, a Polish soccer team whose fans displayed a large banner showing a caricatured hook-nosed Jew wearing a blue and white (colors of the opposing team, not to mention the Israeli flag) yarmulke with the phrase, "Death to the Crooked Noses." These are only a sampling of what is occurring worldwide, as there are far too many incidents on a global scale to cover here.

IS THERE A BULL'S-EYE ON YOUR BACK?

Do these hateful incidents mean Jews need to hide their faith? Absolutely not. Most of what we're seeing is situational hatred fueled by ignorance or planned campaigns to gain public appeal. For instance, in a survey taken in December 2008–January 2009 in seven European countries—Austria, France, Hungary, Poland, Germany, Spain, and the United Kingdom—31 percent of the respondents blamed Jews in the financial industry for the current global economic crisis. Another incident along the same lines involved a YouTube video from September 2008 titled *The Court Jewsters* that blamed current Federal Reserve chairman Ben Bernanke and former chairman Alan Greenspan, as well as other Jews, for the widespread failing of US financial institutions. Is this Jew hatred new? Hardly. Hatred like this is about as old as the religion itself.

The only negative experience that I've had after becoming Jewish occurred after my mother's wedding in Pasadena, Texas. Her fiancé's mother was Catholic and his father was Jewish, so they had this half-way, not-quite-Christian, not-quite-Jewish ceremony. So my brother and I wore our *kippot* and everything. And when we were packing up to leave, a young guy with a girl on his arm approached and said some disparaging comments as he walked by. I'm not surprised considering the location, but I guess I'm the aberration, because I grew up in Pasadena and I don't hate anybody. (Chris, thirty-five, IT director)

FERTILE GROUND FOR ANTISEMITES

Facebook and Twitter are great online platforms to keep current with global friends, colleagues, and breaking issues. But both are also favorite camping grounds for antisemites and the like. Jennifer learned this once she started tweeting and blogging about Israel. Many antisemites challenged her aggressively and hurled unkind names her way. They didn't like the fact that she was writing about Iran's terror proxies, Hezbollah and Hamas. They also didn't like that she called out many Palestinian-led groups that had banded together to delegitimize Israel by undermining its financial and economic stability through a campaign to boycott, divest, and sanction the Jewish state. Luckily, she got a taste of what Israelis and Jews have always faced, and while it was painful, she also saw the other side: a global outpouring from people that support Jews and Israelis.

By establishing herself as a Jewish blogger, Jennifer opened herself up to people that blindly hate us because we're Jews. At the time, she didn't know she was putting herself into a forum where some people hate others just because of the race, religion, politics, or membership to a particular group. As Jennifer says,

I had no experience with this kind of bigotry because I didn't even realize that so many people hate Catholics until I became a Jew. Now I know. It's mind-boggling, but it hasn't deterred me. Instead, I am more adamant than ever to fix what's broken. While I won't change hearts that are already hardened, I hope to make a dent in those on the fence or interested in learning what Jews are all about.

HOW TO AVOID HATERS

Those who perpetrate hate crimes based on religious affiliation strike either persons or their property. Places that are high on the list for religious-motivated hate crimes are places of worship, religious schools, community centers, vehicles, or family homes. Some precautions you can take that apply to everyone include the following:

- *Know your surroundings*—It's wise to research crime statistics for the synagogue you're attending. Chances are good that you can expect future incidents if the area has had previous attacks.
- *Safety in numbers*—Avoid going to synagogue alone whenever you can. Park in visible, well-lit areas, and travel in daylight when possible. Always ask for an official escort upon leaving after dusk or anytime your car is not in plain sight.
- *Be prepared*—Look closely at your surroundings when approaching your vehicle, and always have your keys handy. Those committing crimes are looking for opportunities to strike when people are most vulnerable. Digging for your keys in a pocket or purse or chatting on your phone aimlessly just might give a perpetrator the opportunity. Take charge of your personal security, and don't let anyone have the upper hand.
- *Avoid strangers*—Most of us don't see any reason to avoid people who at first glance seem kind. But consider the fact that those who perpetrate hate crimes may appear nice in order to gain access to you or your property. A good rule of thumb is to avoid strangers that approach you at religious-affiliated functions or buildings or at your home. While it sounds extreme, it will keep you safe. A kindhearted neighbor will leave a note or call if it's important, while a salesperson will leave literature. Someone out to harm you won't do either. Answer your door only to those you've invited or trust.

WHAT CAN YOU DO ABOUT IT?

It's true that the best defense is a good offense. Make it a habit to report antisemitism when you see it, whether it's at work, in a public place, or online. The more people who report it, the greater likelihood the behavior will cease. People are less likely to harass if someone is investigating their actions, and most social media platforms will deny service or deauthorize the user's account. Either way, it's best to make it public.

The Anti-Defamation League has a form on their website that allows you to report verbal or physical incidents or even vandalism. Currently, forty-five states and the District of Columbia have enacted hate-crime laws similar to

ADL's model, and in 1993, the Supreme Court unanimously upheld such laws, ruling that they did not violate First Amendment rights.

While there are risks in becoming Jewish, the same holds true for getting married, vacationing, or myriad other activities. Whether driving a car or commuting via subway or plane, we take risks every day. White supremacists, neo-Nazis, anti-Zionists, and even terrorists (domestic and foreign) will always find a way to exercise their hatred and antisemitic rhetoric. But this doesn't mean you need to hide, adopt a random religion, or become agnostic for fear of practicing what you believe. Local and federal authorities are more than willing to investigate when presented with cases of antisemitism.

REPORTING HATE CRIMES AND BEYOND

Call local law enforcement and visit the Anti-Defamation League's website to research your state's hate-crime statutory provisions. Reporting hate crimes is the first step in fighting back and making sure perpetrators refrain from targeting the places you frequent. Hate crimes instill fear and can have both an economic and psychological affect on establishments, the community, and surrounding neighborhoods. Be vocal about it, and encourage other members and the local community to be vigilant about safety. Hold a meeting or forum where leaders from the organization discuss the incident and invite local law enforcement to reassure those affected.

Children and the elderly also need special consideration when hate crimes occur. Consider the aftermath of emotions after a local news station reports an antisemitic incident at your synagogue. The elderly and youths alike might stay home out of fear. This is a good time to offer them a forum to discuss how they feel and share the facts of the incident and what local law enforcement, the FBI, and organizations like the ADL and the community are doing to counter bias, prejudice, stereotyping, and violence. Putting situations into perspective is a great way to get back on track. We all know that while tragedies occur, these are typically infrequent, isolated cases and not the norm.

YOU'RE NOT ALONE

You've probably heard about the top-notch security at Israel's El Al airline. Well, many American synagogues have taken note too. Some have put up twelve-foot walls around their perimeters and distributed car stickers and ID badges that an off-duty police officer has to verify to allow you access to the property. Many synagogue schools have locks on the door where you announce yourself and get "buzzed in" from an external intercom after identifying you have permission to be there. Anyone picking up a child at a synagogue school not only has to be on a specified pick-up list but may also have to wear a badge, carry a pass card, or have a password handy to gain access to their child. Fingerprint or cornea recognition? Honestly, it might not be that far away. This isn't to make you feel like Evelyn Salt or Jason Bourne, but it shows just how serious the Jewish community takes security threats. We simply don't tolerate them.

A WAVE OF HOLOCAUST DENIAL

Modern times have brought us people that wish to erase the memory of the Holocaust and its eleven million victims by denying it ever happened. Some individuals denying this genocide include Noam Chomsky, David Irving, Norman Finkelstein, and Robert Faurisson. As a result, many countries have made it illegal to deny or modify the Holocaust or have adopted similar statutes that cover it in indirect language (see figure 16.1).

FINDING THE JEWISH ACTIVIST IN YOU

There's a chance you might not be content with the status quo once you're Jewish. After all, Jennifer wasn't. Once she started looking into the issues surrounding Israel and Jews worldwide, she saw so much that needed to change. But there's good news in all this. You don't have to be a superhero or celebrity to become an activist. You simply need to muster enough passion to will a change. Plenty of people do. When in doubt, think of Margaret Mead's quote: "Never doubt that a small group of thoughtful, committed people can change the world. Indeed, it is the only thing that ever has."

Whether you're supporting Israel's right to defend itself, challenging groups that try to delegitimize Israel, calling out the Holocaust deniers, or helping Jewish organizations free Gaza from Hamas or address the Iranian nuke threat, all are important on a global scale.

Here are ten steps that you'll want to take if you're compelled to get involved:

- *Identify your passion*—It's not enough to choose a random cause. It needs to be the one thing that keeps you awake at night. That's the one you need to focus your energy toward.

Figure 16.1

Countries	Illegal Offense	Year Enacted
Austria	Nazism/ Holocaust Denial	1945/ 1992
Belgium	Holocaust Denial	1995
Bosnia and Herzegovina	Holocaust Denial	2007
Czech Republic	Holocaust Denial, Suppressing Human Rights	2001
France	Crimes Against Humanity	1990
Germany	Public Incitement/ Hatred/ Genocide Denial	1985, 1992, 2002, 2005
Hungary	Minimization/ Denial of the Holocaust	2010
Israel	Holocaust Denial	1986
Liechtenstein	Genocide Denial/ Race Discrimination	
Luxembourg	Holocaust Denial	1997
The Netherlands	Hate Crimes	1971
Poland	Holocaust Denial/ Denial of Communist Crimes	1998
Portugal	Genocide Denial	1998
Romania	Holocaust Denial/ Denial of Racist, Fascist Organizations	2002/ 2006
Switzerland	Genocide Denial	1995

- *Channel your passion*—Figure out what you do best and apply it to the issue. For example, if you write, try blogging. If you're a PR guru, use your media savvy to gain coverage and land interviews. If you're a marketer, find ways to market your ideas to a broader audience. If you're a technology whiz, build a website. Whatever your talents are, use them in a way that helps your cause.
- *Research the issues*—Find out where the impasses are and how you can effect change. Learn about existing organizations and how you can help. If your idea is different than the mix, start your own organization or partner with existing groups.
- *Gain real-world experience*—Talk to other activists, experts, and those that have personal experience with the issues and see it from their eyes too.
- *Recruit others*—Talk to your friends, family, synagogue, neighbors, organizations, and community about getting involved in your effort.
- *Act*—Make plans on how your expertise can serve the cause best.

- *Organize events*—Contact community leaders and elected officials that care about the issue you're working on and organize an event where they can speak about it. This is simpler than you think. Most are willing to do it, provided it's a cause they support and you've supplied ample notice. Tip: An impending election helps.
- *Inform the media*—Send a press release to the media describing your event and why it's important and request coverage.
- *Voice your victories*—Take time to note your wins. If you don't, who will?
- *Live what you preach*—It's important to live by example. For instance, if you're an activist for being kosher but you're always eating cheeseburgers, then your credibility is likely in the toilet.

SHOW YOUR *CHUTZPAH*

Hating has never been in vogue, and with any luck, it never will. But you don't have to take it, and you certainly don't have to hide the fact that you're a new Jew. While the world is pockmarked with its share of anti-semites, there are millions who open their arms to Jews. Jennifer recently heard a Christian minister say to a crowd of thousands that Israel might think of itself as a small country of only seven million, but in reality, it can easily add five hundred million Christians to that family. So when you hear stories of Europeans defacing menorahs or Arabs publishing de-meaning cartoons of Jews, or even sporadic acts of violence toward Jews, know that this does not represent the entire world. Hate is wrong no matter where it is, and it's up to those with *chutzpah* to report it, defy it, stay vigilant, and say, "Never again."

CHAI NOTES

- Many people unfortunately hate Jews, but it's unlikely that this blind hatred will find itself focused on you.
- Facebook and Twitter are great online platforms, but both are also favorite camping grounds for antisemites and the like.
- Take precautions when strangers approach you at synagogues, religious schools, community centers, or even your home.
- Make it a habit to report antisemitism when you see it regardless of where it occurs.

- Call local law enforcement and visit the Anti-Defamation League's website to research your state's hate-crime statutory provisions if you're on the receiving end of a hate crime.
- Think El Al. Most synagogues or their affiliated schools don't tolerate hate crimes, so they take extra precautions to keep you safe.
- There are over sixty Holocaust museums worldwide and fifteen countries where Holocaust denial is illegal, yet we have to contend with a modern concern: Holocaust deniers.
- Remember Margaret Mead. All it takes is a few passionate people to change the world.

17

Everyone Matters

יד

"Everyone matters" means different things to different people. To some, it means everybody except those they can't stand. To others, it means everyone except those they can't stand, along with criminals, undocumented workers, and those on government assistance. Yet a fundamental belief in Judaism is that, as Jews, we are responsible for taking care of our world and everyone in it. So does everyone really matter? Absolutely.

This belief is rooted in an idea we covered earlier that God created man and woman in his image. This means everybody. We are *all* a mirror of God. So the next time you get upset at the jerk in the Mercedes who just cut you off on the highway, remember that, like you, he shares the spark of God. Maybe that will help you feel a little better. OK, maybe not. But it should, and after reading this chapter, we hope you'll feel a bit more love toward that guy.

THE GLOVED ONE

The most iconic song of the 1980s is arguably "We Are the World." The song put everything on the table a pop song should. There was a clandestine recording session, egos flying and artists walking out, last-minute edits, and, of course, a catchy tune. It brought star power, too. More than forty of the most recognizable singers in pop music gave their voices to make the song work. In the end, it became the highest-selling single of all time.

You see, this was more than a song. It was part of a fundraiser to feed millions of children starving due to drought and war in Africa. We saw images of them, gaunt and helpless, and *knew* we had to do something. So did Michael Jackson, Lionel Richie, and Quincy Jones. And do something they did. Michael Jackson's lyrics practically pulled money from the wallets of everyone who heard the song. There were people dying and the world had to pull together because we're God's family. Michael could see this, but so many others still can't or won't.

Why did it impact us all so much? Because these children were suffering and we actually *could* help them. The solution was clear. And easy. And the right thing to do. It was a straightforward way for everyone to perform *tikkun olam*—making the world a better place.

For Jews, *tikkun olam* is an ingrained value. As with *tzedakah*, we do it not because we have to, but because we know it's needed. Michael's lyrics went right to the heart of *tikkun olam*. We know it must be done. We have to work together. We can't wait for someone else to do it. We are all a reflection of God, and bringing our love—our actions—will make a difference.

Tikkun olam is mentioned in the Talmud, but not in terms of acts people perform. Instead, it's used to describe ways God brings harmony and stability to the world. Our role in *tikkun olam* comes from Kabbalah; we are expected to fix chaos and disruption in the world. This in turn will improve harmony among nations and with nature, and will ultimately clear the way for the Messiah to arrive.

God made the world, and over time humans have messed it up. We've done it through smoke-belching factories and cars. We've done it through greed and jealousy. We've done it through manifesting hate for others. But God made the world for *us*. So it's clearly up to us to make it all right again. Besides, God's days of major miracles seem to have ended thousands of years ago. While it would be wonderful, we doubt God's going to fix things this time.

WHY SO MANY LAWYERS?

There's an old joke about two Jewish grandmothers meeting on the street. After exchanging pleasantries, one asks the other how her newborn grandkids are doing. The second replies, "The doctor is doing well, but you should see the lawyer!"

Obviously, parents and grandparents want the best for their progeny. But it does seem there's a disproportionate number of doctors and lawyers who are Jewish. There are lots of potential reasons for this, but we like to think that at least the lawyer aspect has to do with the Jewish focus on social justice.

Tzelem Elohim

While other ancient cultures saw people as servants or playthings for "the gods," early Jews saw individuals as the crown of creation. What is so powerful about this value is that when it says we were created in the image of God, there is no "but" or "except" included in the Torah. It doesn't say, "Human beings are created in the image of God, except women," or "except gays and lesbians," or "except people who speak Spanish (or Arabic)," much less "except those who don't like me or think differently than me." In other words, the Torah and Jewish tradition introduced the real power of *tzelem elohim* over three thousand years ago, and there are *no exceptions whatsoever*. Judaism teaches that *every* person is created in God's image, period.

To understand why this is one of the most important values in the entire Torah, all you have to do is imagine what the world would be like if everyone simply believed and acted upon this one idea alone and treated every other person as sacred and important. What a different world it would be. In fact, it would be enough to transform the world if each one of us understood the inherent value and spiritual self-worth that every person holds. How could we hurt each other if we recognized the image of God looking back at us through the eyes of another? Terrorism, wars, genocide would cease to exist. Imagine.

Kol Yisrael Aravim ze Bazeh

This phrase holds important meaning for Jews. It means, "All the Jewish people are responsible for one another" (Talmud, Shavuot 39a). It teaches that all Jews feel a sense of personal responsibility for the welfare of other Jews and traditionally see each other as part of the same family. It's a rabbinic expression that embodies the idea that we described in chapter 2—that what gives Jews our identity is not primarily belief but rather belonging.

It's the deeply felt idea that Jews throughout the world are part of the same spiritual family that traces its origins back to the original biblical family of Abraham and Sarah and every Jew in between. This commitment to each other's welfare, the certainty that we can count on one another no matter how much of the world abhors us, has kept Judaism and the Jewish People alive for millennia.

Mitzvah Goreret Mitzvah

Another important value that the Talmudic rabbis taught is that what we do matters and has an effect on the future, whether for good or for evil. *Mitzvah goreret mitzvah* means "one *mitzvah* brings another *mitzvah* in its wake." It's based on the notion that every time we bring more holiness into the world, that action in turn inspires others to act in kind. It's a kind of Jewish *Pay It Forward* or *Butterfly Effect*. We are taught that every *mitzvah* we perform acts like pebbles in a pond and sends ripples of *mitzvot* into the world.

Knowing this, we automatically choose positive actions so those that are magnified by our *mitzvot* do the same. In Jewish tradition, not only do people matter, but what they say also matters, and what they do matters profoundly.

Love Your Neighbor (or At Least Try)

A rabbi we know in Los Angeles drives around with personalized plates that read, "LEV 19:18." It's her way of announcing to the world what she considers to be the most important teaching of the Torah—namely, the lesson that is taught in Leviticus 19:18: "You shall love your neighbor as yourself."

This idea is much more than simply an encouragement to look kindly upon your neighbor. On a more fundamental and deeper level, it teaches a powerful lesson about how we are to see *ourselves* just as much as how we are to see others. What rabbinic commentators have long taught is that this phrase is really a commandment to love ourselves. After all, if you hate yourself, then we certainly don't want to be your neighbor and have you "love" us the way you "love yourself."

Don't Stand Idly By

Two verses away from the powerful verse we just covered is yet another that many think is one of the most important *mitzvot* in the Torah. Both of these ideas are part of what Jewish tradition has called "The Holiness Code," because they are found in chapter 19 of the book of Leviticus, which begins, "You shall be holy because I your God am holy." This phrase—*Kedoshim te-hiyu ki kadosh ani*—reminds us one of our key challenges in life is to imitate God's holiness in what we say, what we do, and how we act.

After challenging us to "be holy" at the beginning of this chapter, God then goes on to explain what "being holy" might look like in our everyday lives. "Holiness" in the Torah is not so much about prayer, fasting, or even the offerings and sacrifices that seem to be such a prominent part of ancient religious experiences. True holiness is found in all the many ways we interact with other members of our community and all living creatures.

For example, we are told that if we see a stray animal that belongs to an enemy, we must bring it back to its owner. We are commanded to return anything we might find that belongs to another, to pursue justice at all times, not to bear a grudge or seek vengeance, to pay our laborers promptly, and, perhaps most importantly, "not to stand idly by."

This means that in Jewish ethics there is no such thing as an "innocent bystander." You're not considered innocent if you're standing idly by another who is being hurt, exploited, or injured in some way. "Do not stand idly by" means that we have a responsibility to get involved, to stand up for others, to speak out when we see injustice or exploitation of any kind, whether it's life-threatening or not. This *mitzvah* is also one of the ways our biblical ancestors reinforced the importance of both personal and communal responsibility.

Pikuach Nefesh

Nonetheless, *pikuach nefesh* is so important that we are commanded to put aside any ritual rule or law (even relating to *Shabbat*) when in a position to save a life. When rabbinic authorities discussed whether donating organs was consistent with Jewish ethics and law, all but the *Haredi* Orthodox agreed that if donating an organ can save a life, then it's not only kosher but also a *commandment*. To this day, even operations on *Shabbat* are permissible.

A fascinating question related to *pikuach nefesh* is posed in the Talmud. If two people are stranded in the desert and there is only enough water for one, should one drink it and live, or should both share it equally, even if it means both die? Rabbis debated this ethical dilemma at length and ultimately came to the conclusion that it's better for one to live than both to die because the principle of *pikuach nefesh* takes precedence over all else.

It's this principle of *pikuach nefesh* that inspired the Talmudic teaching in the tractate Sanhedrin, "One who saves a single life is counted as if she has saved an entire world, and one who destroys a single life is counted as if she has destroyed an entire world." Every human life is precious, and every human life is a sacred gift from God. That's also why Jewish ethics abhors suicide, because we are taught that just as God gives life, it's God's to take back. So much for armed combat.

MAKING IT YOUR OWN

No matter what branch of Judaism you choose, you'll see that *tikkun olam* and social justice are centerpieces of the community. The key for you is to find the best ways for you to apply these important concepts to your own life. Determine what motivates you and what you do best, then find a way to put them together.

Your synagogue will likely be a source for many opportunities to practice *tikkun olam* or exercise social justice. Recently, while waiting for her twins to finish religious school, Jennifer watched students from a local high school working with synagogue volunteers to create Christmas packages for needy families. There were multiple layers of *tzedakah, tikkun olam,* and social justice in this seemingly simple activity.

Synagogue members were dropping off toys and food. This was a chance for them to participate in *tzedakah.* The synagogue volunteers were passing on their enthusiasm for helping others and their belief in the value of social justice to the high school students, and participating in *tikkun olam* in the process. And, of course, the simple act of giving to improve the condition of the less fortunate is an example of all three ideals.

Check with your synagogue or JCC to learn about activities to improve the community, aid others in need, or address issues of social justice. You'll find campaigns like "sponsor a family," outreach efforts, fundraising walks, Habitat for Humanity days, and more.

Now, are you still going to flip off the guy in the Mercedes?

CHAI NOTES

- *Tikkun olam* means "repairing the world" and is a fundamental belief of Judaism.
- We messed up the world, and we need to fix it.
- Social justice is also a significant tenet of Judaism.
- *Tzelem elohim* is the notion that we are *all* created in the image of God.
- *Mitzvah goreret mitzvah* means "one *mitzvah* will bring another *mitzvah* in its wake."

- *Kol Yisrael aravim ze bazeh* teaches that all Jews are responsible for one another.
- Wars, terrorism, and genocide would cease to exist if people practiced *tzelem elohim.*
- Loving your neighbor means recognizing the divine spark that you and others share with God.
- Not standing idly by means we have a communal responsibility to help anyone getting threatened, hurt, or exploited.
- *Pikuach nefesh* means saving a single life takes precedence over all else.

18

Children of Israel

חי

Israel.

The Promised Land.

The Land of Milk and Honey.

The Land of Israel, the State of Israel, *Eretz Yisrael*.

To Jews, the young country of Israel is the culmination of thousands of years of prayer and yearning. The entire Torah focuses on our efforts to reach this great land God promised our people. *Israel* is, quite literally, the last word of the Torah. In fact, the Torah makes no secret of Israel's significance to the Jewish People, as it mentions it by name over five hundred times. Yet for two thousand years, from 70 CE when the Romans destroyed the Temple in Jerusalem and conquered the last independent Jewish empire until 1948, Jews did not have a true Land of Israel to call our own.

As a new Jew, your new homeland is Israel, regardless of where you live. This incredible, tiny, beautiful, innovative, strong, miraculous, ancient, modern, and (unfortunately) controversial country belongs to every Jew in the world. It is our destiny and our gift. Yet there are many who would like nothing more than to wipe Israel off the map. In this chapter, we'll explain why and, even more importantly, why you should care.

IT JUST *FEELS* DIFFERENT

Ask most who have visited Israel and they'll tell you the same thing. They can't put their finger on it, but the country actually has a different "feel" than any other place they've been. It's not just the people or the architecture or the signs in Hebrew. It's not just the ocean or the Negev (desert) or the forests. It's not just the Arabs, Israelis, Christians, Druze, pilgrims, missionaries, soldiers, children, tourists, or natives. It's everything—and yet something more.

Israel is a true land of contrasts. *Haredi* Jews in long black coats and fur hats, and Israeli youth in bathing suits on the beach. Wrinkled Arab men smoking hookah pipes, and young Israeli Arab girls sporting the latest fashions. Street markets filled with every imaginable sight, sound, and smell, and vast sparkling supermarkets. Ancient ruins and modern skyscrapers. Desolate desert and snow-capped mountains. The country delivers the best of all worlds.

It's most definitely a land of history as well. Just in Jerusalem alone, the majesty and importance of Israel is clear. The Western Wall—all that remains of the Second Temple—emanates holiness. Its cracks contain tiny crumpled bits of paper on which visitors have written their prayers, because we believe this is as close to God as one can get on earth. The golden-topped Dome of the Rock sits above the Western Wall and surrounds a rock that Jews believe is where Abraham almost sacrificed Isaac and where the Ark of the Covenant was placed. It's also the same rock where Muslims believe the prophet Mohammed ascended to heaven on his horse. The Church of the Holy Sepulchre, which some Christians believe stands on the very site where Jesus was crucified, rises from the center of the old city, housing some of the most hallowed spots in Christianity and filled with incense and icons.

It's a land of beauty too. From Caribbean blue seas surrounding sunken Roman columns at Caesarea to sparkling coral reefs in Eilat. From the mountain fortress of Masada to the Dead Sea, the lowest point on earth. From modern cities like Haifa and Tel Aviv to the ancient walled city of Jerusalem. From snow skiing down Mt. Hermon to water-skiing on the Mediterranean. From the natural caves of Rosh Haniqra to the hand-hewn Hezekiah's Tunnel. From the barrenness of the Negev to the richness of Ein Gedi and the Carmel Forest.

But perhaps as a Jew the reason Israel feels different is a bit clearer. It's the one country in the world where you're not a minority. Where stores are open on Easter and closed on Yom Kippur. Where crying and kissing a giant stone block in a huge wall is not only *not* frowned on but nearly expected. Where four thousand years of history culminates with you. It's the Promised Land—the land Moses led us out of Egypt for. The land our ancestors built. And rebuilt. And rebuilt again. The land six million died for. It is—Israel.

BILL SAID IT BEST

In *Romeo and Juliet*, William Shakespeare wrote, "A rose by any other name would smell as sweet." This certainly applies to Israel, as it has had *many* names and loyalties during its raucous and tumultuous history. Canaan. The Kingdom of David. Israel. Samaria. Philistia. Palestine. Israel. Still, chances are you've heard that Israel is a country constantly at war, that if it only would stop occupying Palestinian land, peace would come to the Middle East. Time to set the record straight and put this unfair demonization to rest.

If it were as simple as an issue of "occupation" alone, peace would have arrived decades ago. The primary reason there continues to be war between Israel and the Palestinians is as straightforward as this—no Palestinian leader has ever been willing to publicly state that Israel has a right to exist as a Jewish country. Period. The minute Israel was first declared independent in May 1948 all surrounding Arab countries declared war on the Jewish state, declared their determination to "drive Jews into the sea," and with few exceptions have continued to wage that same war year after year ever since. Israel has been attacked and forced into war by Arab states in 1948, 1956, 1967, 1973, and continuously by terrorists from across all its borders from before 1948 until today.

The only reason Israel continues to "occupy" what is called the "West Bank" of the Jordan River is because it was forced into war in 1967, and after saving its life, it conquered that territory from Jordan. Even though it offered the land back in exchange for peace, the surrounding Arab nations gathered in Khartoum and infamously declared, "No recognition, no negotiations, and no peace with Israel." The Jewish state has repeatedly tried to make peace with the Palestinians, often with the help of the United States and our own presidents. To date, seven Israeli prime ministers have tried to make peace with the Palestinians to no avail. As proof that Israel is not the obstacle to peace, all you have to know is that the minute Egyptian President Anwar El Sadat declared his willingness to make peace with Israel in 1976, Israel went all out. Israeli Prime Minister Menachem Begin gave Egypt back the entire Sinai Peninsula (including its oil wells), dismantled Israeli communities, relocated thousands of Israeli citizens, and demanded nothing in return except peace with its neighbor.

Israel also made peace with the kingdom of Jordan and did so the minute the Jordanians were willing to put down their arms. The same would be true for the Palestinians if they were interested. Israel has offered to give 96 percent of the West Bank for their own state, has already given back the entire Gaza Strip (which terrorist organization Hamas immediately seized), and continues to hold out an olive branch of peace.

Israel has only asked its neighbors to recognize Israel's right to exist and cease attacking civilian men, women, and children with suicide bombings and other terrorist attacks. As many commentators have noted over the years, if the Palestinians and surrounding Arab nations were to put down their arms tomorrow, there would be peace between Israel and the Arabs, but if Israel were to put down its arms tomorrow, there would be no more Israel.

In spite of the constant struggle for survival in a hostile neighborhood, Israel has been one of the most productive countries on the planet. In fact, Israel is one of the smallest countries in the world yet has the most college graduates per capita. It has more companies on the NASDAQ than any country outside North America. Much of the technology that we use today we can thank Israelis for inventing. Those breakthroughs include cell phones, voice mail technology, instant messaging, firewall security software, and Intel wireless computer chips. Motorola has its largest research and development center in Israel, and Microsoft is there too. Anyone using Windows operating systems can high-five Microsoft-Israel for most of its development. The list goes on to include the technology for AOL Instant Messenger: ICQ. Put it this way, if you use a mobile phone, a PC, or instant messaging, you are using a technology originally developed in Israel. This is exactly how Israel earned the title "The Silicon Valley of the Middle East."

But that's not all. Israelis have made countless contributions to our society, including medical breakthroughs allowing surgeons to examine internal organs through miniature video camera capsules. Another Israeli-made device helps restore the use of paralyzed hands. This device electrically stimulates hand muscles, offering hope to millions of stroke sufferers and those with spinal-cord injuries. Young children with breathing problems can rest easier thanks to a new Israeli fuss-free device called the Child Hood. As recently as 2010, Israeli scientists developed a method that can eradicate HIV-infected cells without affecting healthy ones. Consider more facts that make Israel a beacon among nations:

- Israel has more engineers and scientists per capita than any other country.
- Israel produces more scientific papers per capita than any other nation.
- Israelis hold more patents per person than do citizens of any other nation.
- Israel has the world's second highest release of new books per citizen.
- More than 85 percent of solid waste in Israel is treated in an environmentally sound manner.
- Israel holds the largest concentration of high-tech industries in the world per capita.

PEACE OR PIPE DREAM?

On the other hand, history shows a bleak picture when you examine Palestinian actions. For one, their logo says everything you need to know. What peaceful people would sandwich Israel (or any other country for that matter) between two machine guns and place a grenade underneath? Sadly, this violent symbol continues to represent the Fatah party of Palestinian President Mahmoud Abbas.

History is not kind to those that marry themselves to terminal war. In fact, history shows that Palestinians repeatedly use stalling tactics, reject peace offers, and initiate acts of violence to have their demands met. Consider the Camp David Accords (1978–1979) where Sadat, Begin, and US President Jimmy Carter worked on two frameworks to achieve peace. Sadat and Begin even shared the 1978 Nobel Peace Prize. At this time, Begin made a number of far-reaching concessions to achieve peace. Yet the Palestinian response was anything but peaceful. The Palestinians launched a full-scale, preplanned wave of violence known as the Second Intifada. The result was tragic: Palestinians had the blood of 1,184 Israelis on their hands.

Unfortunately, Sadat didn't fare well either for his peacemaking efforts. The Muslim Brotherhood, a known terrorist organization, made sure of that, as authorities linked the group to Sadat's assassination.

Then we can look at the 1993 Oslo Accords that Israeli Prime Minister Yitzhak Rabin worked on with US President Bill Clinton and Palestinian Liberation Organization (PLO) President Yasser Arafat. The following year Rabin, Arafat, and Shimon Perez jointly won the 1994 Nobel Peace Prize. In-

stead of choosing peace, Arafat chose terrorism and instigated a wave of suicide terror attacks in Israeli cities. Arafat was not exactly the peace partner the
White House or Israel had anticipated. Apparently, he wasn't that concerned
about raising a Palestinian state either, as the media widely reported that he
stole billions in aid that his "people" never saw.

Next, Israeli Prime Minister Ariel Sharon disengaged Israeli forces from the
Gaza Strip and northern Samaria in August 2005 in an effort to fast-track
peace. The response from the Palestinians became more volatile. Palestinians
fired more rockets at Israel while Iranian-backed Hamas seized control of
Gaza. The violence had reached a new level. More than ten thousand rockets
and mortar shells hailed on southern Israeli cities.

In 2008, Israeli Prime Minister Ehud Olmert made a generous peace offering to the Palestinians. The Palestinians turned it down and instead continued
ratcheting up violence and their boycott, divest, and sanction (BDS) campaign
while flat out refusing to accept Israel as a Jewish state.

Even today, not much has changed between Israel and the Palestinians.
Since 2010, terrorist factions in Gaza have fired hundreds of Grad missiles,
Qassam rockets, and mortar shells at Israeli cities. Israel, on the other hand,
continues to reach for peace with an outstretched arm. When Israeli Prime
Minister Benjamin Netanyahu asked the Palestinians to acknowledge that Israel is a Jewish state, Abbas replied, "Israel can call itself whatever it wants,"
then walked away from talks. This great divide boils down to Palestinians being unable to change from a mindset of violence and victimization to one of
recognition and peace. Palestinians, like other Arab neighbors, have never
accepted Israel as a Jewish state, and they continue the cycle of hate by refusing to acknowledge Israel on their maps and teaching their children to hate
Israel and Jews through textbooks, TV, and mosques.

At this rate, Palestinians can't achieve peace if they continue to backslide
into violence and intolerance. If the Palestinian Authority can't even enforce
law in both Gaza and the West Bank without Iranian-backed terror proxies
like Hamas seizing control, it's unrealistic to bet on *real* peace occurring between Israel and the Palestinians any time soon. Unfortunately, the United
Nations and neighboring Arab countries are much to blame for inciting hatred of Israel and Jews in the first place. Abbas spent the first few months of
2011 bypassing direct talks with Israel only to seek unilateral declaration via
the United Nations, which will review the request to automatically usher Pal-

estine into statehood in September 2011. By April 27, 2011, the Palestinian Authority (Fatah) announced they ended a four-year rift with Hamas, and made a pact in Cairo to form a national unity government. Making the pact in Cairo is important because the Egyptian government recognized the formerly banned Muslim Brotherhood, which has deep ties to Hamas. Many cite the reconciliation between Fatah and Hamas as tangible proof that the Arab Spring (uprisings across the Arab world) impacted the Palestinians. Subsequently, Hamas declared it does not recognize Israel nor will it negotiate with Israel. Again, Israel is left in a no-win position: it is being tasked to recognize an entity with a terrorist component that doesn't recognize Israel (even though Israel is a UN member state). Until religious tolerance is widespread, a peaceful, progressive Palestine in the near term appears to nothing more than a pipe dream.

ACT FOR ISRAEL

Jennifer must love Israel. She spends her days advocating for the Jewish state that she has never even stepped foot in. Her love for Israel blossomed as a blogger but grew rapidly when she came keyboard to keyboard with tens of thousands of anti-Zionists spreading their messages of hate and delegitimization to Twitter, Facebook, blogs, YouTube, and more. Most spout Hamas, Hezbollah, and Iranian propaganda, and their efforts are polarizing the media and the world against Israel. She began blogging about Israel and world politics in an effort to turn the tide in Israel's favor. Jennifer's experience details her commitment to Israel:

> It really doesn't matter that I'm a Diaspora Jew, as Israel is on my mind 24/7. I think of her when I wake and digest the news that spites her. I think of her during the day when I challenge her enemies and advocate for her rights online. I think about her when I blog about her efforts toward real peace while her enemies turn public opinion against her. I think of her every time BDS propagandists call for universities, corporations, and organizations to ban products like hummus but fail to portray Israel as a "pariah" state. I think of her each time a world leader steps up to blame her for "crimes" she didn't commit while ignoring neighbors that engage in genocide, human rights abuses, and acts of war like it was child's play. I think of her whenever I Facebook my Israeli relatives and wish the world was on their side. I think of her whenever her enemies delegitimize her and downplay her amazing contributions to the world. I think of her

when I clasp my *chai* necklace and kiss it in her honor. I think of her whenever I smell challah baking or eat falafel, latkes, *hamantaschen*, or *gelt*. Who wouldn't? I think of her when my kids pray to *Hashem* and sing in our synagogue choir. I think of her whenever I look into my husband's eyes and see that his soul yearns for peace in our eternal homeland. I think of her whenever I talk to my father-in-law, named none other than Israel. Who couldn't? I think of her when I see my kids play together with their classmates—Christian, Jewish, Muslim, Sikh, agnostic—and wonder why adults can't get along. I think of her and wonder how anyone could rightfully demonize the only true democracy in the Middle East that happens to be the only Jewish state on the planet. She calls my name every time I light *Shabbat* candles and attend services with my family. Israel and I are one. Two halves of the same whole. This lifelong bond formed the day I converted, and it grows stronger each day. For this, I will always defend Israel and her people until I take my last breath. *Am Yisrael Chai!*

As you can see, Jennifer's passion for Israel runs deep. So deep that she and her husband along with a handful of others started a digital advocacy group for Israel called, appropriately enough, *Act for Israel*. And while you might not go as far as starting an organization, you will learn about Israel in your conversion class, and there are a number of things you *can* do to help the world understand the Jewish state better and develop a greater tie to her.

Plant a Tree

No matter how young you are, or how long you've been Jewish, chances are the idea of planting a tree in Israel is not new to you. For more than one hundred years, the Jewish National Fund (JNF) has planted more than 240 million trees all over Israel, all purchased by individuals in honor of weddings, *b'nai mitzvah*, and more. While the forests of Israel belong to Israel, JNF ensures they are environmentally sound and focuses on diversification by planting native trees such as oak, carob, redbud, almond, pear, hawthorn, cypress, and Atlantic cedar. To its great credit, Israel was the only country in the world that began the twenty-first century with a net gain in the number of trees over the twentieth century.

Consider planting a tree in honor of becoming a new Jew. In December 2010, a devastating fire swept Mount Carmel, destroying over five million trees and taking forty-four lives, so the need to continuously support the JNF is greater today than ever.

Buy an Israel Bond

Want to help grow Israel's economy and infrastructure? Buy a bond! Since 1950, Israel has sold bonds to raise funds for all sorts of projects. Past investments have included roads and railroads, port facilities, immigrant absorption, and more. You can buy Israel bonds online, but sometimes the best way is through your synagogue's annual High Holy Day appeal. While your synagogue doesn't share in any of the money raised (they have their own hat to pass), you can support Israel during an appeal by simply folding down a paper tab on a pledge card.

Read

For a country its size, Israel has a lot of news outlets. The *Jerusalem Post* is probably the most well-known English-language daily paper, but there is also *Haaretz*. Both offer very comprehensive websites. And if you're on the Internet, you can visit YnetNews or Arutz Sheva (Israel's Channel 7). Each has its own unique perspective and political slant. Reading from these gives you a sense of Israel from an Israeli perspective. It also introduces you to the wonderful, entertaining world of Israeli politics.

Become an Advocate

There are literally hundreds of groups dedicated to sharing the truth about Israel and countering delegitimization efforts. Join one! Volunteer your time to help spread the message on Twitter or Facebook, write emails to politicians, participate in rallies and events, or simply show your support. You'll learn a lot and help Israel in the process (see Resources).

Visit Israel Yourself

This is perhaps the most rewarding of all options. To truly know Israel, you have to visit the country. You need to walk the same streets our ancestors walked, pray at the *Kotel*, eat falafel on a street corner, ride a camel, float in the Dead Sea, and climb Masada at sunrise. Short on time? No problem, Israelis are flexible. You can eat a falafel on camelback near the *Kotel* if that works better. Bottom line: everything you do in Israel connects you to her history and your destiny. Don't delay. Start planning your trip today and visit often.

Tweet Your Prayers

Times are tough and if you're like many, your immediate future may not entail an overseas trip to the Jewish state. If this describes you, or your schedule is too hectic to travel to Israel in the near term, have no fear. First, there's an iPhone app that gives you the next best thing: it's a webcam that allows you to zoom in on the Western Wall. Then there are several online services that help Twitter users connect to the Western Wall from wherever they are in the world. How? Now you can tweet your prayers to one of several online services who will then place your confidential tweet right into the *Kotel* wall. Imagine that!

ALL CORNERS OF THE GLOBE

Jews have come from all corners of the globe. Various communities have emerged since the first Babylonian exile in 586 BCE and the second exile by the Romans in 70 CE, with specific geographical names that often reflect a unique Jewish culture, language, diet, music, liturgy, and literature. All of these communities share their identity as part of *Am Yisrael*, the people of Israel, regardless of their specific location on the map. As the term *Israel* evolved from the time of the Patriarch Jacob to include all the Jewish People, Jews have considered themselves to be part of "Israel the people" from biblical times until today.

As Jews, our daily life along with our religious practice is greatly influenced by the societies where we live. On one hand, we are influenced by larger societal trends, but on the other, we are affected by events that are unique to our Jewish experience. This "double consciousness" is a by-product of living in a larger society yet experiencing the deep connections in our intimate culture.

AM YISRAEL CHAI!

It's true you can say *Am Israel Chai!*, visit Israel, advocate for Israel, and even consider yourself a child of Israel without ever becoming Jewish. If your heart of hearts tells you this is where you should be, then we support your decision. Ideally, the best reason for picking up a *siddur* (and ultimately converting) is simply because the beliefs, ideas, values, traditions, customs, celebrations, and way of life mirror your true sense of self in the most authentic way possible. You may have come to this conclusion as a result of being exposed to Judaism or its traditions through a friend, a course, an organization, a spouse or partner, or maybe even on your own. Likewise, you may be single, partnered, or married.

Yet conversion is an intensely personal decision, and one that you want to make thoughtfully and carefully. There are many implications to consider when choosing Judaism. In short, it includes fulfilling your spiritual needs; the lifestyle you want; your beliefs; your way of life; your feelings about Jews and Judaism, Israel, and antisemitism; and your willingness to cast your lot with that of the Jewish People. But it also affects those around you, your family of origin, your colleagues, and even your friends.

Ultimately, the best reason for becoming Jewish is simply because the ideas, values, traditions, customs, celebrations, and way of life allow you to express your true sense of self in the most authentic way possible. Regardless of the particular spiritual path that led you to *Becoming Jewish* and perhaps ultimately making the decision to convert, we hope that the information in this book has inspired you to find your own sense of wholeness, personal fulfillment, and joy. If we can continue to help you along your spiritual path beyond this point, we encourage you to mine our book resources, inhale our terminology list, and visit our related websites at BecomingJewishBook.com and InterfaithRabbi.com.

Remember, becoming Jewish is a lifelong journey filled with constant opportunities for self-discovery and spiritual growth. Conversion is just a starting point that opens a door to a whole new dimension of richness. Enjoy the energy and commitment that you're bringing to the tribe. *Mazel tov!*

CHAI NOTES

- Israel is the Jewish homeland.
- Israel is a land of many contrasts.
- Israel is a highly productive, intellectual country that has made huge contributions to the world.
- While there has been a Jewish presence in Israel for over three thousand years, the state of Israel was only established in 1948.
- Many Arab neighbors, including the Palestinian people, have refused to accept Israel as a Jewish state.
- Seven Israeli prime ministers have tried to make peace with the Palestinians to no avail.
- There are many ways you can take action to support Israel. Plant a tree, buy a bond, read Israeli news, become an advocate, and visit the country.
- Jews have lived in every corner of the world and represent every race.

- The term *Israel* evolved from the time of the Patriarch Jacob to include all the Jewish People.
- The best reason to convert is because Jewish customs and traditions mirror your true sense of self in the most authentic way possible.
- Becoming Jewish is a lifelong journey filled with constant opportunities for self-discovery and spiritual growth.
- Visit BecomingJewishBook.com and InterfaithRabbi.com for more guidance along your spiritual path.

Appendix 1

Thirty-Nine Types of Work Forbidden on Shabbat

Carrying

Burning

Extinguishing

Finishing

Writing

Erasing

Cooking

Washing

Sewing

Tearing

Knotting

Untying

Shaping

Plowing

Planting

Reaping

Harvesting

Threshing

Winnowing

Selecting

Sifting

Grinding

Kneading

Combing

Spinning

Dying

Chain-stitching

Warping

Weaving

Unraveling

Building

Demolishing

Trapping

Shearing

Slaughtering

Skinning

Tanning

Smoothing

Marking

Appendix 2

Sample Conversion Courses

ORTHODOX

Note: Unless otherwise stated, the convert is required to master all of the following areas. The tutor should sign and date the appropriate sections when the study of that unit has been completed.

I.   Blessings
        Required Text: *The Laws of Berachos* (Artscroll)
        a. Various blessings on foods
        b. *Beracha Acharona*
        c. Various blessings, such as thunder, oceans, etc.
II.   *Taharat Hamishpacha*
        Tutor will choose preferred text.
III.   *Shabbat* and *Yom Tov*
        Required Texts: *The Shabbos Kitchen* and *The 39 Melachos* (Chait)
        Illustrated Guide to Halacha
        a. Concepts and examples of 39 *Melachot*
        b. D'Oraissa and D'Rabbanan
        c. Categories of *Muktza*
        d. Cooking and warming foods
        e. Candlelighting
        f. When cooking is permitted on *Yom Tov*

      g. *Kiddush, Havdalah, Lechem Mishnah,* etc.

IV.   *Tefillot*

    Required Text: *Artscroll Siddur* (or an equivalent English-language *siddur*)

    The World of Prayer

    a. Requirements

    b. Priorities

    c. When and in what manner talking is prohibited

    d. Knowing your way around the *siddur*

    e. Additions and omissions on special occasions

    f. Understanding and ability to read basic *tefillot* including:

        A. All of the *Amidot*

        B. *Shma Yisroel* (all paragraphs)

        C. *Birkat Hamazon*

        D. *Al Hamichya*

        E. *Borei Nefashot*

        F. *Hallel*

        G. *Shabbat* services (particularly the structure of the services and the meaning of major prayers)

V.   A. For Men

    a. Blessings on the Torah

    b. *Kiddush* and *Havdalah*

    c. Leading *Birkat Hamazon*

    d. *Tzitzit* and *Tefillin*

    B. For Women:

    Required Text: *Halichos Bas Yisroel* (Feldheim)

    a. Haircovering

    b. General *Tzniut* (*kol isha*, etc.)

    c. Modesty in dress

VI.   The Jewish Calendar

    Required Text: *Book of Our Heritage* (Feldheim)

    a. Knowledge of all the *Yomim Tovim* and fast days, including:

        A. Meaning of the day

        B. All pertinent practical *halachot*

VII.   *Kashrut*

    Required Text: *The Laws of Kashrus* (Wagshall)

     a. Understanding of kosher and *glatt* kosher meats
     b. Understanding of kosher cheese and *cholov yisrael*
     c. Separation of meat and milk and waiting in between
     d. Common kitchen *shailot*
     e. Kashering
     f. *Tevillat Keilim*
     g. Taking challah
     h. Bugs
     i. Meat and fish
     j. Kosher fish
     k. *Starn Yeinum*
     l. *Bishul Akum*

VIII. *Hashkafa*
     a. Study of the 13 *Ikarim* of the Rambam
     b. *Mishneh Torah*
        A. *Yesodei HaTorah, perek* 1 and part of 2
        B. *Hilchos Teshuva* 2, 3, and 5
        C. *Hilchos Avodah Zarah perek* 1
        D. *Hilchos Melachim perek* 11 and 12

We also recommend that you consider teaching select portions from works such as the *Kuzari*, *Tanya*, or other works of *Chasidus* and *hashkafa* of your choice.

IX. Torah Knowledge
Suggested Text: *Artscroll Chumash*
The student is encouraged to attend classes as often as possible. The tutor should make a point of briefly mentioning the *Parshat Hashavua* on a weekly basis and assigning reading of the *Parsha* as homework.

X. Hebrew
The RCC Gerut program assumes that every candidate will make a maximum effort to acquire Hebrew reading skills and will be able to (a) read the most basic prayers such as the *Shema* and *Amidah* in Hebrew and (b) follow *Shabbat* synagogue services in Hebrew. Conversion candidates will be tested on their Hebrew.

XI. Jewish History
Overview of Jewish History Curriculum: *Crash Course in Jewish History* by Rabbi Berel Wein. Available on tape or CD.

This syllabus focuses primarily on the *halachot* that the convert must master in detail. As far as other areas of Jewish knowledge are concerned, the RCC's policy is that the candidate for conversion must be knowledgeable in all matters of daily life and sufficiently aware of when and how to ask a competent Rav when unusual circumstances arise.

XII.   Torah Ethics

Study of some basic concepts of Jewish ethics and values

a. *Pirkei Avos, perek* 3 study and discussion of the text

b. *Orchos Tzadikim*, introduction

c. *Mesilas Yesharim*, introduction and *perakim* 1 and 2

We also recommend assigning any of the three of Rabbi Baruch Chait's illustrated series on *midot*, which are delightfully engaging for young and old alike. The pictures and story line are a superb platform for study and discussion of ethics and interpersonal relationships according to Torah.

Source: Anonymous

REFORM

Civil Date	Hebrew Date	Topic	Important Dates
*10/18/10	11 Cheshvan 5771	Shabbat I	
10/25/10	18 Cheshvan 5771	Shabbat II	
11/01/10	25 Cheshvan 5771	Pesach I	
11/08/10	2 Kislev 5771	Pesach II	
11/15/10	9 Kislev 5771	Yom HaShoah	
11/22/10	16 Kislev 5771	Yom Ha'Atzmaut	
*11/29/10	23 Kislev 5771	Chanukah	12/02 Chanukah
12/06/10	30 Kislev 5771	Rosh Hashanah	
12/13/10	7 Tevet 5771	Yom Kippur	
01/10/11	6 Sh'vat 5771	Sikkot/Simchat Torah	
01/24/11	20 Sh'vat 5771	Shavuot	
01/31/11	27 Sh'vat 5771	Jewish Peoplehood	
*02/07/11	4 Adar I 5771	Birth	
02/14/11	11 Adar I 5771	Jewish Education	
02/28/11	25 Adar I 5771	Conversion	
03/07/11	2 Adar II 5771	Marriage	

| 03/14/11 | 9 Adar II 5771 | Purim | 3/20 Purim |
| 03/21/11 | 16 Adar II 5771 | Death | |

* Students may enter the class *only* on these dates.
Source: Temple Shir HaMa'a lot

CONSERVATIVE

1. Sept. 9   High Holy Day Workshop (2 hrs)
2. Sept. 16   Converting to Judaism (2 hrs—incl. Calendar/Sukkot—No Hebrew)
3. Oct. 7   *Shabbat*
4. Oct. 14   Prayers—Structure of *Siddur*, Overview of Services [JCC Tour]
5. Oct. 21   Overview of Jewish History, Classic Jewish Texts, Jewish Book List
6. Oct. 28   Beliefs: God/Revelation/Torah/*Mitzvot*
7. Nov. 4   Beliefs: Life after Death/Messiah/Resurrection
8. Nov. 11   Beliefs: Reward and Punishment/Theodicy
9. Nov. 18   Beliefs: Extra session
10. Dec. 2   Hanukkah (night of 12/4)
11. Dec. 9   Prayers: *Shema* and Its Blessings (incl. *Mezuzah, Tzitzit, Tefillin*)
12. Jan. 6   Prayers: *Amidah*
13. Jan. 13   Prayers: *Amidah* (cont'd)
14. Jan. 27   Kashrut
15. Feb. 10   Ethics: Love Your Neighbor/Speech

Special: February 17—*Yom Limmud*—Citywide Jewish Day of Learning @ Emanu El
16. Feb. 24   Ethics: *Tzedakah/Gemilut Hasadim*
17. Mar. 2   Ethics: Honoring Parents/Aged, *Bikur Holim*
18. Mar. 9   Antisemitism/Christianity and Judaism
19. Mar. 16   Purim [Visit Holocaust Museum—*Yom Hashoah* Is May 2]

Special: March 23—Purim Carnival
20. Mar. 30   Passover (4/19) [Kroger's Tour]
21. Apr. 6   Passover: The *Seder*
22. Apr. 13   Life Cycle
23. May 4   Israel (Independence Day is May 8)
24. May 11   Life Cycle

25. May 18   Shavuot (5/23) (incl. Ruth as Convert)

Source: Congregation Beth Yeshurun

RECONSTRUCTIONIST

October 20	Introduction: Starting a Journey
November 3	*Shabbat*: Patterns in Time
November 17	Theology: Relationship with Divine
December 8	Chanukah
January 12	Life Cycle: Sex, Marriage, Divorce
January 26	Reconstructionist Thought
February 5	(*Shabbat* morning) *Minyan*—JA&A Prayer Workshop
February 9	Prayer
February 23	Life Cycle: Death and Mourning
March 9	Jewish Texts: Bible
March 23	Passover
April 6	Holocaust
April 20	Jewish Attitudes toward Israel
April 29	JA&A *Shabbat*—dinner at 6 p.m.

Source: Kehillat Israel

Glossary

Aaron: Moses's brother and the first high priest of the Israelites.

Abraham: The first Jew, and father of all three major world religions.

Adonai: Hebrew for "Lord." Used as a name for God.

Afikomen: Ceremonial piece of the middle matzah from the Passover *seder*.

Aliyah: Hebrew for "going up." Has two distinct definitions: in synagogue, *aliyah* means going up to the *bimah* to read from the Torah; if used as "making *aliyah*," it refers to moving to Israel and becoming an Israeli citizen.

Anti-Defamation League (ADL): Organization established to monitor and address issues of antisemitism and racism.

Antisemitism: Statements or actions against Jews. While it is true that Jews are not the only "Semites," antisemitism is defined specifically as anti-Jewish activity.

Arabic: The predominant language used in countries of Arab descent. One of the two official languages of Israel, and the language of the Koran.

Aramaic: An early language that shares the Hebrew alphabet and that was used in Canaan. Some books in the *Tanakh* are written in Aramaic.

Ashkenazi: European branch of Jews. See *Sephardi* for the other main branch.

Avodah: Sacred service or worship.

Bar Mitzvah: The culmination of Jewish education a boy demonstrates at age thirteen. Typically involves leading *Shabbat* prayers, reading the Torah, and reciting a *Haftarah*.

Bat Mitzvah: The culmination of Jewish education a girl demonstrates at age twelve. Typically involves leading *Shabbat* prayers, reading the Torah, and reciting a *Haftarah*.

BCE: Before the Common Era. A nondenominational way to refer to BC (Before Christ).

Bedeken: Prewedding ceremony in which the groom veils the bride.

Bedouin: A desert-dweller, often who has only semipermanent ties to a location.

Bereshit: The first book of the Torah, Genesis. Hebrew for "In the beginning."

Besamim: Spices.

Bet Din: A three-person Jewish rabbinical court. The *bet din* determines whether a potential convert is able to become a Jew. (Plural form: *batei din*)

Bikur Cholim: Visiting the sick.

Bimah: Hebrew for "stage." Literally, the stage a religious service occurs on.

B'nai Mitzvah: Multiple *bar* and *bat mizvot*.

Bris: Ashkenazi pronunciation of *brit*.

Brit: Short for *brit milah*.

Brit Milah: Ritual circumcision conducted on Jewish boys eight days after birth.

Bubbe: Yiddish for "grandmother."

Bube: Bob Saget's paternal grandmother.

Bulbul: Hebrew slang for "penis."

Cantor: A Jewish religious leader who specializes in Jewish music and liturgy. The cantor's role is to sing or chant prayers during services. Sometimes called the *Hazzan*.

CE: Common Era. A nondenominational way to refer to AD (Latin *Anno Domini*, meaning "Year of our Lord").

Chabad: A *Hasidic/Haredi* movement of Orthodox Judaism founded in Brooklyn, New York.

Chai: Hebrew for "life." In *gematria*, the letters that form *chai* total eighteen, which makes eighteen an auspicious and "lucky" number for Jews.

Challah: Braided egg bread served at *Shabbat* and on Rosh Hashanah (when it is traditionally round to symbolize the circular path of a year). (Plural form: *challot*)

Chanukah: Festival of Lights. Commemorates the victory of the Maccabees over the Greeks and the rededication of the Temple in Jerusalem. The available oil to light the menorah in the temple was enough for only one day, but it miraculously burned for eight days until more oil was available.

Chanukiah: The special nine-branched menorah used on Chanukah. One branch is for the *shamash*, or "helper." The remaining eight symbolize each day of the festival.

Charoset: Mixture of apples, nuts, wine, and cinnamon eaten during the Passover *seder*. Symbolizes the mortar used by the Israelites to make bricks.

Chavurah: Literally, a group of friends. (Plural form: *chavurot*)

Chuppah: Wedding canopy.

Chutzpah: Yiddish for "guts" or "nerve."

Circumcision: Removal of the foreskin covering the head of the penis.

Congregant: Member of a synagogue.

Conservative: A modern sect of Judaism that seeks to preserve Jewish tradition and ritual, yet interprets doctrine and laws in a more flexible way than Orthodox Judaism.

Crowns: Ornamental pieces placed on top of the upper handles of a Torah scroll.

Day: In Judaism, the "day" begins at sunset. This is because in Genesis it is written, "And it was evening and it was morning—the first day."

Dead Sea Scrolls: A collection of manuscripts written between 100 BCE and 70 CE that contain segments of the Torah as well as descriptions of life and activity during that time frame. They were found in caves in the Qumran area near the Dead Sea in 1947 by a Bedouin boy looking for his goat.

Deuteronomy: The fifth book of the Torah.

Diaspora: Jewish communities outside Israel.

Dogma: Code of belief.

Dreidel: Four-sided top used at Chanukah. Each side features a Hebrew letter—*Nun, Gimel, Hay, Shin* (or *Pay* in Israel)—which together stand for the Hebrew sentence *Nes gadol haya sham (po)*, or "A great miracle happened there (here)."

Eid: Islamic feast day. Eid al Fitr is celebrated at the end of Ramadan.

El Al: The national airline of Israel.

Eliezer Ben-Yehuda: The father of modern Hebrew.

Elijah: Biblical prophet who, according to tradition, will return to announce the coming of the Messiah.

Ellis Island: The first stop, in New York Harbor, where millions of immigrants began their entry to America.

Erusin: Jewish betrothal ceremony.

Esther: The Jewish queen of Persia who saved the Jews from mass execution. Esther is the star of the Purim celebration.

Etrog: A citron, which is a large, fragrant lemon-like fruit used along with the *lulav* to celebrate *Sukkot*.

Exodus: The second book of the Torah.

Gaza: Disputed strip of land along Israel's border with Egypt.

Gefilte Fish: A Passover staple made from ground whitefish, matzah meal, and spices.

Gemara: The collected conversations, discussions, arguments, and commentaries that rabbis in rabbinic academies both in Israel and Babylonia conducted based on their study of the *Mishnah*. This is the second part of the Talmud.

Genesis: The first book of the Torah.

Get: Jewish divorce decree.

Gilad Shalit: Israeli soldier captured at age seventeen by Hamas terrorists and held in captivity without access to family or aid. At the time of publication, Gilad had been in captivity for more than five years.

G'milut Chasadim: Acts of loving-kindness.

Gregorian Calendar: The 365-day calendar traditionally used in Western culture.

Haftarah: A portion of the *Tanakh* read after the Torah on Saturday mornings that has a contextual link to the Torah portion.

Haggadah: Hebrew for "telling." The book used to guide the Passover *seder*. (Plural form: *Haggadot*)

Hajj: Muslim pilgrimage.

Halachah: Jewish law.

Haman: The "bad guy" of the Purim story. Advisor to the king of Persia who wanted to kill all the Jews.

Hamas: Palestinian organization based mainly in Gaza that is dedicated according to their charter to the elimination of Israel.

Hamentashen: Triangular filled pastries eaten on Purim.

Hametz: Leavened bread, cake, cookies, etc.

Hamotzi: Prayer said over bread.

Hamsa: A downward-pointing, hand-shaped symbol believed to ward off the evil eye or bring good luck.

Hanukah: An alternate spelling of Chanukah.

Hashem: Name used by traditional Jews instead of God to show respect.

Hatafat Dam Brit: Ceremony performed for male converts who have already been circumcised that symbolizes the religious aspect of circumcision. It involves drawing a small drop of blood from the penis and reciting the prayers for circumcision.

Havdalah: Service that marks the end of *Shabbat*.

Hebrew: The language of the Torah, the Jewish People, and Israel.

Hebrew Bible: See *Tanakh*.

Hezbollah: Radical Islamist organization based in Lebanon that is dedicated to the Islamification of the country and the elimination of Israel.

High Holy Days: The major holidays of Judaism: Rosh Hashanah and Yom Kippur.

Holocaust: The Nazi's systematic roundup and murder of six million Jews (and five million non-Jews) during Hitler's reign.

Holocaust Denial: The false statement that the Holocaust did not exist, was fabricated, or was a Jewish plot. Often used to justify delegitimization of Israel.

Holy: To make something holy is to set it apart from other things, to make it special and ultimately important.

Interfaith: Involving different religions.

Isaac: Son of Abraham who was nearly sacrificed as a sign of Abraham's loyalty to God.

Israel: The name given to Jacob after defeating an angel in battle. Also the name of the Jewish homeland, established in 1948.

Jacob: Isaac's second son, who tricked his brother, Esau, out of Isaac's death-bed blessing.

Jerusalem: The holy city of the Jewish People and the capital of Israel.

Jew by Association: A person married to a Jew who practices Jewish traditions but has not converted.

Jew by Birth: In Orthodox and Conservative circles, the child of a Jewish mother. In Reform and Reconstructionist circles, the child of a Jewish parent.

Jew by Choice: A person who has converted to Judaism.

Kabbalah: The mystical practice of Judaism that explores the nature of God, the afterlife, numerology, and more.

Kaddish: Literally, a prayer exalting the holiness of God. Generally, *Kaddish* refers to the mourner's *Kaddish*, recited when mourning for a loved one.

Karpas: Greens eaten during a Passover *seder*. Usually parsley.

Kashrut: The laws of Jewish cooking, cleaning, and eating.

Kavvanah: Intention.

Ketubah: A Jewish marriage agreement. (Plural form: *ketuvot*)

Kibbutz: A communal farm.

Kiddush: Hebrew for "sanctification." The prayer over wine.

Kiddush Cup: Ornamental cup used when chanting the *kiddush.*

Kiddushin: Hebrew for "wedding."

Kipah: Skullcap worn in synagogue and by some Jews at all times. (Plural form: *kippot*)

Kishka: Eastern European food made from meat, blood, and grain stuffed into an intestine casing.

Kosher: Hebrew for "fit" or "proper." Common word describing *kashrut.*

Kri'a: Tearing a black ribbon or one's garment to symbolize mourning.

Ladino: The language of Sephardic Jewish culture spoken throughout the Spanish empire, as well as in Turkey, North Africa, and to some extent in France and Greece.

Latke: A potato pancake fried in oil and traditionally served at Chanukah.

L'Chaim: Hebrew toast—"To Life!"

Leah: The first of Jacob's wives.

Lechem: Hebrew for "bread."

Leviticus: Third book of the Torah.

Lubavitch: *Hasidic/Haredi* Orthodox group based in Brooklyn, New York. Members are recognizable by their fifteenth-century-style black garb.

Lulav: Literally, in Hebrew, a "palm frond." More commonly refers to the combined bundle of palm, myrtle, and willow branches used in *Sukkot* celebration.

Maccabees: Band of brothers who led a successful revolt against Antiochus' Greek army and recaptured and rededicated the Temple in Jerusalem.

Machzor: Communal prayer book for Rosh Hashanah and Yom Kippur.

Magen David: Hebrew for the "Shield of David." Also known as the Star of David or Jewish Star.

Maimonedes: Rabbi Moshe ben Maimon (RAMBAM), a great Jewish sage of medieval times.

Maror: Bitter herbs eaten during a Passover *seder.* Usually horseradish or arugula.

Matisyahu: American-born, *Hasidic* reggae musician, known by his Hebrew name (given name is Matthew Paul Miller), who has released many albums, including a Top 40 hit, "King without a Crown."

Matriarchs: The "Mothers" of Judaism: Sarah, Rebecca, Rachel, and Leah.

Matzah: Unleavened bread eaten at Passover to commemorate the bread our ancestors made in haste during the Exodus.

Matzah Ball Soup: Chicken soup with large fluffy delicious dumplings made from matzah meal, eggs, and spices.

Matzo: Alternative spelling for matzah.

Mazel Tov: Hebrew for "Good luck." Generally used as congratulations.

Menorah: A traditional candelabrum with either seven or nine branches. A nine-branched menorah is called a *chanukiah*.

Mensch: A good, righteous person.

Meshuggah: Yiddish for crazy or senseless.

Mezuzah: A small box and scroll placed on doorposts of Jewish homes. (Plural form: *mezuzot*)

Mi Chamocha: A *Shabbat* prayer that glorifies God.

Midrash: Torah commentary written between 400 and 1200 CE in the form of anecdotes and stories.

Mikdash Me'at: Hebrew for "small sanctuary," describing the home as a religious and spiritual center for your life.

Mikvah: Ritual bath. (Plural form: *mikvot*)

Milkhama: Hebrew for "war."

Minyan: A quorum of ten people (men in Orthodoxy) required for certain prayers.

Miriam: Moses's sister.

Mishnah: A collection of sixty-three tractates arranged in what are called six "orders" and that were originally the "oral law" developed by ancient rabbis. This is the first part of the Talmud.

Mitzvah: Hebrew for "good deed." (Plural form: *mitzvot*)

Mohammed: Prophet of Islam.

Mohel: Ritual circumciser. (Plural form: *mohelim*)

Moses: Prophet who led the Jews out of Egypt to the Promised Land and delivered the Torah from God.

Moshiach: Hebrew for "messiah."

Motzi: Hebrew for "bring forth [bread]." A short way to refer to the *Hamotzi* prayer.

Mount Sinai: The place where Moses received the Ten Commandments from God.

Nefesh: According to Kabbalah, the base part of the human soul linked to animal instincts, emotions, and cravings.

Neshamah: According to Kabbalah, the higher soul that allows us to be aware of God's existence and presence, and the part of us that exists in the afterlife.

Neshamah Kedoshah: According to Kabbalah, the "holy higher soul" we receive when we have a *bar* or *bat mitzvah*.

Neshamah Yeseira: According to Kabbalah, a special "extra" soul we obtain on *Shabbat* if we are observant.

New Testament: The primary books of Christian theology.

Nisuin: Jewish marriage ceremony.

Numbers: The fourth book of the Torah.

Numerology: The study of occult and magical use of numbers.

Old Testament: The Torah plus the Psalms of David and prophetic books. In Judaism, this is referred to as the *Tanakh*.

Oneg Shabbat: Hebrew for "Delight in the Sabbath." An *Oneg Shabbat* or *Oneg* is a celebration of the *Shabbat* often held at the conclusion of Friday-night services.

Orthodox: Most traditional branch of Judaism. Orthodox follow all *halachah*.

Oy Gevalt: Yiddish for "Oh my goodness!" or "Oh gosh!"

Palestine: The historical Greek name attributed to the land that is now Israel.

Parchment: A writing material made from prepared sheep- or goatskin. The Torah is handwritten on scrolls of parchment.

Passover: The Jewish holiday celebrating the exodus from Egypt.

Patriarchs: The "Fathers" of Judaism: Abraham, Isaac, and Jacob.

Patrilineal Descent: The concept that Judaism can be passed from the father, not just the mother.

Pesach: Hebrew for "Passover."

Pikuah Nefesh: Saving a life.

Pirke Avot: A book of the Talmud.

Proselytize: Attempt to gain followers and converts.

Purim: Holiday celebrating restoration of religious freedom. Celebrated with costumes, revelry, and reading of the scroll of Esther.

Qumran: The city near the Dead Sea where the Dead Sea Scrolls were found.

Rabbi: A Jewish religious leader and teacher.

Rachel: Jacob's second wife.

Ramadan: The Muslim month of fasting.

RAMBAM: Abbreviation/title given to Rabbi Moshe ben Maimonedes (see *Maimonedes*).

Rebecca: Isaac's wife.

Reconstructionist: A modern branch of Judaism that views Judaism as a constantly evolving culture.

Reform: A modern branch of Judaism that integrates Jewish beliefs with modern life.

Rosh Hashanah: The Jewish New Year.

Ruach: Hebrew for "spirit." According to Kabbalah, the part of the human soul that defines our morality and ethics.

Ruth: A Moabite woman who became the first recorded Jewish convert.

Sabbath: The day of rest. Observed from Friday sundown to Saturday sundown.

Sarah: Abraham's wife.

Seder: Literally means "order." The traditional meal of Passover during which the story of the exodus is retold.

Seder Plate: A ceremonial plate placed at the center of the table during a *seder*. It holds the primary symbolic items of the *seder*.

Semite: A person whose ancestors originally came from the Middle East. Includes Jews and Arabs.

Sephardi: Branch of Jews descending from medieval Spain, Portugal, North Africa, and the Middle East. Can be used of Jews who use the liturgy and customs of Spanish Jews, whether or not they have a historical or ethnic connection to Spain. (Plural form: Sephardim)

Shabbat: Hebrew for "Sabbath."

Shabbat Shalom: Traditional *Shabbat* greeting. Literally means "Peaceful Sabbath."

Shalom: Hebrew for "Hello, goodbye, peace."

Shalom Bayit: Peace in the home.

Shamash: "Helper" candle for lighting the *chanukiah*.

Shanah Tovah: "Happy New Year." Traditional Rosh Hashanah greeting.

Shavuot: Festival memorializing God giving the Torah to the Israelites.

Shehecheyanu: Prayer that marks the arrival of a special event.

Shema: The cornerstone prayer of Judaism that asserts there is one God.

Shevarim: A broken, sighing *shofar* blast of three short calls.

Shiva: The seven required days of mourning at home. Often referred to as "sitting *shiva*."

Sh'mini Atzeret: The "Eighth Day of Celebration" of *Sukkot*.

Shoah: Hebrew for "Holocaust."

Shofar: Ram's horn blown on Rosh Hashanah and Yom Kippur.

Shomer Shabbos: Fully observant "defense" and keeping of the Sabbath.

Shul: Yiddish for "school." Refers to synagogue.

Sidur: Prayer book.

Sifrei Torah: Hebrew for "Books of the Torah."

Simchat Torah: The holiday that marks the completion of reading the Torah and beginning the reading again, ensuring a circular cycle.

Sofer: A scribe who handwrites Torah scrolls.

Sofit: Hebrew for "ending." Several Hebrew letters have a different form when at the end of words.

STA"M: The form a script a *sofer* uses to write *Sefer Torah*, *tefillin*, and *mezuzot*.

Star of David: The six-pointed star often used to represent Judaism. See *Magen David*.

Sufganiyot: Jelly donuts eaten on Chanukah.

Sukkah: A temporary "booth" built for *Sukkot*. Must have three walls and a loose ceiling one can see the sky through.

Sukkot: Festival of "booths." Reflects both the harvest and the temporary living quarters of the Israelites during the exodus.

Synagogue: A Jewish place of worship.

Tallis: Ashkenazi version of *tallit*.

Tallit: Traditional prayer shawl worn on *Shabbat* mornings and High Holidays.

Talmud: The collection of ancient rabbinic analysis and stories that forms the basis for *halachah*. Formed by the combination of the *Mishnah* and *Gemara*.

Tanakh: The collected thirty-nine books of the Jewish Bible. Contains the Torah, the Prophets, and the Writings (Torah, *Nevi'im*, *Ketuvim*).

Tefillin: Phylacteries wrapped around the arms and placed on the forehead as part of morning ritual. Typically used in Orthodox and some Conservative movements.

Tekiah: One long *shofar* blast with a clear tone.

Tekiah Gedolah: a single unbroken *shofar* blast held as long as possible.

Tel Aviv: The largest city in Israel.

Temple: Holy place. When capitalized, usually refers to either the First or Second Temple built in Jerusalem.

Teruah: The alarm—a rapid series of nine or more very short notes on the *shofar*.

Tikkun Olam: The Jewish philosophy of making the world a better place.

Tish: Groom's table.

Tisha B'av: Holiday commemorating the destruction of both the First and Second Temples in Jerusalem and the expulsion of the Jews from fifteenth-century Spain.

Torah: The holy books of Judaism believed to be written by God and passed down from generation to generation. Contains the five books of Moses: Genesis, Exodus, Leviticus, Numbers, and Deuteronomy (*Bereshit, Shemot, Vayikrah, Bamidbar,* and *D'varim*).

Transliteration: Hebrew written in the English alphabet so those who do not read Hebrew can still recite prayers.

Tu B'shvat: Jewish "New Year for Trees," similar to Arbor Day.

Twelve Tribes: Jacob had twelve sons, from whom the Israelites organized themselves into "tribes" during the exodus from Egypt and even geographically after settling in Canaan.

Tzedakah: Hebrew for "righteousness," but refers to what we generally call the moral obligation of charity or helping those in need.

Tzitzit: Strings tied at the fringes of garments, including *tallit*, to honor God's commandment to do so.

Ushpizin: Yiddish for mystical/spiritual guests.

V'ahavta: The prayer that declares the *mitzvah* of writing God's words on the doorpost.

West Bank: An area west of the Jordan River that Israel took from Jordan in 1967. Since then, this land has been under continuous ownership dispute.

Yad: Hebrew for "hand." Refers to the stylized pointer used for Torah reading.

Yahrtzeit: Anniversary of a death.

Yamim Noraim: The ten "Days of Awe" between Rosh Hashanah and Yom Kippur.

Yarmulke: Yiddish for *kipah*.

Yeshiva: A school for studying Torah and Talmud. (Plural form: *yeshivot*)

Yiddish: A language of Ashkenazic Jews used commonly until the mid-twentieth century. Yiddish is a fusion of German and Hebrew and uses the Hebrew alphabet.

Yihud: Separation. Refers to private time a bride and groom spend immediately following their marriage.

Yom Ha-atzmaut: Israel independence day.

Yom Hashoah: Holocaust memorial day.

Yom Kippur: Day of Atonement.

Yom Limmud: A community day of learning.

Yom Tov: Holy day.

Zayin: Hebrew letter *z*. Also Hebrew slang for "penis" due to its shape.

Zionism: The movement for establishment of a Jewish state in Israel.

Zohar: Hebrew for "radiance." The set of Kabbalistic writings of Rabbis Akiva, Yochai, and Abba.

Resources

We've selected the most useful resources for supporting you through the conversion process, and for assisting you in your life as a new Jew. Refer to this list often—it will help you as you progress through conversion and beyond. And visit our resources page at BecomingJewishBook.com for the most up-to-date recommendations.

JUDAISM
Orthodox
Orthodox Union
Phone: 212-563-4000
Website: OU.org
The OU represents over eight hundred synagogues across North America. Their "circle U" kosher supervision label is one of the most recognized in the world.

Chabad
Phone: 718-774-4000
Website: Chabad.org
Chabad is a branch of *Hasidic* Jewry that integrates aspects of Kabbalah into Jewish ritual and prayer. The group has centers worldwide, including many on college campuses.

Conservative

The United Synagogue of Conservative Judaism (USCJ)
Phone: 212-533-7800
Website: USCJ.org
The USCJ is the association of over seven hundred Conservative congregations in North America.

The Conservative/Masorti Movement
Phone: 212-870-2216
Website: Masorti.org
The Masorti Movement is the Hebrew name for Conservative Judaism in Israel. The organization is an umbrella for Conservative synagogues and groups and also acts as a legal advocate for Conservative Judaism in Israel.

Reconstructionist

Reconstructionist Rabbinical College (RRC)
Phone: 215-576-0800
Website: RRC.edu
RRC is the federation of over one hundred Reconstructionist congregations and groups across North America.

Reform

Union for Reform Judaism (URJ)
Phone: 212-650-4000
Website: URJ.org
The URJ is the union of over nine hundred Reform congregations across North America and the Caribbean.

Prayer Delivery

Tweet Your Prayers
Website: TweetYourPrayers.info
Site that allows you to use Twitter to send a prayer directly to the Western Wall. Simply send a tweet to @TheKotel, and it will be printed and placed directly in the cracks of the Wall.

The *Kotel*
Phone: 212-725-0598
Website: English.TheKotel.org
This is the site for the Western Wall Heritage Foundation. On the site, you can get lots of information on the wall and the archaeology around it, as well as a live webcam of the *Kotel* (except on *Shabbat* and holidays).

JEWISH EDUCATION
My Jewish Learning
Phone: 212-695-9010
Website: MyJewishLearning.com
MyJewishLearning.com is the leading transdenominational website of Jewish information and education. It offers thousands of articles on all aspects of Judaism and Jewish life and is geared toward adults of all ages and backgrounds.

JEWISH LIFE
Jewish Community Centers of America (JCCA)
Phone: 212-532-4949
Website: JCCA.org
The JCCA is the umbrella organization for the Jewish Community Center Movement, which includes more than 350 JCCs, YM-YWHAs, and campsites in the United States and Canada.

JDate
Website: JDate.com
JDate is an ideal destination for Jewish men and Jewish women to make connections and find friends, dates, and soul mates, all within the Jewish faith.

Jewcy
Website: Jewcy.com
Jewcy is an online magazine focusing on ideas that matter to young Jews today.

Jewlicious
Website: Jewlicious.com
Jewlicious is an often offbeat blog about Jewish culture and issues. As they describe themselves, "We're basically the Jews that you meet, when you're walking down the street. We're the Jews that you meet each day."

Hillel
Phone: 202-449-6500
Website: Hillel.org
Hillel is the foundation for Jewish Campus Life. The group provides opportunities for Jewish students at more than five hundred colleges and universities to explore and celebrate their Jewish identity through its global network of regional centers, campus foundations, and Hillel student organizations.

Aish
Website: Aish.com
Aish's goal is to give every Jew the opportunity to discover their heritage in an atmosphere of open inquiry and mutual respect.

JEWISH HISTORY
Jewish Virtual Library
Website: JewishVirtualLibrary.org
This is the most comprehensive online Jewish encyclopedia in the world, covering everything from anti-Semitism to Zionism. So far, more than thirteen thousand articles and six thousand photographs and maps have been integrated into the site.

Yad Vashem
Website: YadVashem.org
Yad Vashem is the Jewish people's living memorial to the Holocaust and is located in Jerusalem. It was established in 1953 as the world center for documentation, research, education, and commemoration of the Holocaust. One of the key components of their website is a database of Holocaust victims' names so that they will never be forgotten.

United States Holocaust Memorial Museum
Phone: 202-488-0400
Website: USHMM.org
The United States Holocaust Memorial Museum is America's national institution for the documentation, study, and interpretation of Holocaust history, and it serves as this country's memorial to the millions of people murdered during the Holocaust.

Judaism 101
Website: JewFAQ.org
Judaism 101 is an online encyclopedia of Judaism, covering Jewish beliefs, people, places, things, language, scripture, holidays, practices, and customs.

Center for Jewish History
Phone: 212-2914-8301
Website: CJH.org
The Center for Jewish History is a world-class venue for exhibitions, cultural ideas, and public scholarship rooted in the rich collections of five distinguished Jewish collections.

JEWISH CHILDREN
The PJ Library
Phone: 413-439-1981
Website: PJLibrary.org
The PJ Library program supports families in their Jewish journey by sending Jewish-content books and music on a monthly basis to children from ages six months to five, six, seven, or eight years depending on the community.

Akhla: The Jewish Children's Learning Network
Website: Akhla.com
Akhlah provides Jewish children and their families access to the prayers, stories, and rituals that have bound Jews together around the world and through the ages.

HEBREW
Hebrew-English Translation
Website: translate.google.com
This is a terrific site for translating words, phrases, or entire web pages. While not perfect, the results are generally enough to understand the key points.

Rosetta Stone
Website: RosettaStone.com
Rosetta Stone offers one of the most widely praised self-paced language-learning methods.

eTeacher Hebrew
Phone: 888-563-7370
Website: eTeacherHebrew.com
eTeacher provides live online learning through desktop videoconferencing. The hallmarks of eTeacher's language courses are live online instruction, flexible hours, and the convenience of learning from home or office.

JEWISH CHARITIES
Jewish National Fund
Phone: 888-JNF-0099
Website: JNF.org
Over the past 109 years, JNF has evolved into a global environmental leader by planting 240 million trees, building over 210 reservoirs and dams, developing over 250,000 acres of land, creating more than 1,000 parks, providing the infrastructure for over 1,000 communities, bringing life to the Negev Desert, and educating students around the world about Israel and the environment.

Israel Bonds
Website: IsraelBonds.com
Since 1950, proceeds provided by the bonds organization have been used by Israel's Finance Ministry to support key economic projects, many of which were essential to solidifying Israel's postindependence economy, including the following:

- The National Water Carrier
- Dead Sea Works
- Communities in Galilee and Negev
- Port construction and expansion
- Road and rail networks
- Immigrant absorption

American Jewish World Service (AJWS))
Phone: 212-792-2900
Website: AJWS.org
AJWS is dedicated to alleviating poverty, hunger, and disease among the people of the developing world regardless of race, religion, or nationality.

The Jewish Federations of North America
Phone: 212-284-6500
Website: JewishFederations.org
The Jewish Federations of North America represents 157 Jewish Federations and 400 network communities, which raise and distribute more than three billion dollars annually for social welfare, social services, and educational needs for Jews worldwide.

American Jewish Committee (AJC)
Phone: 212-751-4000
Website: AJC.org
AJC promotes pluralistic and democratic societies where all minorities are protected. AJC is an international think tank and advocacy organization that attempts to identify trends and problems early—and take action. Their key focus areas are the following:

- Combating antisemitism and all forms of bigotry
- Promoting pluralism and shared democratic values
- Supporting Israel's quest for peace and security
- Advocating for energy independence
- Strengthening Jewish life

Hadassah
Phone: 888-303-3640
Website: Hadassah.org
Hadassah promotes the unity of the Jewish people. In Israel, Hadassah initiates and supports pace-setting health care, education and youth institutions, and land development to meet the country's changing needs. In the United States, Hadassah enhances the quality of American and Jewish life through its education and Zionist youth programs, promotes health awareness, and provides personal enrichment and growth for its members.

ISRAEL
Israel Ministry of Tourism
Phone: 888-77-ISRAEL
Website: GoIsrael.com
This site provides trip-planning information including suggested itineraries, various themes for visits, key attractions, and accommodation information.

ISRAELI ACTIVISM
Act for Israel
Website: ActForIsrael.org
Act for Israel is the leading digital platform for pro-Israel activism. The group relies on the latest Internet-based technology to win the war of ideas. They believe that Israel has the right to live in peace and security, and that all people deserve the right to live in dignity. Their goal is to share this centrist position with a wide audience to correct misinformation, end demonization, stop delegitimization, and give Israel a much-needed voice.

Anti-Defamation League (ADL)
Website: ADL.org
The Anti-Defamation League was founded in 1913 "to stop the defamation of the Jewish people and to secure justice and fair treatment to all." Now the nation's premier civil rights/human rights agency, ADL fights antisemitism and all forms of bigotry, defends democratic ideals, and protects civil rights for all.

Middle East Media Research Institute (MEMRI)
Website: MEMRI.org
MEMRI explores the Middle East through the region's media (both print and television), websites, religious sermons, and school books. MEMRI bridges the language gap that exists between the West and the Middle East, providing timely translations of Arabic, Farsi, Urdu, Pashtu, Dari, Hindi, and Turkish media, as well as original analysis of political, ideological, intellectual, social, cultural, and religious trends in the Middle East.

Simon Wiesenthal Center
Website: Wiesenthal.com
The Simon Wiesenthal Center is an international Jewish human rights organization that confronts antisemitism, hate, and terrorism; promotes human rights and dignity; stands with Israel; defends the safety of Jews worldwide; and teaches the lessons of the Holocaust for future generations.

StandWithUs
Website: StandWithUs.com
StandWithUs is an international organization dedicated to bringing peace to the Middle East by educating about Israel and challenging the misinformation that

often surrounds the Middle East conflict. Through brochures, speakers, programs, conferences, missions to Israel, campaigns, and Internet resources, they strive to ensure that Israel's side of the story is told on university campuses and in communities, the media, libraries, and churches around the world.

ISRAELI NEWS
Jerusalem Post
Website: JPost.com
Israel's best-selling English daily and most-read English website. *Centrist*

Haaretz
Website: Haaretz.com
Israel's leading Hebrew newspaper. The website offers both English and Hebrew versions. *Left*

Ynet News
Website: YNetNews.com
This is the English-language sister-site to YNet, Israel's largest and most popular news and content website. *Right*

Arutz Sheva
Website: IsraelNationalNews.com
Website for an Israeli media network that includes Internet and radio broadcasts. *Far Right*

US JEWISH NEWS
Jewish Week
Website: TheJewishWeek.com
The *Jewish Week* of New York is the largest Jewish weekly in the United States.

Jewish Journal
Website: JewishJournal.com
The *Jewish Journal* of greater Los Angeles is the largest Jewish weekly outside New York City.

Jewish Daily Forward
Website: Forward.com
Originally a Yiddish newspaper, the *Forward* is now an English-language weekly from New York.

POLICY THINK TANKS
Jerusalem Center for Public Affairs (JCPA)
Website: JCPA.org
JCPA is a multidisciplinary, independent nonprofit think tank for Israel policy research and education, bringing together the best minds in the political, strategic, diplomatic, and legal arenas.

Jewish Telegraphic Agency (JTA)
Website: JTA.org
JTA provides in-depth coverage of political, economic, and social developments affecting Jews in North and South America, Israel, Europe, Africa, and Australia.

Reut Institute
Website: Reut-Institute.org
The Reut Institute is a policy think tank designed to provide real-time, long-term strategic decision support to the government of Israel.

Index

Earth Day, 82
Easter, 38, 43, 154, 204
Eastern Europe, 20, 131
eco-*kashrut*, 123
Efron, Zac, 171
egg, roasted, 90, 94
Egypt, 12, 58, 82, 91, 118, 126, 129, 205, 209; Exodus from, 92; liberation from, 88–89, 90, 136
Eid, 2, 38, 43, 154
eighteen, significance of, 125. *See also* *chai*
Eilat, 20
Ein Gedi, 204
Ein Sof, 174
El Al, 189
e-learning. *See* online course
Elijah, 92; cup of, 92–93; opening door for, 92
Emerson, Ralph Waldo, 32
England. *See* United Kingdom
English, 61, 63
Ephraim, 74
equality, 21
Eretz Yisrael, 203
erusin, 144, 150
Esther, Queen, 12, 82
ethical monotheism, 125
etrog, 81, 134
Eucharist, 27
Eve, 17, 143, 149
Exodus, Book of, 58, 91

Facebook, 15, 16, 136, 187, 209, 211
family, 7, 77, 127, 133; dynamics, 42; and friends, 31–32, 37–45. *See also* *taharat hamishpachah*
Farrakhan, Louis, 183, 185
Farsi, 9

fasting, 28, 80, 120
Fatah, 207, 208–9
Faurisson, Robert, 190
FBI. *See* Federal Bureau of Investigation
Feast of the Tabernacles. *See* Sukkot
Feast of Weeks. *See* Shavuot
Federal Bureau of Investigation (FBI), 189
Federal Reserve, 186
Ferdinand, King, 83
Festival of Booths. *See* Sukkot
Festival of Lights. *See* Chanukah
Fiddler on the Roof, 118
financial industry, 186
Finkelstein, Norman, 190
First Amendment, 189
fish, 122, 123
Fisher, Isla, 9
flags, 81
flash cards, 60
forced conversion, 83
forced paganism, 84
foreskin, 12, 112
Four Questions, 91–92
France, 131, 186, 191
freedom, 88, 93
Free Gaza Movement, 185
funeral. *See* burial

Gaelic, 35
gay, lesbian, bisexual, and transgendered (GLBT), 19, 21, 146
Gaza flotilla, 186
Gaza Strip, 206, 208
gefilte fish, 8, 29
gelt, 87
Gemara, 129, 130
gematria, 174
Genesis, 58, 68, 81, 114, 119, 125, 143, 175